KARAGIOZIS

KARAGIOZIS

Culture & Comedy
in Greek Puppet Theater

LINDA S. MYRSIADES AND
KOSTAS MYRSIADES

THE UNIVERSITY PRESS OF KENTUCKY

Editorial and Sales Offices: Lexington, Kentucky 40508-4008

Library of Congress Cataloging-in-Publication Data

Myrsiades, Linda S.
  Karagiozis : culture and comedy in Greek puppet theater /
Linda S. Myrsiades and Kostas Myrsiades
    p. cm.
  Includes bibliographical references and index.
  ISBN 0-8131-1795-X
  1. Shadow shows—Greece. 2. Karagöz. I. Myrsiades, Kostas
II. Title.
PN1979.S5M96   1992
791.5—dc20   92-9927

For Giorgos Haridimos

Contents

Acknowledgments

The authors would like to thank Giorgos Haridimos, nine times president of the Karagiozis Players Association, who has generously, during a sixteen-year period, shared his art and his expertise, his indigenous theory and native criticism of the Karagiozis performance, and his hospitality with us. Mr. Haridimos introduced us to his family, both at home and at the theater, involved us in setting up exhibits of his puppets, stage properties, posters, and stage, and allowed us backstage to observe and record the preparation and presentation of his performances. He submitted to myriad interviews, largely by Kostas Myrsiades, with whom he shared professional and personal confidences that enabled us to see the performance from the inside, as the player knows it.

This work was facilitated by a variety of grants over a period of several years that West Chester University has generously provided. This aid, including travel grants, released time, and funding for project materials from the Faculty Development Committee and the College of Arts and Sciences Development Award, not only kept a difficult undertaking from becoming intolerable but also ensured the successful completion of this manuscript. We are further indebted to the expertise of the Inter-Library Loan Office staff at WCU, which made available sources that were difficult to access.

The Karagiozis figure, designed by Giorgos Haridimos and executed in cardboard.

Enter Karagiozis

The Karagiozis tradition dates from at least 1799 in Greece, but it has its origins in the Ottoman empire. Turkish theater historians have bemoaned the loss of this satiric and political performance in Turkey over the last generation, but few believed the end in Greece would follow so soon.

Part I of this book provides an extended study of critical issues that have been debated but have not been conclusively addressed in the numerous critical studies of the Karagiozis performance that have appeared in Greek. These issues require comment and resolution if we are truly to engage the performance in both its particular historical moment and its political and social context. In Chapters 1-4 Linda Myrsiades has taken up these issues: the performance as the non-canonical expression of an unofficial social world, as a gender statement that stands as a homologue for the split social vision of the culture in which it exists, as a form of folklore that expresses the pluralism of different social strata as well as interactivity along the rural-urban continuum, and as an indigenous performative event that is determined by its economic, geographic, political, and social contexts. In Chapter 5 Kostas Myrsiades describes the background of Giorgos Haridimos, the last of the great Karagiozis players in Greece.

Part II presents an oral translation directly from a 1973 tape made of Giorgos Haridimos's classic performance of the inestimable *Karagiozis Baker* text. Kostas Myrsiades checked the transcription of the tape line for line with the player, who elaborated at critical points on scenic effects, audience reaction, historical references, and alternative presentational strategies.

This publication of a live Karagiozis performance is thus the first of its kind in Greek or in translation. It represents an important change in the collection and dissemination of Karagiozis texts, which have been printed exclusively in reduced form, either dictated by a player or put together by a publisher from typical scenes rather than an actual performance. This translation provides, as a result, an opportunity to study oral compositional techniques in performance as they naturally occur as well as to observe the actual effect of the presence of an audience on the conduct of the performance. The translator, Kostas Myrsiades, not only preserves performance rhythms and original performative divisions but also replicates linguistic and paralinguistic playing techniques of the oral performance style in translation.

The key to producing a translation of a Karagiozis performance lies in the language of the performance, for the critical cultural component in translating the Karagiozis text is the performance's colloquial speech. The demotic language of these texts represents a culmination of the development of popular speech in Greece. It has been challenged by purist Greek, or Katharevusa, a form of educated speech used by the upper classes and officials since early Byzantine times. It has accommodated itself to the various foreign tongues spoken by Greece's many invaders, including the Franks, Slavs, and Turks. It is continually modified by dialects of the various regions of Greece—those of the Ionian and Dodecanese islands, Macedonia, Rumeli, and Thessaly, among others. The spoken language of the Greek people thus distinguishes both historic period and geographic area through the variety of its expressions (those generally common to the Greek language, those peculiar to certain sections of Greece, and those of Turkish origin), its foreign-derived vocabulary (historically Italian, Slavic, and Turkish, but in modern times also French, German, and English), and its local forms and pronunciations (e.g., Vlacho-Greek, Italianate Greek, Turco-Greek, Athenian, Cretan, and high or purist Greek).

The language of the Karagiozis text capitalizes on the rich potential of idiomatic demotic Greek through the range of the performance's characters: Barba Giorgos (Uncle George) the Rumeliote, Omorfonios the Corfiote, Manusos the Cretan, Dionisios of Zákinthos, Stavrakas from Piraeus, Gerasimos the Cephalonite, Pip the Corfiote, and Karagiozis the Athenian, for example. Moreover, it clearly plays on distinctions of power and status in its handling of Katharevusa. On the one hand, high Greek is reserved for heroes, rulers, and leaders; on the other, it is ridiculed by Karagiozis, the political leveler. Finally, language establishes a clear historical frame for the action. Set in the Ottoman period, the texts use a colloquial Greek characterized by more frequent Turkish expressions than are common in modern Greek popular speech. It encompasses as well the wide variety of languages of the Ottoman empire in the Arab, the Jew, the Vlach, the Albanian, the Persian, and the Armenian.

The performance, furthermore, consciously exploits in its oral delivery those language differences that distinguish characters by time period, geographic region, level of education, roles, and individual psychology. Just as Turkish pashas, beys, and viziers use a polite form of speech that is slightly antiquated and interspersed with Turkish phrases to create an impression of the Ottoman period, so modern figures like Stavrakas and Kolitiris use an Athenian argot that reflects modern times in the lower-class urban world of the piazza. Regional characters exhibit characteristics of a conservative country culture itself dated by several centuries. Characters like San Na Leme and Omorfonios use tag phrases to identify themselves and to punctuate rhythmically their otherwise nondescript speech, while Kolitiris stutters under the tutelage of his abusive father Karagiozis. Whining pitch patterns for Omorfonios and Dionisios and accelerated speech rhythms for Dionisios and Stavrakas add up to a highly variegated aural world. The translator who specifies the language values of the performance thus has an opportunity to convey in translation much of the original performance value of the Karagiozis text.

Other vocal peculiarities and performance rhythms require representation in translation as a means of preserving performance values. Karagiozis, for example, speeds his pace as he comes to the end of long speeches that build to a climax. This quality can be recaptured by short, noninformational terms set into run-on constructions. Verbal exchanges during beatings are expressed in measured tempos that coincide with the rhythmic sound of the hitting of a stick against a piece of wood. Regular metrical patterning of these expressions in translation and metrical balancing of rhymed exchanges between characters can recreate performance effects. Equally, the exploitation of progressively developing rhythms in pun sequences or in series jokes (one joke can go on as long as fifteen paired exchanges, as in Karagiozis's quizzing of his sons in the prologue to the performance) can replicate oral effects that are not available to translators who work from print texts rather than performances.

Other effects that deserve attention include interrogative narrative rhythms, in which the player uses one character's interrogating of another to punctuate informational scenes and thereby to maintain audience interest through dialogical interaction; matching inversions of word order, whereby one character mirrors his partner's speech; and formulaic constructions, which establish within stock scenes clear structural predictability both for transmission and for composition. By paying such attention to the particular problems of translating from performance, the translator need not agonize over the potential loss of effect in translating the speech of such a character as Dionisios, whose vocal pitch, rhythm of speech, use of foreign words, and dialectical peculiarities constitute his comic effect much more completely than does the material content of his speech. Translating from the oral performance, the translator thus remains sensitive to nuances of pitch, speed, stress, projection, and vocal range, making it more likely that such language values as run-ons, syllable separations, up glides and down glides, and nasal and gutteral vocal qualities will be recaptured in the translation language.

Content problems in translation from performance are, by contrast, more predictable, if only because they are more commonly recognized by translators used to working from print texts. Structural considerations in translation themselves affect performance content. Thus repetitive content cannot be eliminated, and variations and balances must be preserved. Telegraphed scenes, audience asides, various forms of breaking the theatrical illusion, and other performance techniques designed to keep the audience apprised of the ongoing action, to comment on the plot, or to acknowledge and respond to both audience presence and audience preference for more or less of a particular character or scene cannot be edited out of a performance translation, no matter how digressive such techniques may appear. Indeed, the not infrequent mistakes made by a player who introduces a motif he later chooses to abort, who stops in the middle of a speech or scene to begin it again more effectively, or who has one character correct or adopt another's dialogue or function when a plot has gotten off track because of inattention or a player's change of mind should also be maintained in translation as a means of illustrating oral compositional techniques at work.

Clearly the most satisfying way for the translator to reflect performance values is to provide a direct translation from an actual performance, for in performance the text is set in its proper situational context. When the text is translated in its performance context, the translator works to capture not only the context of the event but also the texture of the performance, aspects of the performance that are affected by the authority with which a player performs a text, the Karagiozis player's performance of all the roles in a performance, and the player's sense of his own role or purpose. Some perform to express the purity of their art, others as exponents of a family tradition, and yet others out of social conscience, to change minds or influence attitudes.

Until the 1989 retirement of Greece's preeminent Karagiozis player, Giorgos Haridimos, one could stroll from the Pillars of Olympian Zeus through the old Plaka quarter of Athens to Lysicrates Square directly below the Acropolis on any weekend to attend a classic Karagiozis performance in Haridimos's Family Laic Theater. In this small open-air theater, now a fashionable tourist café, one had the opportunity, through the seventies and eighties, to witness an entertainment form that has been popular among the Greek people since the beginning of the nineteenth century. An oral form passed from generation to generation by masters to their recruited pre-teen apprentices, the Karagiozis performance found itself in decline by the middle of the twentieth century. By that time the original masters of the form and many of their equally talented students had died. Other forms of entertainment, especially film, supplanted it, and the more than 150 players who had once criss-crossed Greece performing Karagiozis through its villages and cities dwindled to a handful located largely in populous areas such as Patras and Athens. Karagiozis soon appeared as thirty-two-page booklets, competing with Mickey Mouse comic books, and as fifteen-minute episodes on television. By the late fifties Karagiozis had become a children's entertainment.

A shadow puppet form, the Karagiozis performance developed in Greece over two centuries, using local character types, costumes, and dialects; folk anecdotes; contemporary events; topical humor; themes and motifs of classical, hellenistic, and Byzantine origin; and Greek legends, songs, and dances. It was modeled on a fourteenth-century Turkish prototype, Karagoz, which itself found its roots in fool lore and the classical mime, the dominant form of entertainment in the eastern empire from the fourth century B.C. to A.D. 1400. The Turkish performance was introduced into occupied Greece certainly as early as the eighteenth century and quite possibly earlier. Christianized, sentimentalized, and Europeanized in the last half of the nineteenth century, Karagiozis is a product of an oral tradition that, by adding

ΚΑΛΗ ΟΡΕΞΗ! Περάστε ἀπ' τό μαγερικο — συγ-
γνώμην, ἀπό το «Θέστρο Αὐλαια» τοῦ Πειραιως —
αὔριο το πρωί στίς 11, με πολλην ὀρεξη Ὁ φίλος

ΚΑΘΕ ΚΥΡΙΑΚΗ ΠΡΩΪ 11-1
ιΤο ΘΕΑΤΡΟΝ ΑΥΛΑΙΑ ΠΕΙΡΑΙΩΣ
ΠΑΣΣΑΛΙΜΑΝΙ ΤΗΛ
422-019

ΚΑΡΑΓΚΙΟΖΗΣ ΜΑΓΕΡΑΣ

ΓΕΛΙΑ ΠΟΛΛΑ

ΧΑΡΙΔΗΜΟΣ

Γιωργος Χαρίδημος ὑπόσχεται, οὕτως ἤ ἄλλως, ἀπ'
τα πολλά τά γέλια, θά σάς ανοίξη τήν ὀρεξη, με'
τήν ὡραία γαστρονομικη κωμωδία χ Ὁ Καραγκιόζης
μάγερας». Μιά ἀπόλουση.

A newspaper
advertisement for
Giorgos Haridimos's
performance of
Karagiozis Cook.

suspensefully arranged historical materials to the traditionally comic
Turkish plays, became a vehicle of national expression and a medium
for the Greek people to explore their own identity.

Patterned oral composition linked Karagiozis to an oral tradition
that from Homer through the Byzantine Akritic cycle to modern
klephtic ballads has formed a resilient part of Greek life. Preserved
through oral transmission, the Greek performance in its basic comic
patterns as well as in the content and psychology of its tragicomedies
resisted domination by literary drama and the corrupting influences of
the print medium. It has, however, borrowed from the former since the
last half of the nineteenth century and has been conditioned by the
effect of a reading, rather than a purely listening, audience since 1921,
the date of the first published Karagiozis script. Unashamedly folk in

its origins, the Karagiozis performance kept faith with the oral tradition in which it was rooted with a tenacity that is all the more admirable considering the competing influences it had to endure.

The main body of the most common type of Karagiozis performance consists of a series of stock scenes tied together by a string of stock types introduced in a predictable series and loosely related to some central theme. The comedies aggregate popular stock scenes and extend the comic tricks of individual characters, filling in their comic frame with repetitions for comic effect and the unsophisticated humor of beatings, confusion, disguises, and mockery. The repertoire of puppet figures in Haridimos's troupe was established in the performance tradition between 1890 and 1910. It consisted of twenty-five regularly appearing figures, twelve of which constitute the core of the troupe. Karagiozis is the humpbacked fool-hero of the performance who wears the rags of the poor Greek and turns the world of the rich and powerful upside down. His sidekick, Hatziavatis, represents the acquiescent Greek. He speaks in the elevated Katharevusa, or purist Greek, and acts as an intermediary for upper-class Turks. Barba Giorgos (Uncle George), a country bumpkin, represents the rustic mountaineer or shepherd of Rumeli. Feared by all, he wears the skirts of the Greek mountain fighter.

The eldest son of Karagiozis, Kolitiris, is physically a miniature version of his father and represents the street urchin of Athens. Karagiozis's wife, Aglea, or Karagiozena, takes on the role of the nagging wife; like her children, she is a physical replica of Karagiozis. From the island Syros, Stavrakas is associated with the harbor tough of Piraeus, whose taverns and drug dens he frequents. Omorfonios of Corfu is an elegant idiot, a pseudo-intellectual fop with a huge head who lisps like a spoiled child. Dionisios, an Italianate Greek from Zákinthos, is a member of a fallen aristocratic family; he plays the role of the dandy who apes Western fashions. The Jew is a merchant from Salonika; clever, capricious, powerful, and arrogant with his peers, the Jew is obsequious to his betters. Veligekas is the first officer of the serai and the enforcer of the pasha's rule; an arbitrary and cruel figure, he mistreats Karagiozis and intimidates the Greeks. The bey plays the role of the old man who is duped; he generally appears in the opening scene of the play, initiating the action by his search for someone to provide a service or fill a position. The pasha is the highest member of the Turkish ruling class depicted in the performance. Representing

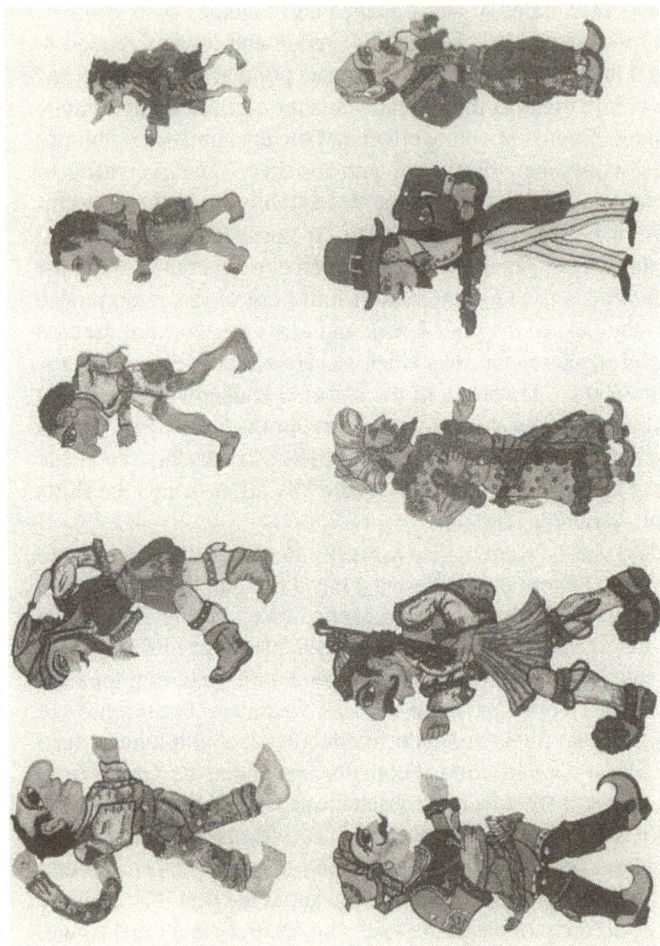

A troupe of Karagiozis Shadow Theater puppets designed by Mimis Mollas and executed in plastic for a performance kit for children. Left to right, top row: Karagiozis, Hatziavatis, Kolitiris, Skorpios, Pitsikokos; bottom row: Veligekas, Barba Giorgos (Uncle George), the Pasha (Veziris), Dionysios (Nionios), the Bey.

authority and stability, he is generally a just and moral man, although he is not above deception.

On a clear night inside Haridimos's open-air theater, one could sit on any of a hundred folding chairs neatly placed in rows on a clean earthen floor swept nightly by Haridimos himself. Admitting several dozen tourists and regulars—in earlier days in his father's Piraeus theater, he is known to have drawn audiences of 3,000—Haridimos would begin to perform from a repertoire of some sixty-five texts, mostly comic, that he considered classic performances. His full repertoire contained four hundred oral texts, including a number of historical texts whose material and length no longer held the interest of even the most ardent Karagiozis audiences; some, over six hours long, required three nights to perform.

Haridimos's stage (*skini*), an easily dismantled booth in touring versions of the performance, was a permanent elongated rectangular structure of stone and wood about five and one-half feet high and seventeen feet wide. Set on a small raised platform that gave the booth as much as two or three feet of additional height, the apron (*podia*) was decorated with Haridimos's own drawings of puppet figures. The strip over the cloth screen, the *erio* or *kambot,* carried the player's name. A shelf one foot to one and one-half feet wide was set three feet off the floor of the *skini* behind and below the bottom edge of the screen, both as a walkway for the performing puppets and as a place to set the lamps used to illuminate the figures. Nine to twelve shelf lamps stood about one foot away from the screen between the player and the screen and were complemented by three overhanging lamps hung from the top of the *skini* on projecting pieces of wood. These overhanging lamps created an even wash of light to illuminate the set pieces, which were attached to the screen with staples. Haridimos also used a pulley system, employing two screens, or *tavles,* one acting as a set scene and one waiting ready behind the *erio* for a scene change. Each screen had its own tracks or grooves, so that the new screen with its preset scene could descend simultaneously with the ascent of the old screen.

The entire Karagiozis performance occurred behind these white cloth screens. Standing at some distance behind the screen, the performer manipulated the puppets against the screen with twenty-inch-long sticks (*sustes*). The audience, sitting in front of the screen, could only see the puppets' shadows emanating through the white cloth. The spaced lights focused on the cloth made available all puppet details

The interior of the stage showing automatic scene changes (*Kapiamento*), brought to Thessaloniki by Harilaos and to Athens by H. Haridimos.

Two set pieces that appear at the opening of a performance: to the audience's left, the hut of Karagiozis; to the right, the Pasha's serai.

and colors to the audience. Behind this screen, Haridimos was aided by two apprentices, who made sound effects, set and changed scenes, and worked supernumerary puppets, although the voices of all puppets used were done solely by the Karagiozis performer. In these reduced performances sound and light effects were kept simple and at a minimum; clapping one's hands, slapping together two pieces of wood wrapped in a rag, or hitting a piece of tin indicated various stage events. Haridimos replaced the singers and orchestra—violin, bouzouki, clarinet, hand drum, and santuri—used at the height of the performance's popularity, with recorded music.

One evening's performance began with the traditional prologue, in which Karagiozis picks a fight with Veligekas, enlisting the support of Uncle George, who soon disappears. These antics over, Haridimos moved without a break into a modern form of the prologue, in which Karagiozis quizzes his three sons (Kolitiris, Skorpios, and Pitsikokos) on a variety of topics. Concluding, he instructs his eldest son, Kolitiris, to announce the evening's main performance: "Honorable ladies, honorable gentlemen, mademoiselles, and our beloved children, good evening to all of you./ This evening our theater will present the old, classic comedy of the shadow theater, / My Father the Baker."

PART ONE
Karagiozis in Context

CHAPTER ONE

Official and Unofficial Culture

The Karagiozis shadow puppet theater performance was born out of an Ottoman subterfuge responding to an Islamic prescription that only permitted the artistic representation of human figures when they appeared as shades cut with holes to allow the spirits to escape. Subsequently, in both its Turkish and Greek forms, that is, as Karagoz as well as Karagiozis, the performance has capitalized on its association with the mime grotesque, the carnival fool, divine madmen, and psychological shadow figures. Freed from conventional standards of behavior, the Karagiozis figure has been tolerated for four hundred years as an antithetical, even anathematical expression that frames the norms by means of which social institutions exist, even as it stands for the outer boundaries of disorganization, anarchy, and chaos.

We can thus profitably examine the Karagiozis performance through the struggle between unofficial and official culture that occurs in history in general and in Greek society in particular. Mikhail Bakhtin has elaborated this distinction between elite and popular culture in terms of the unofficial culture of carnival humor, the purity of whose festivities was mitigated in Europe by the Middle Ages but not in Greece until the passing of the Ottoman empire. Bakhtin begins from the premise that in a preclass or prepolitical order the serious and comic aspects of the world were considered equally sacred and official. But in a consolidated state and class structure, the equality of the two became impossible. Comic forms were transformed to an unofficial level, where they became more complex expressions of folk consciousness and culture. Such were carnival festivities.

The basic carnival nucleus of what Bakhtin (1968) calls the pure marketplace culture belongs to the borderline between art and life where there are no distinctions made between actors and spectators. All are participants. Carnival is not, as a result, an object to be viewed by the people. The people live in it and through it; its very idea embraces all the people. Carnival is thus the people's second life, a festive life organized on the basis of laughter, a utopian realm of community, freedom, equality, and abundance.

The true festival spirit is indestructible. It suspends hierarchical ranks and precedence in its affirmation of the equality of all and its denial of the official spirit that consecrates inequalities. This suspension of hierarchical ranks leads to a special type of communication in everyday life, communication that is free, without distance, playful and dynamic, and full of changing, undefined forms. It affirms gay relativity and the logic of the world turned inside out, which shifts values from top to bottom, resulting in comic crownings, turnabouts, and a parody of the extracarnival life. Whereas feasts are linked to crises and breaking points, to death and revival, change and renewal, their focus remains eternally positive. They focus on rebirth, not in the abstract but in experienced reality, for the ideal and the real in carnival are merged. Moreover, the focus is on the collective rather than the individual. The laughter is that of all the people, at all the people; it is an experience of wholeness rather than of isolated events. Universal in scope, it is ambivalent, triumphant, and mocking.

Bakhtin's emphasis on wholeness prohibits looking at folk humor and its familiar and abusive speech separated from the maternal womb of carnival ritual. Fold humor must be studied within the unity of folk culture, inside its variety and heterogeneous character, and not as isolated fragments or expressions. By extension, images of the human body—eating, defecating, experiencing sexual acts—must also be seen as part of the indivisible whole. This concept, referred to as grotesque realism, describes the bodily element as deeply positive and universally shared, not as private, egotistical, and separate from other spheres of life. The material bodily principle is contained not in the individual but, again, in the collective. Grandiose, exaggerated, and immeasurable, it embodies the positive characteristics of fertility, growth, and overabundance, which are celebrated by transferring the high spiritual abstract ideal to the material level of earth and body.

Grotesque realism represents the essential process of degradation, such that abusive language, curses and oaths, are essential to understanding its expressions. Here, the lower body is seen as a deeply positive expression of universal nature, as the regenerative function of the earth and the womb seen through the belly, the breasts, the buttocks, and the genitals. As Bakhtin expresses it, "it is an incantation of this world at the absolute lower stratum, as the swallowing up and generating principle, as the bodily grave and bosom, as a field which has been sown and in which new shoots are beginning to sprout" (1968: 27).

Time and ambivalence represent the two indispensable traits of the grotesque image, which is itself a phenomenon in transformation, an unfinished and continuing metamorphosis. The two poles of transformation are seen as the old and the new, the dying and the procreating, the beginning and the end, understood as recurring events in a natural cycle following the phases of reproductive life.

In this scheme, over the course of time the unofficial world became officialized. A canon of consciously established rules and norms grew up to circumscribe the noncanonical carnival phenomenon, turning a changing, ambivalent experience into one that was fixed and immutable. Official festivities tended to sanction or reinforce existing patterns of moral norms and prohibitions. Having lost their festive life, they became serious and affirmed stable, unchanging, perennial truths that had already been established as eternal and indisputable. The assertion of such a canon led to the descent of carnival to a low comic level in which carnival forms narrowed and the state encroached on festive life to turn it into a parade. Carnival freedom was transformed into a mere holiday mood; it lost its living ties with folk culture and became a literary form.

An important distinction to make here is between popular culture and mass culture. Whereas there are two points of convergence and areas of overlap, these two cultures do have different ideological bases and serve different purposes. Popular culture represents an expression of unofficial culture. It is to a large extent oral, emanating from the nonelite subordinate classes through forms that may once have been official, such as Church rituals, civic pageants, and community fairs, and expressing the disorderly values of the lower classes (Burke 1978). It is not restricted to rural culture, although identified with it, and not to be confused with national culture, although a component of it.

Mass culture, by contrast, represents an expression of official culture, simplified and in print, that acts as a force of order and transmits elite values. It appears in the city, representing a social system that benefits the urban elite more than the poor. Here the invasion of the educated elite arose and penetrated popular culture more deeply than it did in the countryside (Michembled 1985). Insofar as popular culture when it appeared in the city was more frequent, more ambiguous, and more heterogeneous than in rural areas and resisted authority more successfully, the elite offered a form of its own more alienating culture to the masses. Not only did the process represent the repression of popular culture (Bakhtin 1968; Burke 1978; Frow 1986; Herzfeld 1982; Kiurtsakis 1985; Michembled 1985; Underdown 1985), but it also served as an index of the modification of the power structure. It moved toward political centralization of the absolute state, imposing unity on diversity in a fragmented world. Pluralism was rejected for unity and regional differences for uniformity in one unique, unified cultural reality in which subjugation of the soul was seen as the work of the Church, and subjugation of the body as the work of the state (Michembled 1985).[1]

Acting as a surrogate for popular culture, cheap print chapbooks or peddlers' literature (*vivliarakia*) arose to act as an intermediary language or discourse between popular and elite cultures. Cutting the people off from their roots even as it capitalized on prominent aspects of popular culture, this mass surrogate for popular culture spread the ideology of learned culture in simple terms, building on the moral values of the elite class and its dominant ideological models and assimilating its culture to the popular milieu (Burke 1978; Michembled 1985). If popular culture had been a system of survival for the lower classes, it would soon have few means of resistance against the values of this new world.

The elite, nevertheless, represented a secondary audience for popular culture and had traditionally participated in it in both rural and urban settings (Myrsiades 1986b), sharing many popular attitudes. They had not only influenced popular culture by bringing to it literary themes and bourgeois attitudes, but they also carried popular culture back into their own elite culture through epic narratives, dances, and songs (Burke 1978; Michembled 1985; Underdown 1985). On the other hand, popular attitudes to urban life and elite culture themselves ranged from highly traditional resistance to change to commitment to and even identification with the urban world, responses inspired by certain aspects of village life itself. Still, popular culture in the urban setting distinguished its own identity from mass culture as an unofficial culture of the subordinate classes of the city, at the same time maintaining clear ties to rural traditions and behaviors through an interactive rural-urban relationship. In this sense, it can be referred to as a culture of the poor. The urban poor has more in common with the rural poor than it has with other urban classes, including the bourgeois or elite classes. Seeing in popular culture a jobless, low-caste, newly arrived population, the bourgeoisie and elite created an isolation that increased solidarity among the poor while strengthening neighborhood ties and ties with the rural villages that ensured heterogeneity within that solidarity.

In some forms and to varying degrees, popular culture survived, having nevertheless lost some of its regenerating powers. Behind their masks, these carnival forms continue to negate uniformity, similarity, and conformity, and they remain tied to transition, metamorphosis, mockery, and the violation of boundaries, liberating people from inhuman necessity, destroying pretense, and freeing human consciousness for new potentialities. One can trace this continuity of carnival forms in the Karagiozis performance (Kiurtsakis 1985), affirming the ability of later forms of marketplace humor to continue to express the unofficial ideology that comic humor still makes possible in the face of officializing strategies of the state culture. Taking up Bakhtin's argument and applying it to the Karagiozis performance as it developed in Greece, one can draw a fundamental distinction between Karagiozis in the mountains (the heroic texts) and Karagiozis in the city (the comedies). Indeed, Giannis Kiurtsakis considers the rural-based texts, with their roots in Byzantine and Ottoman festivals, consistent with the carnival spirit and representative of collective and deathless Romiosini, or, as he defines it, the essential Greekness of the Greek people. The urban texts, by contrast, find their roots in three places: the life of the international city, inherited from the Ottomans; modern social and political forces that resulted from internal and external migration—from the Greek countryside to Greek cities, from Anatolia to Greece, and from Greece to Canada, the United States, Australia, South Africa, and Germany; and the urban underclass as it came to be constituted in Athens.

A critical aspect of the distinction Kiurtsakis draws between rural and urban culture involves the collective-individual antithesis expressed by the heroic and comic texts. The heroic texts, in Kiurtsakis's view, express the collective body through the Karagiozis figure. While its life responds to a variety of laws implicit in that collective and takes on a wide range of the masks or personae of that collective, the

Karagiozis figure is identified with the history of a human type that is deathless, an empty ego that is Everyman and whose mythic truth is that it provides a comic form of the whole *laos,* or people, the body of the laos in its wholeness. Karagiozis summarizes a people. In this sense, Karagiozis embraces the common human fate of the history of a people, a whole culture and universal allness at the same time. Here, man is one with nature in the larger drama of cyclical death and renewal that leads to constant rebirth.[2]

Extending Bakhtin's analysis, we can see Karagiozis's physical anomalies, asymmetries, and deformations—primarily his phallus, humpback, and long arm, but also his long nose and insatiable mouth—as typical embodiments of the grotesque form in carnival humor (Kiurtsakis 1985). The grotesque leads man to a form of otherness that permits him to have intercourse with the world of spirits, with demonic powers. Karagiozis himself is regarded as an anthropomorphic mask that participates equally in the character of the best and spirits.[3]

Kiurtsakis (1985) has fit Karagiozis to this concept by regarding him as the symbolic embodiment of the undying laos. Karagiozis has died as a concrete individual only to be married/resurrected in the larger collective concept of the undying people as a whole. The irony of Karagiozis is that whereas he represents himself in a number of texts as having no other job but dying, he has not yet ever died, affirming the relativity of death and the deathlessness of the grotesque body.[4]

In this view, Karagiozis in the heroic texts symbolizes the continuity and growth of the collective life of Romiosini each time death mows its ranks and Karagiozis, in the midst of it all, continues to feast (Kiurtsakis 1985). Karagiozis is not here merely counterposed as an antisocial force against the heroic ideal of the Greek captains who revolted against Turkish rule in 1821; rather, his experience exists at a deeper level, for he does not fight in a war but against war, against death itself embodied in war, using the reason of life embodied in food.

In Kiurtsakis's view of the comedies, by contrast, death becomes a simple biological fact, a simple individual end for one incapable of rebirth. The comic texts cease to represent the collective and become identified with factions, points of view, or, more pertinently, the individualism of the lower class, which sets itself against the rest of society in its struggle, not to achieve wholeness, but merely to survive.[5] Individual misfortune is lifted out of the social picture as an isolate. Man is separated from the natural context and set against others in a battle of class antagonism. Here we lose the sense of the equality of all that exists in the mountains, the sense of abundance, and the sense of rebirth, and, devolving, see only social injustice and individual survival. The movement from the mountains to the city has thus become a movement from heroism, symbolism, and the collective to pessimism, reality, and the individual.

The critical element that led to the move away from the carnival spirit in the Karagiozis performance is described by Kiurtsakis as the sense of estrangement created by migration to the modern Greek city. Building on the discontinuity posed in anthropological descriptions of a rural-urban dichotomy, Kiurtsakis identifies agricultural society with unofficial culture and urban society with official culture. In agricultural society, sufficient control was exerted by family and collective life that neither daily vulgarities nor orgiastic festivities proved threatening. In the city, such controls had dissolved, and the anonymous urban environment gave rise to themes of male sexual hunger. Formal bourgeois moral law came into play as the urban family circle narrowed, collective ties loosened, and man became alienated from nature. In response, an ideology of decency arose in the city to privatize sexual life and censor vulgarity, internalizing the ethic of the urban upper class and Europeanizing influences.

The city, described by Kiurtsakis as the source of this estrangement, has a special configuration. It is not a prototypical city like the city of the Middle Ages that spontaneously concentrates a new social collective and celebrates a homogeneous national urban class and culture that yet has laic roots. Nor is the city, like the industrial cities of the nineteenth century, the product of a mass agricultural exodus at a time of radical economic and social transformation that supplies industrialized centers with a great proletarian work force. Rather, the modern Greek city is seen as the result of the quantitative and qualitative changes imposed on the Ottoman city by two phenomena: the creation of the Greek state and the European orientation of postrevolutionary Greek society. This city constitutes a model of foreign organization and control superimposed on a traditional social body.

Karagiozis is thus, in Kiurtsakis's view, the creation of a preindustrial society, like the English Punch and the French Guignol. Like the modern city, the Karagiozis tradition declines with industrial decline and the decline of the proletariat, which it came to express, when it diverges from the universal carnival spirit to become an embodiment specific to modern Greek urban life. In particular, Kiurtsakis examines the comic Karagiozis texts in which he identifies Karagiozis as the comic hero of the unemployed lumpen proletariat. Motivated by an ethic of survival, that proletariat remained unable to exert the most elementary force of protest against the system that oppressed it.

Kiurtsakis refers to the comic texts as encapsulating a time without future, a place of broken social ties and barren competition. The comedies thus represent a static place of changelessness. Stories end where they began with no way out. Yesterday, today, and tomorrow are leveled in an endless present. The wheel of time has failed to turn and remains stubbornly in the same spot. For Karagiozis and all those who live on the screen, all is the same and remains the same. Time is uniform; now is the same as before.

In the heroic texts, by contrast, Kiurtsakis finds hope of a better future, of liberation, of resurrection. The bitter pessimism of the comedies is matched by the joyful celebration of the heroic text that envelops the laos in a vision of social change that is utopian, if elusive. In contrast to the hostile law of the capitalist marketplace, the precapitalist agricultural economy represents a positive natural experience, for in the mountains the comic hero engages successfully in a contest in which he turns hierarchical values topsy-turvy.

Thus the modern heroic texts of the agricultural social world of the Turkish Occupation expressed, in Kiurtsakis's view, the collective myth of laic ideology, a free mountain world of abundance and equality expressing the bodily values, collectivity, and the cyclical patterns of nature that renew life and restore a sense of wholeness. Here man defies the fires of battle to defeat death. The Karagiozis heroic texts are, as a result, not merely a celebration of the heroes of 1821 but are, at a deeper level, about the anonymous laos itself, the collective body symbolically reproduced in Karagiozis's grotesque body. The laos is the collective force of deathlessness that underlies history.

Within the Karagiozis tradition, the language of carnival thus expressed change, representing deep unofficial comic-historic knowledge, and stagnation, representing superficial local ahistorical (or dehistoricized) official knowledge. Kiurtsakis holds that Karagiozis is meant to tie together these two worlds, that of the city and the mountains, the klepht and the city dweller. Combining in himself both hero and antihero, he captures both extremes of the human personality. He links the experience of the present tense, the specified past, and some exotic other time; he organically joins the group and the individual, the history of all and the situation of the individual, stagnation and change, in one self. Karagiozis's role is to assert the village within the city, the freedom of the mountains to counter the slavery of occupation. He represents, as a result, a combination of the rural and the urban, the official and the unofficial, the Romeic and the Hellenic. Rather than a synthesis, however, he expresses the coexistence of the continuity and the discontinuity of the laic experience and ideology, the contradiction in which the laos lives.

Heroic drama is thus balanced with comic completion to redress its one-sidedness and to re-create the wholeness of meaning that is the central message of the symbolic laic myth of 1821: life struggle and victory. Without the mocking complement of the comic mirror, the seriousness of heroism is empty language. It takes the two together to find the wholeness of carnival spirit that gives us a broader, richer horizon rediscovered in the reality of everyday life. In other words, comic and heroic values are not oppositional, but complementary and interchangeable in the highest sense of an interactive dialectic. The parody of Karagiozis comedy, especially as seen intermingled in the heroic works, is thus not only denigrating but also affirming. It does not merely denounce by dethroning that which is high, but it affirms by enthroning that which is low, to rise up to a still higher form.[6] The characteristic comic reversal of hierarchical status was retained in both the history and comic texts as a statement of Karagiozis's fundamental topsy-turvy ethos, which, temporarily, as in the comedies, or permanently, as in the histories, insisted on a disorderly challenge to authority.

The debate between official and unofficial culture can be viewed in yet another light, specific to Greek society, in its Hellenic and Romeic guises (Herzfeld 1982). The differences between official and unofficial cultures are those between the nation-statism of the Karagiozis heroic texts and the pragmatic vagaries of everyday life that characterize the Karagiozis comedies. In its Romeic face, Karagiozis represents the interiorized view by means of which Greece describes its own Ottoman habits, attitudes, and customs.[7] The comedies are based on a restricted code that depends heavily on contextual cues for interpretation; it is a code best represented by demotic language that elevates the emergent and local truths of everyday practices as an alternative vision to that of official ideology. Speaking of the essential weaknesses of the human condition and its flawed descent, of social and cultural ambiguity, it makes marginality and inferiority central to its introspective discourse.[8] Social outsiders and exponents of the evil otherness of the female, negative side of origins are incorporated in this inclusive view of Greek society.

In its Hellenic face, Karagiozis represents the exterior view that Greece presents to those outside its boundaries and that regulates all those within as "one of us." The elaborated context-free code exemplified by Katharevusa, a form of social rhetoric more easily adapted to abstract thought, is here appropriated by the history texts. The insider's knowledge of received absolute truths provides a realm of certainty that arises out of the positive origins of ancient Greece, origins that speak of self-worth and the extroverted self-display of male exclusiveness (Herzfeld 1982, 1987).

As paired alternatives, the Hellenic and Romeic poles appear in each other throughout society, although differently at different levels, demonstrating the interactive nature of the cultural dialectic. This dialectic, which Herzfeld calls disemia, cuts through a series of concentric social circles leading from the state down to the level of the individual.[9] Thus, official and unofficial ideologies exist at every level, and the dialectic itself is repeated in every circle of the series. By this argument, conflict cannot be appropriately described as class conflict or as the individual against the state but must be discussed incorporatively as occurring throughout society and at every level. As a result, unofficial culture can be viewed as a form of insubordination at the top as well as at the bottom of the social ladder. It is a form of Babel that goes right to the top of the tower, a multileveled pluralism that is pansocial, so that self-interest, like individual heroism, affects the highest as well as the lowest levels of political activity.[10] Here certainty and absolute knowledge are a mere appearance, for not only are they merely ideological constructs of the official view, but they are also themselves relative concepts based on the existence of fundamental oppositions at all levels, the shared and interactive nature of those oppositions, and the fact that the identity of outsiders and insiders as well as boundaries themselves are functions of one's perspective.

The tower itself figures the irreducibility of discourses to a single system of totalizing structural order or a coherent construct (Derrida 1985). Thus it is in a persistent state of deconstruction, and the need for translation between discourses is imposed on what must be regarded as a permanent state of confusion in which the imposition of order is itself a temporal aberration. The plurality of these discourses, the unsystematic conflict of tongues that Bakhtin (1968) calls hetero-glossia (see Morson 1986), necessitates a polylogue that takes into account other perspectives. Each discourse itself represents an opposi-tional form in any dialogue in which it is engaged, each dialogue rep-resenting the struggle of one subject to incorporate another (Hirsch-kop 1986). The principal "engine of change" is the conflict implicit in the varieties of speech (Morson 1986).

Social knowledge, like oppositional interactions, is thus negotiable. This very negotiability represents the inner face of Greek political experience and is related to social differentiation, segmentation, and heterogeneity at all levels. The inner face represents a mode of social knowledge inside the hierarchical order that is not suppressed by the state as long as it remains an internal expression of self-description and not an external presentation of self. Official unity is the face that divided insiders present to outsiders.

Thus the larger social question becomes internalized in the Kar-agiozis performance itself. Self-knowledge as alienation and the most deeply experienced sense of historical otherness are retained in the comedies, which represent a form of social experience that respects heterogeneity and pluralism. Self-presentation, which legitimates po-litical and cultural differences under the guise of unity, is permitted to influence the heroic texts, which thus come to represent a form of official interpretation that imposes unity and homogeneity. In the comedies, the Karagiozis performance still stands as an obstacle to reducing difference—the mark of otherness—and an obstacle to replacing the distinctiveness of social experience with a generalized, officially shaped structuring of that social experience.

Thus, whereas official ideology sees Karagiozis texts as corrupted and divisive refractions of the national identity it sponsors, unofficial tradition has already internalized in the comedies the nation's adulter-ated past, just as the later heroic texts internalized the Europeanized present. In Greece, as a result, Eurocentric identity confronts an alterity in itself (Herzfeld 1982), so that the nation is caught between the condescension of imposed Europeanization and the humiliation of internalized Orientalism. The Karagiozis performance as a whole finds less difficulty in accepting the dichotomy of these alternative visions because of its own pluralistic and incorporative unofficial base in the comedies. Exclusive and absolute, official ideology is less accepting of the "muted" unofficial view.

In a deeper sense, by incorporating two realms usually kept separate, Karagiozis blurs boundaries, thus deconstructing our perception of the world and leaving it open, as well, to further dissolution. It is here that unofficial ideology has its most devastating effect, holding open an alternative view that speaks to an opposite but equal truth of freedom, even anarchy. The negotiability of unofficial against official ideologies and strategies is best served by Karagiozis's disorderly and uncontrolled challenge to the dominant, or Turkish, statist ideology of order and control by reversing the dominant pattern and turning hierarchical status topsy-turvy (Kiurtsakis 1985; Danforth 1976). The Karagiozis figure embodies the negotiability of Greek society through the variety of masks he wears, behind whose voices he performs a series of changing roles and yet remains in himself a static figure with his own persona. The madness of these contradictory shifting roles is its own form of reason, a deeper sense that lies behind the figure's nonsense, the wisdom of festival, a stable form behind change. Karagiozis is thus not one figure, or even many figures, but a plurality that, taken together, make up the substance of his person. He is thus the comic symbol of the multiform condition of humanity, bounded within the chronological and spatial frame of modern Greek life.

Within these varied approaches to understanding the dialectical relationship of official and unofficial culture, it becomes apparent that several contradictions need to be explored. The first difficulty arises over the use of the concept of collectivity. The term may be used to discuss Karagiozis as an Everyman and the laos as the people as a whole (Kiurtsakis 1985), but such a usage does not reflect the degree of heterogeneity and pluralistic differences that we find in both the Karagiozis performance and popular culture at large. Whereas Bakhtin might refer to the equality of all within the constraints of carnival humor, that equality speaks to the loss of rank, to the destruction of hierarchical order, not to lessened differences of interest or to dissolution of factions or groups whose members find themselves mutually identified by some attribute such as age, occupation, sex, or regional

characteristics. Unity never means homogeneity or singularity of inter-
est in unofficial culture as it does in official culture.

The Karagiozis audience does not, as a result, represent a collective
understanding of shared assumptions commonly held, as Kiurtsakis
suggests. Rather, it represents the plurality of interests of the hetero-
geneous groups the performer addresses (Caraveli 1980, 1982). The
Karagiozis performance responds to more than one class or interest (it
is endemic to culture), to more than one kind of society (industrial as
well as peasant), and to more than one setting (urban as well as rural).
Consequently, notions of class consciousness and collectivity are
diffused, acknowledging not only intraclass dispute and the failure of
class consciousness but also a plurality of interests among folk groups
as well as between folk groups and the larger social order. Thus
Karagiozis expresses differentiated sensibilities and specific ways of
life in contrast to abstract cultural universalism. Moreover, the Romeic
guise of the Karagiozis performance is the guise that in the nineteenth
century was identified with the Turkish occupation. As a result,
Romeic texts were attacked for their pluralism, not for their collec-
tivity of expression (Myrsiades 1986a). Ironically, the Romeic guise of
unofficial culture appeared historically in the comedies, which Kiurt-
sakis identifies as urban and thereby as part of official culture. Actu-
ally, the comedies were being performed in Greece for almost a
century before a truly urbanized base developed in Greek towns and
cities in the first decades of the twentieth century. In addition, the
influence of official culture on the Karagiozis performance was not felt
until the end of the nineteenth century, a period during which we find
the heroic texts, not the comedies, being developed as responses to
national sentiments expressed by the literate elite of Greece (Myr-
siades 1986b).[11]

It becomes apparent that Kiurtsakis's ascription of unofficial humor
to the heroic performance and official humor to the comedies requires
revision. On the one hand, the comic text was denounced in the
nineteenth century by the literate Europeanized upper class, not for
its satire or its strong political or social statement in Greece, but for its
freedom in expressing Bakhtin's bodily principle—its openness, its
sexuality, its irreverence, its egalitarianism (Myrsiades 1986a, 1986b).
Since heroic or history texts were not developed until the 1890s, the
comedies, themselves derived from Turkish Karagoz prototypes, ex-
pressed these carnival characteristics. This historical identification of

the original carnival spirit with the comedies disputes Kiurtsakis's theoretical identification of the comedies as devolved and nonconforming with the carnival spirit.

On the other hand, Karagiozis came to be regarded as a metaphor for a nation struggling to overcome its external enemies, obliterating its Ottoman origins and thus removing an embarrassment as well as an obstacle to a Eurocentric ideology (Herzfeld 1987). In this view, Karagiozis represents a form subverted by official strategies and affirms the postrevolutionary state, having become an instrument of the same literate upper class that had earlier condemned it. This scenario is supported by the ultimate development of heroic texts. Historically, they were strongly based on patriotic postrevolutionary performances in the live theater that, built on the model of European drama, were written by Greeks who subscribed to a Europeanized ideology. Moreover, whereas the comedies were regarded as "polluted" with Oriental vulgarities (consistent with carnival humor), the heroic texts, in both language and themes, were "purified" (consistent with Bakhtin's notion of the co-optation of unofficial ideology by official ideology once a state culture develops). Thus, Kiurtsakis's identification of the heroic texts with carnival humor is contradicted by the history of the development of the form. In sum, whereas aspects of official and unofficial culture exist in both the comic and heroic texts, if one looks at them diachronically it is clear that the unofficial Romeic guise is most completely expressed in the comedies, and the official Hellenic in the heroic texts.[12]

The final difficulty lies in the notion of time. Carnival is described as made up of recurrent events placed in a cyclical time frame. The implication here is of a self-contained system that operates mechanically, so that today's upside down becomes tomorrow's right side up. This frame is opposed to the urban time frame in which man is described as trapped in an endless present, a timeless, stagnant, forever now. Neither time frame acknowledges the diachronic reality of the Karagiozis performance as it existed in its historically specific context. Moreover, the self-contained nature of both time frames fails to account for the interactive influence of context on performance. Thus neither notion is responsive to the open systems nature of the performance, which participates in an active exchange with social reality and expresses flexibility to external demands through its unstable boundaries. By contrast, the Romeic-Hellenic dichotomy used to describe the dialectic of unofficial and official culture offers an explanation by means of which the Romeic expression is described as heavily dependent on its context for interpretation and the Hellenic expression is characterized by its context-free code, allowing discussion of both the presence and absence of an active exchange with the performance environment.

Placing Karagiozis in the context of the dialectic between official and unofficial culture allows us to understand the form as both an individual expression of the larger conflict inside human culture and as a homologue for the larger social realm not only of Greek society but of human culture itself (Kiurtsakis 1985). Karagiozis thus represents one code or sign system through which elements of this opposition are balanced against each other (Herzfeld 1982, 1987).

By investigating Karagiozis, we can study the diachronic nature of the larger debate, which strikes at the deepest sources of culture (Alexiou 1984). It is important, however, to recognize that in the Karagiozis performance the diachronic motive, the force that pushes the system forward, is the Romeic, or deconstructive, force that requires ongoing adaptation to and interaction with dynamic historical and environmental forces in response to the larger context in which it presently exists and with which it must in the future become congruent. The Romeic expression of the Karagiozis performance is, in sum, a trope for the transformational aspect of the social dialectic. In the diachronic sense, Karagiozis is both rooted in historical experience and shaped by social organization. It is particular to a given society and responsive to the plurality of interests that make up the social order (Fox 1980). It operates through interactive processes in which relationships take priority over objects and engages in the active formation of its own audience (Williams 1977), representing a form of indigenous folk expression arrived at without the mediation of the culture industry (Zipes 1979, 1984). Even as it participates in the act of social exchange that goes on in the oppositional practices of everyday life, it emphasizes destabilizing influences and social misalignment. As an alternative form of reality, its function is to act symbolically to negotiate pluralistic interests and thus to engage social contradictions (Abrahams 1972). It also provides a ground through which emergent ideologies can exert their force (Jameson 1981).

The Romeic expression represents an open system that has a tendency to break up, as neither is it goal-oriented nor does it act as a coherent organism. Rather, it is held together by the dialectical tension between disharmonic interests in the intermittent construction and deconstruction of social organization that oscillates throughout society (Blau 1964). Such alienation and conflict are seen as essential to social affairs, for they help achieve social relationships and lead to innovation (Merton 1957). Indeed, insofar as conformity to regulation can be dysfunctional, the Romeic face not only admits the ability to generate changes in social forms of organization and to maintain flexibility by allowing parts of the form to operate autonomously to respond to external demands (Gouldner 1955), but it also admits the possibility of breaking the bounds of the form to lead to new forms. The most common themes of the Romeic expression are, as a result, uncertainty and unstable boundaries, which function as the necessary conditions for survival as the form seeks congruence with its environment.

Because the interior of the form represents an arena for conflicts between a plurality of interests, its dysfunctions are cumulative and self-reinforcing and become increasingly embedded as they resist the imposition of formal unity. Leading to different ends, the pluralism of the form is dysfunctional to a single harmonic end. As a result, survival is at once protected and threatened by the flexibility of the form.

Since there seems to be no limit to the degree of conflict the Romeic expression will tolerate, it becomes the ultimate engine of both change and instability. The Hellenic expression, by contrast, becomes the means through which sufficient limits ensure stability in the form. Driving toward integration of parts, maintenance of the form as a whole, and order, it exerts a positivist and determinist influence. Operating on the bureaucratic model, it tends to conformity and unity, to preestablished goals, as it stabilizes needs in terms of the whole.

Because it runs the risks of rigidity and defensiveness and because it fails to allow the form to spend the force of its aspirations (Blau 1964; Gouldner 1955; Merton 1957; Selznick 1979) or to negotiate its boundaries, the Hellenic expression can be as dysfunctional as the Romeic expression. The form thus needs both expressions. Once differentiated as individual interests, it must once again become an interdependent whole to be fully effective.

The Karagiozis performance as a whole neither resisted the call of Europeanization in the history texts nor rejected the Ottoman elements of its comedies. It absorbed both truths in an incorporative holistic statement, more generous than that found in cultural forms favored by the literate classes of modern Greek society. In this sense, the Karagiozis performance participated in the carnival dialectic, which saw larger meaning in the acceptance of antitheses and a recognition of their interaction.

CHAPTER TWO

Karagiozis
as Urban Folklore

Anthropological discourse has raised the issue of a dichotomy be-
tween official and unofficial culture as an opposition between rural
and urban, rural acting as a trope for unofficial culture and urban for
official culture. It has, nevertheless, been difficult to separate discus-
sion of urban folk culture from concepts of traditional values, beliefs,
and expressions. Thus, much of urban anthropological and folklore
research has involved searching for survivals of rural folk culture in the
city, looking for preservation of some idealized past. In some sense, we
are looking for continuity or adaptations of rural traditions in the city
and not for specifically urban forms of folk culture.

On the other hand, if we look to the city as a unique social system,
opposing it to rural traditions in a dichotomous relationship, we risk
missing the undeniable backward-and-forward interactions and influ-
ences between the country and the city, although we do begin to
appreciate that different levels of culture exist. Moreover, opposing
urban to rural systems has led to the assumption that urbanization
inevitably destroys or displaces folk culture as part of an evolutionary
process. In this argument, rural areas express homogeneity, tradition,
stability, and continuity, whereas urban areas express heterogeneity,
social change, ephemeral human relationships, and a complex divi-
sion of labor. Following this line, urban traditions are seen as expres-
sions of modern groups of people in the broader context of the cultural
conglomerate of the city, a cultural level that mediates between the
rural isolation of individual ethnic cultures and the level of a unitary
national culture (Moore 1975). Looking at the city and the countryside
as different but interactive systems inside a larger social whole,
however, represents an alternative position that enables us to consider
both the dichotomous and the continuous elements of rural and urban

folk cultures with a better understanding of how they fit into what some view as a national level of culture.[1]

During the Ottoman period, most Greeks lived in small villages. Cities were then merely small market and manufacturing centers serving agricultural regions. Migration, however, was (and had been for several centuries) common both within rural areas and across national boundaries, indicating continuous local and extralocal interaction (Costa 1988). The shift to administrative centers did not occur until after the War of 1821, a time nevertheless characterized by regional fragmentation and little real movement into cities from rural areas (Sutton 1978, 1983). Indeed, from 1834 to 1846, when Athens grew from a village of one thousand to a city of thirty thousand, more people left Greece than moved into Greek cities (Vermeulen 1983). Until 1860 most movement involved repopulating the islands and countryside then under Greek control. The mid–nineteenth century did begin to see an acceleration of rural-urban migration. Until 1870 this largely consisted of merchants, landowners, and politicians moving to Athens and Syros.

From 1870 on Greece experienced a progressive loss of its rural population (Sutton 1983), with most migration after 1880 directed toward Athens (Vermeulen 1983), which at this time had a population of less than fifty thousand (Dubisch 1977). By 1896 28 percent of Greece's population lived in urban areas (Sutton 1983). Athens alone, between 1896 and 1907, held 7 percent of the Greek population, and by 1928 it held 28 percent (Dubisch 1977). It had doubled in size since 1920, at which time the populations of all twenty-two of Greece's other largest cities taken together equaled only 75 percent of the capital's population. By 1928 the percentage of Greece's population that was urban had leveled off at a little less than a third. Thus, two periods appear to account for bursts of urban growth in Greece: the period from 1870 to 1896 and the one from 1920 to 1928.

Historically, migration in Greece began with wealthy entrepreneurs, older children, and educated villagers who wished to connect the village to new sources of power (Sutton 1978). They set up networks so that relatives could join them, capitalizing on connections established by the first wave of migrants. The second wave profited from kinship links and patronage in the cities to locate jobs much like they had had in the villages, to locate in neighborhoods in which fellow villagers had settled, and to join regional associations both to aid those back in the village and to support those already in the city (Vermeulen 1983). These neighborhoods were usually working-class and poor. They supported a culture of the poor (Lewis 1965, 1973), which, neglected by the government, found solidarity in its isolation without developing a sense of class or a proletarian consciousness, for basically these neighborhoods supported the petit bourgeois notions of the migrants who settled there (Vermeulen 1983).

The political context of the twentieth century was itself rooted in the post-1821 years, in which the leading role was given to the bourgeoisie. Throughout the nineteenth century the urban population was largely uninvolved in production; even in the urban growth years of 1870-90, the proletariat remained an insignificant force. In the 1920s, with the inflow of already urbanized refugees from Anatolia bringing cheap, skilled labor and industrial development (Vermeulen 1983), social fragmentation, a still undeveloped economy, and foreign ownership of large firms acted as a barrier to the organization of labor (Mouzelis 1976, 1978). Although an urban proletariat with a class character did develop during the interwar years, it was small, and its growth was restricted. Moreover, not only did patronage play a central role in a political party context, but entrepreneurs and civil servants also made up the bulk of the population (Vermeulen 1983).

The impression created is thus that Greece, at least by 1870, was in the process of urbanizing, that by 1896 it had experienced its first wave of significant urban migration, and that between 1920 and 1928 it completed the process of mass migration and urbanization. Still, Greece in 1930 was 67-percent rural (Dubisch 1977; Sutton 1983) and had hardly produced even an urban work force; 93 percent of manufacturing establishments each employed fewer than five persons (Vermeulen 1983). Not only were family, kinship, and patronage the dominant social forms in the small rural villages of the Ottoman period, but they still represented the primary forms by means of which twentieth-century Greek migrants lived in urban areas (Sutton 1983). The use of dowry and arranged marriages (du Boulay 1983), the practice of traditional religious observances (Hirschon 1983b), continued control over female sexuality, the loyalty of family members, and the continuity of rural sexual roles in working-class neighborhoods (Vermeulen 1983) suggest that villagers did not cease to be villagers by moving to the city (Dubisch 1977).[2] Such phrases as *village urbanites, peasant cities,* and *the urban village* are legitimately used to describe cities like Athens, which do not repeat the history of Western cities. They do not fit the model of disorganized, superficial, and alienating social life that anthropologists who view the urban experience as destructive of rural traditions and life have used to describe cities.

The city served as an economic resource for rural Greek communities, as it relieved pressures on village families and land, offered economic opportunities, and provided additional village income (Dubisch 1977) through villagers who, prior to 1940, largely viewed life in the city as a temporary strategy for survival and did not see the city itself as a permanent or ultimate residence (Sutton 1983). Villagers viewed this provisional migration as a move to another part of their environment, a move in which they kept significant ties with their home communities (Dubisch 1977). This wave of migration had the effect of spreading rural networks of familism, localism, and patronage over wider geographic areas. The interactive process that developed was a system in which migration changed urban life, which then fed back to change rural life (Sutton 1983; Southall 1973). Subsequently, greater regional disparities appeared between developed and less-developed areas. With second-generation migrants, gaps grew between the city and the countryside, as these networks drew people out of the villages more often than they returned services to it (Sutton 1983). Greeks of the diaspora, by contrast, actively supported the urban areas of Greece they covered state deficits, invested in the economy, and contributed to private education (Vermeulen 1983). With the great inflow of Greeks from the exterior, Greek cities thus faced a massive social dislocation.

It is important here to specify our discussion of Greek cities. First, smaller cities differed in critical ways from larger economic centers such as Athens. Those that did not experience a large influx of migrants remained largely provincial, whereas those that accepted migration came to have as much as 50 percent of their population made up of migrant groups. Truly urban centers were reduced to a handful— Athens-Piraeus, Salonika, Patras, Volos, Larissa, and Kaválla—with Athens as the center of activity and the focus of mass migration. None of these cities were highly industrialized, for the same forces were at work here as in politically dependent nations: centralization, dependence on foreign government, and lack of economic development (Sutton 1983). Nevertheless, migration was to set off a process that reinforced the processes set in motion by the creation of a Greek state. It contributed to a centralized state, decreased local power, shifted the population balance to industrial centers, and led to fuller participation of peasants in the political systems of the new state, thus basically reinforcing the new system without substantively challenging its inequities.

One could argue that, to some extent, the rural-urban continuum facilitated stable growth of the city and that the rural traditions and systems used by migrants in their neighborhoods, voluntary associations, and social networks maintained among them a sense of stability and continuity that diffused their sense of alienation or isolation in the urban context and permitted them to adapt gradually, over several decades, and with little dislocation from their rural bases. Migrants expanded kinship patterns first into the suprafamilies of their neighborhoods and then created new spiritual kinships through work, school, church, and intermarriage with other neighborhoods (Sutton 1983). Gradually they separated from the political patronage networks of their villages, but without changing their political ideology or reorganizing politically in the city. The political shifts that were to occur came first among their children and later and more significantly among Anatolian refugees who had no networks in the cities and no ties to home villages.

In sum, what we find in Greek cities from 1870 to 1928, the period of critical importance for the development of the Karagiozis performance, is not a whole community with high moral density—agreement and conformity with norms and customary patterns of behavior (Southall 1973)—but social life that occurs in small universes (Lewis 1965, 1973), neighborhoods that break the city into small cohesive communities that rely on adaptation of traditional systems for survival (Hauser 1965a; Southall 1973). The city was ethnically heterogeneous, and the lower class had more in common with village groups than it had with other groups or classes in the city, so that the urban and rural poor could be considered in many ways part of the same system (Lewis 1965, 1973; Southall 1973).[3] The middle and upper classes, distinguished by education or wealth, were certainly more urbanized than the poor. Clearly, the poor did not share with them the status of birth, the power of wealth, or the prestige of intellectual or professional pursuits; this suggests a stratified society (Hauser 1965b).

The heterogeneity of the Greek city was founded on two processes:

the formation of little villages within the city as regional neigh-
borhoods, cooperative within themselves but reflecting the ghettoiza-
tion of the city as a whole (Gulick 1975), and the use of the city as a
rural resource with continuous feedback between rural and urban
areas. This heterogeneity is not class- but ethnically based (Lewis
1965, 1973), both through internal migration and its maintenance of
regionally associated neighborhoods and through the return of Greeks
of the diaspora from Anatolia and Egypt (and later from Germany,
Australia, South Africa, the United States, and Canada).[4] Discrimina-
tion against and isolation of these migrant groups ensured their co-
hesiveness and prevented homogeneity within the city as a whole. Two
forces ensured heterogeneity. First, the lack of economic development
in Greek cities made it unlikely that simple, self-sufficient commu-
nities would be absorbed into a larger society of high moral density.
Second, continuity with rural life in towns rapidly swollen with local
migrant groups made identification with urban life difficult. With
clear divisions between these ethnically diverse groups, a form of
urban tribalization becomes more likely. With unstable economic
class or social status and the presence of clientage, populism develops
in which ethnic division rather than class is again favored as an
organizing principle (Barnton 1973). Finally, it becomes clear that
heterogeneity is based on an urban pluralism sponsored by varying
village-based reactions to the new urban context. Different origins
gave rise to different urban adaptations, ranging from greater degrees
of urban identification to greater insistence on traditional patterns of
behavior as a means of survival. These responses cannot be said to
have arisen entirely in response to the urban environment (Suzuki
1964; Keyser 1975). As Sutton (1988) has made clear, community
unity or urban homogeneity had no basis in Greek village life for yet
another reason. Because villages emptied and were created over time
in rural Greece—an ongoing process for several centuries—integra-
tion of families into any community was largely provisional. Families
clearly differed in their loyalty to the village. Moreover, there is no
question that family loyalties preceded community loyalties.

In the face of change, however, cities had to prove capable of
integrating diverse or heterogeneous forms into what has been called
diversity in proximity (Moore 1975). This integration creates out of
multiple cultures a distinct urban level of culture. In these terms, the
city does not weaken or continue rural cultures but represents another

identity. We can look at the city as a process of developing an equilibrium between a pool of cultures, identified essentially as lower-class ethnic subcultures, within the context of the urban setting, structure, and process. The critical factor for this study is that Karagiozis, if it is urban folklore, must express the tension of the heterogeneous groups that make up the urban environment (Laba 1979).

In the urban context, folklore operates within the constraints of a social system that does not itself constitute a whole shared cultural meaning but in which subcultures exist with their own shared symbols and meanings. Because folklore is not merely an alternative reality but a process, it is important to understand how it functions in the urban context. Is it an equilibrium of conflicting subcultures? A mechanical equilibrium assumes a mechanism that, once disturbed, returns to its original state. It ignores friction within the system and fails to acknowledge the influence of outside forces (Turner 1968). Moreover, it assumes that catastrophes do not happen within the system. Is the function of folklore, then, to resolve, or even to integrate, cultural conflicts? Resolution assumes some form of reduction of conflict, and integration assumes the ability of subcultures to interface; both prospects are made less likely by the cohesiveness and separateness of the ethnic and regionally based cultures we find in the city (Hymes 1967).

An alternative prospect, capitalizing on the features of a cybernetic system in which both order and change, equilibrium and disequilibrium, play equal parts, seems more promising (Turner 1968). Here, two directions of movement, change and restoration to a steady state, prove responsive to the nature of the rural-urban continuum. Finally, the backward-and-forward interaction along that continuum is paralleled by input, gain, and feedback features. This dynamic model of the interactive process of popular culture shows promise as well for explaining transformational issues that have been elsewhere described as resolved by the imposition of a dominating, hegemonic, elite order. We can speak, rather, of a variety of interpenetrating force fields rife with struggle that lead not to a balance or power or the forceful imposition of power, but to an imbalance that then leads to continuing adaptations, interdependence, and change.

In this sense, the truest understanding of popular culture is as a pluralistic dialectic between different subcultures (Bakhtin 1981). Popular culture thus represents, rather than an ideology of fixed meanings, a polylogue between several meanings that express the true heterogeneity of the social forms themselves rather than the mere content of their symbolic expressions. In this sense, popular culture relates itself to several other internal structures that inform it and with which it is engaged. It is not merely embedded in a simple oppositional relationship to a ruling class culture (Frow 1986).

Now we can begin to determine whether there was sufficient urban development or a city culture sufficiently unique to be called urban in Greece at the time the Karagiozis performance is thought to have established itself as an urban form. In particular, in relation to Kiurtsakis's argument about the urban nature of the Karagiozis performance, we must determine whether conditions were present to enable the development of a proletarian class in the Greek city. Alternatively, it is important to consider whether cities might not have been basically large villages or combinations of villages, peasant cities so continuous with rural culture that to call them urban in Kiurtsakis's sense would be misleading.

Applying our analysis to an understanding of Karagiozis as urban folklore, we find that several themes emerge from our general outline. The city is not treated by migrants as a negative, hostile, alienating force that stands in a dichotomous relationship with rural life. The continuity between rural and urban worlds is expressed by traditionally based subcultures that establish themselves as village islands in the urban landscape to create a heterogeneous, pluralistic world that does not form a unified class of the urban poor. Nor does it stand in a clearly oppositional relationship with the urban elite.

The urban Karagiozis audience was essentially made up of city peasants from a second wave of rural migration that entered into established kinship networks. Audience members did not possess wealth, education, or social status. Taking jobs much like those they had in the village, they did not become part of an urban proletariat. The Karagiozis audience at the height of the Karagiozis performance (1910-40) was only provisionally a part of the city, not only because permanent migration had not yet become a dominant pattern but also because the social dislocation of the Asia Minor Disaster made stability from 1920 to 1928 itself provisional. Only gradually over this time period did urban Greeks begin to expand and then separate from their traditional networks. Only gradually did patronage, kinship, and family systems become significantly modified. Only with the impetus of the Asia Minor refugees did political shifts begin that were ultimately to be long-lasting.

It is clear from our discussion that the essential conditions for complete or systemic urbanization were not present in Greek cities during this period.[5] Role differentiation and specialization and division of labor had only a partial or patchy effect on the city, just as the possibilities for integration and centralization were limited. Karagiozis capitalized on its audience's regional differences, its rich pluralism, its populism, its heterogeneity. Rural and urban values were shared in the performance through a common sense of family, kinship, status, and patronage structures. In this respect, the Karagiozis performance maintained a parochial rather than an urban perspective, capitalizing on the villages within the city and only tentatively acknowledging the urban changes forced on Greek society. Karagiozis thus stood as an incorporative statement of both the interdependence of the rural and urban worlds and the heterogeneity of urban life within the larger national culture. The debate between official and unofficial culture, between elite and popular ideologies, took place within this urban context.

It is useful here to consider why some cultural critics regard Karagiozis as urban folklore of the proletarian class. Was it because its Turkish progenitor, Karagoz, grew up in Istanbul, which by the sixteenth century had reached a population of 700,000? But Karagoz was not exclusive to the Turkish capital; it maintained rich points of contact in its truest origin, court and popular festivals held throughout Ottoman lands. Thus it is linked more appropriately to popular culture in a more general, even rural, sense. Was it because Karagoz was extensively performed in the city and used the format of the city quarters as its setting? But that setting itself illustrated the concept of villages in a city, that is, of an elaborated market town rather than an industrialized urban center. Was it because Karagoz was sexually and politically free-thinking? But such free-thinking was itself an attribute of rural carnivals or popular festivals, of unofficial popular culture, and not specifically attributable to an urban center.

Karagoz spread into Ottoman-held Greek lands; the first recorded instance of this occurred in 1799. Its history of players touring throughout the countryside belies again the notion of the performance identified with an originary urban base. Pluralized through wide travel and its itinerant nature in the countryside, the transformed performance, now Greek Karagiozis, may have been easily adaptable to the urban environment of Greek towns and cities without having grown out of an urban folk culture. Certainly the itinerant history of the Greek form in Greece after the revolution of 1821, as well as the village status of Greek cities up through 1870 and until 1896, does not suggest a convincing picture of the urban develpment of the Greek performance as originally, or even essentially, an urban form (Myrsiades and Myrsiades 1988).

Finally, the Karagiozis performance in its final twentieth-century stage of development was characterized by the addition of an urban stationary style to supplement its earlier provincial touring style. The urban style did not, however, develop until urban centers had sufficient population density to support a full summer season. Players then settled for long periods in one location and developed a full repertoire of performance texts. Individualization of performance styles developed, competition increased, theaters grew up, and the performance stabilized in its new urban location. Evidence of the establishment of such theaters and the subsequent development of an urban performance style dates from about 1920, when Antonios Mollas had established himself in Athens and successfully exploited neighborhood audiences there. Not until 1920 did a sufficient number of theaters emerge in Athens to support a variety of permanent urban players, and not until 1930 did players themselves maintain their own permanent theaters in any numbers (Myrsiades 1988a). Audiences grew from an average size of 200 to 300 in the 1910s to as many as 800 to 1,000 in the 1920s. Published scripts began to appear in significant numbers from 1924 to 1930; as many as 400 may have been put into print during this period. The repertoire expanded rapidly from an average of 10 to 20 performance texts in 1910 to 40 to 60 in 1930 and ultimately to at least 150 to 200 works by 1940. By 1930 a four-month summer season was possible, and it eventually grew to a six-month season extending from Easter through October.

Some might argue that the earlier touring style was essentially urban. Indeed, it originated in the coastal city of Patras and was performed in Corinth, Volos, Larissa, Kalamata, Tripoli, Argos, Lamia, Pyrgos, and Préveza. But such cities remained essentially provincial towns up through the end of the nineteenth century. Moreover, they served as geographic reference points from which players developed tours of surrounding towns and villages. Indeed, a number of players depended for their livelihood on a few nights in villages and towns rather than on extended stays in provincial cities right up through the early decades of the twentieth century.

In discussions of its function as urban folklore, scholars have compared Karagiozis favorably with a form, *rebetika,* that has itself been widely accepted as true urban folklore. Rebetika reached their zenith in essentially the same time period as did the Karagiozis performance. Many of the songs were recorded in the 1930s, essentially during the same period that the Karagiozis performances were being published. By 1936 the rebetika had to pass censorship. During the German occupation of World War II, none were recorded, and after the war systematic commercialization ensured that by 1955 the original spirit of the rebetika had been lost and the songs were incorporated into the superficial tradition of urban popular music (Petropoulos 1975). Parallel developments in the Karagiozis performance included the proliferation of pirated and commercialized texts, censorship by the occupation government, and the devolution of the form to a children's performance.

Until the late nineteenth century, differences between the music of urban and rural areas were slight. Indeed, creators of rebetika had themselves been villagers who left their homes to travel to developing ports and industrial towns and who encountered disappointing and alienating urban experiences. The separation of the rebetika into a separate urban song type, away from their points of contact with Byzantine and Turkish music as well as Greek folk songs, did not, however, occur until the early twentieth century (Dragoumis 1975). What was produced with this separation was a music of the fringes presenting the symptoms of urban individualism. Erotic and bitter songs, they were accepted by neither the Greek establishment nor the middle class.

Although the songs of the rebetes have been identified as songs of the working classes by several students of the form (Petropoulos 1968; Kyriakidou-Nestoros 1976), their individualism and political indifference make them an unlikly source of proletarian attitudes or sentiments. Whereas they shared with a form like Karagiozis some understanding of the psychology of the urban poor, they represent more than anything else the psychopathology of a marginal slice of that life in its most alienated expression. Indeed, the rebetika perspective assumes a negative urban model of disorganization and social injustice, which, as we have discussed, did not describe the social life of the bulk of the urban lower classes. The lower classes may, nevertheless, have participated in such a world through their acceptance of rebetika songs.

The rebetes themselves were *manges,* or marginal figures, whose first appearances were as brigands, or *listes,* after the War of 1821 (Petropoulos 1978). By the end of the nineteenth century, when an urban class began to develop, we meet a type called the *koutsavakis,* again a marginal, sometime criminal type from the Ionian islands and Turkey. By the early twentieth century and into the 1920s, under the influence of the urban Asia Minor refugees, the rebetes were identified as clearly urban underworld figures. Rebetes lived in isolation, frequenting bordellos, drug houses, jails, and bars. They were drug addicts and prisoners who emanated from the lowest social class and resided principally in Piraeus and Athens, having originated in Syros and the Asia Minor cities.

Rebetes entertained themselves with whores, camp followers, and sexually liberated women, forswore family life even as they maintained a pathological attachment to their mothers, and expressed the ambiguity of a life lived on the edge of social existence (Petropoulos 1968). One psychoanalytic study refers to the theme that threads its way through the labyrinth of rebetic life as an impotent eroticism of uncontrolled shadows that prevented both sexual satisfaction and creative union. *Erotas* became a source of misfortune and sickness from which the rebeti wished to flee. For the rebeti, women other than his mother were crazed and faithless assassins who attacked his manhood. Narcotics, which provided the easiest release from the oppressive present, dragged the rebeti into a spiraling decline. Once augmented, sexual desire proved unstable, and the *rebeti* fell deeper into his addiction until an increased alienation from life led to a dominant instinct for death. Isolated from his surroundings in a state of paranoid and schizophrenic withdrawal, the rebeti devolved into perversion, vagrancy, and corruption (Papayiannis 1977).

Psychoanalytic examination thus presents the rebeti as a shadow figure who moves in the dark, outside of time and space, humiliated and dangerous, without a taste for life. He represents the psychosocial product of a certain limited aspect of his times, taking on many of the pathological attributes of contemporary life and marked by the despair and desperation wrought by the negative social, political, and economic pressures of his historical moment (Papayiannis 1977). Sociological analysis of the rebeti (Damianakos 1976) leads to some of the same conclusions, but with an emphasis on the collective identity expressed by the rebeti rather than his marginality and the uniqueness of his expression. In this case, rebetes were taken as an expression of the lumpen proletariat. In this perspective, rebetika had a dichotomous relationship with traditional culture, which it replaced, and was itself co-opted by mass culture in the process of commercialization. Mass culture serves as an intermediary between the unitary values of elite culture and the heterogeneity of popular culture, marketing the former through the values of the latter on behalf of a larger national culture.

Comparison of Karagiozis with rebetika as expressions of urban folk culture demonstrates that Karagiozis had a significantly longer independent existence as a defined form that did rebetika. Thus it is less likely that Karagiozis, a full century after its first appearance in Greece and several centuries after its origins in Turkey, would adopt in the 1920s a proletarian persona that represented a partial expression contradicting its holistic perspective. Moreover, the developed forms of both Karagiozis and rebetika in the twentieth century represent different kinds of responses to different experiences in the same historical period. Karagiozis assumed a view of the family neighborhoods of urban life that was broader, more heterogeneous, more integrative and incorporative, whereas rebetika accepted a negative model of urban life lived at its margins. Where rebetika lost the taste for life and escaped life's struggle, Karagiozis embraced it with a voracious appetite. The impotent sexuality of rebetika, sexuality without issue, divorced from nature and family life, is overcome by the fertile, reproductive sexual energy of the Karagiozis fool-hero, whose very nature—exemplified by his long arm, hump, and big nose, all phallic expressions—exudes sexuality. If rebetika regarded women as avenging themselves against men and saw them as objects of lust, Karagiozis regarded them as nags, scolds, disobedient daughters, and old hags, but ultimately as part of the natural order of the family. The apathy and indifference of rebetika is supplanted by an involved caring in Karagiozis, the end of which is neither jail nor death, as in the rebetika, but festivals, weddings, victory, and resurrections. If rebetika are timeless and spaceless, Karagiozis is rooted in place, very much a part of the present moment. The psychopathology of rebetika is replaced in Karagiozis by the inspired and socially enriched madness of the divine ritual fool. The darkness of the rebetika soul is balanced by Karagiozis bathed in light, in life.

Kiurtsakis's comparison of Karagiozis and rebetika requires that we accept the comic texts as an urban form that essentially reflects the proletariat's negative experience of city life in a setting characterized by class conflict. The argument of this chapter denies such a characterization for the Greek city, challenging the basis of Kiurtsakis's comparison of Karagiozis with rebetika. Karagiozis, rather, functions in the urban setting as a form of both official and unofficial culture. It is unofficial as a continuing expression of popular culture in the urban setting, and it is official insofar as it has been influenced, through the heroic texts, by forms of mass culture promulgated by the learned elite. In neither guise, however, does it serve as a negative and defeated force of individualism. Instead, it expresses heterogeneous forces of struggle, which, while they negotiate for survival, continue to turn the world on its head, unnerve the status quo, and preserve the dialectic of alternative forms that gives meaning to a more inclusive perspective that Kiurtsakis seems unwilling to allow Karagiozis in its urban expression.

Protected in villagelike enclaves, the urban Greek does not experience the degree of anonymity and estrangement described by Kiurtsakis as characteristic of the comedies. Nor is urban life deprived of some degree of collectivity, family life, and kinship networks. The differences between rural and urban life, in sum, indicate by degree and type as much continuity as they do dichotomy, certainly not the degree of alienation and isolation that is necessary to Kiurtsakis's argument. Indeed, Kiurtsakis himself appears to have accepted such a position in his description of the modern Greek city as a model of foreign control and organization imposed on a traditional social body. What he has not accepted is the contradiction offered by identifying the performance as a product of preindustrial society and as a form intimately tied to industrialization and the proletariat. In what sense can he assume the presence of a Westernized, industrialized, capitalist, class-identified proletariat in such a traditional social body? What force of history or social development allows Karagiozis to become the hero of such a proletariat? In essence, Kiurtsakis has not effectively dealt with inherent contradictions arising from the double origin of the Greek city: quantitative and qualitative changes imposed by Ottoman rule before the revolution and the European orientation of Greek cities after the revolution. Without a massive social transforma- tion, which Kiurtsakis rejects, how does one account for such radical change in urban development when the city itself is, in his terms, essentially a static place of changelessness?

Indeed, it is clear that radical transformation of the Greek city did not occur until 1922 and that until such radical transformation oc- curred, that is, until industrial capitalism was dominant in Greece, the class character of the cities was not possible. The great migration of 1922 created the necessary preconditions for industrial develop- ment of the type that would lead to the development of a proletariat by doubling Greece's population and territory, providing for an influx of foreign capital, and contributing to the development of the institu- tional framework for a transformation to a capitalist society. Until 1922 Greece was characterized by intraclass disputes emanating from a large state apparatus that oversaw a fragmented political oligarchy. This oligarchy stood at the head of an extensive patronage network that was itself based on special interest groups. The influx of massive numbers of workers into the cities in 1922 saw those disputes transformed into conflict between the masses and the dominant classes. Industrial capitalism thus shifted the political agenda of Greece from irredentism and monarchy to safeguarding the bour- geois order from the incursion of the masses into active politics (Mouzelis 1978).

Such a scenario places changes in the Karagiozis performance resulting from the economic influences of urbanization and the politi- cal influences emanating from the imposition of mass culture by the learned elite once again in the third decade of the twentieth century. Such a late development in the Karagiozis performance makes any description of the performance as essentially urban folklore, and in Kiurtsakis's case urban folklore of the proletarian class, untenable. What the transformation of the Greek city under industrial capitalism did accomplish, however, was to provide the performance with a larger audience, enable it to expand to a larger number of theaters, and allow it to resist the influences of official culture for a more extended period of time. Karagiozis might neither have originated as urban folklore nor developed as the handmaiden of urbanism, but it certainly capitalized on the growth of the city as a stable performance location and took the opportunity to generate a more substantial repertoire. Consistent with its function of negotiating heterogeneous impulses to address social conflicts, it also adapted itself to the urban environment not only by creating a responsive urban style but also by performing within the urban context interactively with its audience.

We thus find that two themes inform our understanding of Karagiozis as an urban performance: interactive feedback between rural and urban areas, and the failure of the modern Greek city to develop a rigidly Western industrialized profile. In the first instance, the Karagiozis performance proved responsive to both its rural and its urban audiences by maintaining a provincial touring style and an urban stationary performance style. The same player often performed both in different locations: in a permanent theater in the city in the summer and touring in the villages in the winter. The heterogeneity of urban neighborhoods up to the 1940s presented players with traditionally based audiences in the cities, helping to maintain, again, the interplay between urban and rural influences in the performance. This interplay ensured the continued force of the Romeic comedies and enabled the performance to resist becoming the handmaiden of the bourgeois urban elite. By contrast, however, the lack of a defined urban proletariat until late in the history of the form ensured that the performance would not become the political expression of a truly urbanized lower class.

Second, we find that to the extent that essentially urban features, such as role differentiation, division of labor, political centralization, and interdependence of the social and economic orders, did exist in Greece, they resulted in some integration of the urban subcultures, leading thereby to the development of an urban performance style that responded to the urban elite and generated an urban audience. Moreover, the presence of the urban elite in the Karagiozis audience as a secondary consumer of popular culture facilitated the performance's responsiveness to the force of the new elite as a representative of official culture through the development of Hellenic texts and themes.

Nevertheless, it is not realistic to claim, as some have, that the Karagiozis performance is a form of urban folklore, for neither did it originate in an urban setting nor did it stand as a homologue for urban reality. It is, rather, more appropriately described as a discourse that embodies the alterity of urban and rural forms, accepting their differences but expressing as well the interactive nature of their dialogue. Indeed, the source of the richness of the Karagiozis performance rests in its incorporative and not its exclusionary nature as a statement, in its symbolic reality as the grounds on which the larger social dialectic is acted out, or, as Marx put it in another context, as the sack in which the potatoes are kept (see Hirschkop 1986).

CHAPTER THREE
Gender in Karagiozis

Official and unofficial ideologies have been described as gender-based. Muted official culture is identified with the passive female orientation of Ottoman domination. Limited to the private world of the domestic domain, it represents the inner world of self-knowledge, that which a culture admits only to itself. Dominant official culture is identified with the active male, Eurocentric world of postliberation Greece. Extended to the public social world, it represents the outer world of self-presentation, the honor that a culture exhibits to outsiders (Goffman, 1959; Herzfeld 1987). Maintaining ties between such dichotomies as that between official and unofficial culture and other levels of analysis, including the family, kinship relationships, and village and urban life, enables us to link male and female relationships to larger social issues.[1] The linkage of male-female, honor-shame, public-private, and exterior-interior can thus be extended to the disparate images posed by the Hellenic and Romeic models.

In the Romeic guise of the Karagiozis comedies, not only are women restricted to the domestic sphere, but they are denied the cultural recognition that comes with access to the public sphere of social action. Men, presumed to be more powerful than women, monopolize positions of authority in formal institutions. Since women wield power informally, without directly participating in these institutions, and since they assume responsibility for child-rearing, they are not accepted into adult activities, nor are they acknowledged as adults until their old age.[2] Their world is thus largely restricted to that of their female kin and the associations they build up among other women.

In the Hellenic expression of the heroic Karagiozis texts, the position of women as wives and mothers is presented positively and is culturally valued both within and without the domestic domain. Here, where women have control over resources or make the same contribution to subsistence production as men, their status is higher. When women assert power beyond the domestic domain, it often occurs in the absence of the male in the subsistence sphere, so that women are forced to ensure the family's social survival. We find this in the heroic texts when men leave home and escape to the mountains to fight for the liberty of the homeland. A positive legitimated change in female status occurs in public life in terms of female control over resources, the importance or demand for female goods, the political participation of female actors, and cultural recognition of female solidarity groups or alliances (Sanday 1974).

In the Karagiozis comedies, however, where male status in the large society is low, as occurs with workers and peasants who must serve a boss or where men are not much more autonomous in the public realm than women are (Ardener 1981), female solidarity in the domestic domain becomes a significant unauthorized force (Lamphere 1974). Segregation of women being a precondition to their inequality, women are kept powerless by being kept out of the powerful arena of the public domain (Sanday 1974). Nevertheless, the domestic domain itself represents a source of power, albeit not a legitimate one (du Boulay 1986). Thus power takes on two forms: culturally legitimate authority in the public sphere, which is acknowledged and which is largely proscribed for women in the Romeic guise (it is not, in any case, accepted as the norm), and the informal power to gain compliance in the private sphere, which is not acknowledged and which women in the Romeic guise exercise. It is clear, however, that without an assertive male presence, women's power in the household extends by default into the community at large through such mechanisms as their ability to control information, influence public opinion, and mediate between neighborhood and kin groups (Dimen 1986; Friedl 1967; Rogers 1975).[3] In the comedies, where decisions are made by avoiding legitimately constituted institutions and where, as a result, informal structures can have great importance, women become key informal actors (Friedl 1967). Particularly when "real" power is thought to lie outside the community, informal power becomes an important infrastructure in the peasant context (Rogers 1975). In this sense, women have access to the only effective channel of power open to villagers, and women, holding a good deal of informal influence and power, mitigate the influences of culturally legitimated male authority (Rosaldo 1974).

In the Romeic perspective, the symbolic power of men, maintained in the myth of male dominance, is thus overestimated (Rogers 1975) and has little relevance in the everyday world. In fact, male dominance in daily life is an appearance that neither men nor women believe represents the actual situation. Nevertheless, each sexual group behaves as if it believes the other accepts the myth as reality. But since most important interactions occur in the face-to-face contact of community life and since in peasant society the domestic unit is of primary economic, political, and social importance, informal, indirect forms of power represent a force at least as significant as formal, authorized forms of power. Moreover, male authority does not exhaust available means of acquiring and using power, for while men may hold legitimate authority, women hold unassigned powers that result in shaping events, exerting pressure, controlling information, and giving rewards (Rosaldo 1974; Lamphere 1974).

Prevailing perceptions about gender roles in the Karagiozis comedies lead to the treatment of women as the "other." That is, they are excluded from the male world of articulated social differences, and they gain status only through their association with men. Moreover, whereas men achieve rank and are individualized as the result of explicit achievements, women's differences, seen as the product of such idiosyncratic characteristics as temperament, personality, and appearance (Rosaldo 1974), do not liberate them from being seen in generalized terms as a collective group. Men participate in the larger social world, whereas women are considered irrelevant to the formal social order. Since men define the social order, women in the comedies are understood as a threat to that order and are regarded as anomalies. Because the social system rarely accounts for their interests and because their power is opposed to formal norms (Collier 1974), women are seen as deviants (Tiffany 1984). Indeed, the more omnipotent male authority is, the more it is threatened by women (Denich 1974). Thus men project conflicts among men onto women so that they can deal with them in ways less subversive of the dominant group.

The community thus regards the exercise of power by women as either a trivial activity (Dubisch 1986) or an illegitimate interference, not as an integral force. Women's greatest power, their sexuality, has the greatest potential to threaten men's honor, if it is not controlled, at the same time that it has the greatest potential to support it, if it is disciplined by shame. It does so by either lending the male reputation and prestige—the recognition of honor by others—or denying it

(Campbell 1966). Since the family is seen as having been instituted by God, that which corrupts marriage or kinship is identified as the work of the devil. Pollution, as a result, is woman's responsibility, for she is viewed as naturally predisposed to evil and, like Eve, responsible for man's fall.

Honor is not, in any case, isolated as a gender issue in the comedies. It is an economic issue as well. In the village, honor has been described as dependent upon numbers and wealth, so that extremely poor families are denied the recognition of honor (Campbell 1966), leading to the insecurity of the nuclear family in the village reputation hierarchy. This insecurity leads to agons of honor (Péristiany 1976), for the conceptual framework of the village is based on obligations of families linked by honor (Péristiany 1966). In this context, male culture acts to restrain the potentially destructive force of unrestrained female sexuality as a means of ensuring social organization (Hirschon 1978). This process is protected by passing women from the protection of the father to that of the husband with little exposure to the outside world. Only with the advent of marriage does feminine sexuality "open." In the same way, women are permitted a fuller use of space, for they are now permitted limited access to certain outdoor areas, including the village fountain and cemetery. Women must, however, continue to seek access to the outside world largely through their husbands or risk bringing shame to the family by shaming him. This is both a source of power for women and a threat against men, who are thereby encouraged to accord women greater authority in the domestic domain (Hirschon 1978).[4]

Although men are accorded the function of controlling nature and expressing culture, they are themselves permitted to exhibit uncontrolled sexuality and violence. The charter for male behavior in the Romeic view of the comedies allows men a freedom and lack of confinement that stands in striking contrast to the code adopted for women (du Boulay 1986). As long as the house is secure, men are permitted great latitude in the expression of their sexuality without undermining their spiritual superiority to women. Women are considered responsible for men's desires, since they arouse them, and must take steps to control their physical allure. Women are regarded as able to control their sexual drive, whereas men respond to a physiological imperative over which they have no control (Hirschon 1978). There are, however, limits to this freedom, for just as women are constrained by a code of obedience to men, so must men serve the honor of the house. Their failings are put in the context of the responsibility they bear, and their weaknesses, because they affect male influence in the public sphere, are given a value not accorded those of women (du Boulay 1986). In any case, the faults of men never justify those of women, who are considered both cursed by the innate weakness of Eve and responsible for the excess of men.

As a facet of the larger social discourse, "female" is, finally, identified with "low" Romeic characteristics: cunning, illiteracy, intimacy, closeness to nature, lack of control, privacy, and concealment. This identity is closed off, shielded from outsiders as it speaks of national inferiority and subordination (Hirschon 1978). Through Eve, women are linked to the fall of the Greeks at the hands of the Turks. There exists at both the local and national levels of this disemic structure (Herzfeld 1986, 1987) an ambiguity that allows the Romeic (female) to subvert the Hellenic (male) order, just as the Greeks (males) subverted Turkish (female) rule, leading to paradoxical role changes. In the least ambiguous statement of this oppositional view, women's fallen state speaks analogically to the fallen state of mankind in general.

Karagiozena, or Aglea, the voracious protector of home and brood, represents the dominant Romeic female role in the comic Karagiozis performance, as well as the most substantial statement about women made by the performance as a whole. Karagiozena functions as a central point to which the audience refers itself in its judgment of the other female figures. As the female counterpart to Karagiozis, she is at the hub of a wheel within his larger wheel, the domestic circle of a concentric series of social circles. She prides herself on being a *nikokira,* mistress of the house, an economical homemaker, and mother hen. But she is seen by both her husband and the male world outside her home as a jealous nag, an aggressive personality with a false sense of her own social rank, and a woman of loose morals whose husband, in the end, must be content with the cuckold's horns.

Deeply rooted in the harsh, earthy world of the common class, Karagiozena has adopted a survivor's psychology that is pragmatic and self-aggrandizing. One means of survival is to convince the world of one's social standing or status. Whereas Karagiozis's solution to that problem is to trick his betters in situations where he can effect a status reversal (as a pretend dragon-slayer, doctor, or magician or in a contest of wits), Karagiozena simply bullies the weak, asserting superior rank where no real difference in rank exists. In Kostas Kareklas's *Gossip,* she brushes aside neighborhood women to take a place at the well and beats them when they complain.

With her value tied to her family's fortune and not to her own inherent worth, the married woman, through Karagiozena, soon becomes identified as the cause of domestic discord and the bane of a man's existence. She is the butt of snide remarks and sexual humor. A possession, she is of value only as a reflection of her husband's worth. Indeed, she appears almost exclusively in scenes with her spouse, borrowing his social space. As a sign of the arbitrary manner in which she is regarded, Karagiozis's comment "Better a woman lose her eye than her name" can be considered typical. Once more, a woman's inherent worth is denied as a relevant issue.

Like her social value, Karagiozena's sexual value is identified with property. The challenge to her womanhood centers not on her role as a mother or housekeeper—functions that she performs well—but on her reputation as a faithful wife. In this capacity she can most add to or detract from the social stock of her male consort. It is here that Karagiozena performs poorly, particularly in those plays in which the Turkish influence is still strongly felt. That the most despised of men in this Christian culture, a Jew, is introduced as her lover in Vasilis Vasilaros's *Karagiozis in America* and that her behavior is spoken of in the Turkish pasha's palace itself are evidence of the serious light in which her indiscretion is held. Indeed, the Jew, one of the regular figures in the Karagiozis troupe, is murdered in Karagiozena's bed by an irate Karagiozis, and his body is dumped into the street like a dog's. Karagiozena is returned to Karagiozis's regime.

While Karagiozena's sexual exploits are decried in the performance, Karagiozis's are indulged. In Dimitris Basios's *Karagiozis Don Juan,* the humpback goes directly from a quarrel with his wife to a garden tryst with several young women. In the same player's *Karagiozis Exiled,* this strangely attractive grotesque is conspired against and ultimately exiled because of his success with a rival's girlfriend. In spite of having repudiated Karagiozis's rights as a husband, Karagiozena demonstrates in Markos Xanthos's *Karagiozis Fisherman* that she is both jealous and paranoid:

Karagiozena: So, who's this woman? What do you want with her, you?
Karagiozis: Just wait a minute, wife. Hold off with your jealousy and look
   after the woman, and let's see if there's time for us to save her.
Kara.: Get out of my way so I can take a look. Bah, she's wet, too? How
   come? *(She revives the girl and tries to chase Karagiozis away.)*
Kar.: Don't be frightened here, Mamsell.
Kara.: Shut up, you mutt! Would you look at him. Get out of here; there's
   nothing for you to do here. Would you look at him. Get out of here.
Kar.: Just a minute, wife. Why should I get out?
Kara.: Get out, you! What is it you want, eyeing first one woman and then
   another, you old orangutan!
Kar.: Aha! Jealous again, eh, wife?
Kara.: Get out, I tell you, or I'll take off my belt and let you have it . . .
Hariyie: Who saved me [from drowning]? Who might this good man be?
Kar.: Moi, miss.
Kara.: He's married, lady. He's my husband.
Kar.: And who asked you, you misshapen slipper, if I'm married or not?
Kara.: Pipe down, you. No one's talking to you. Do me the favor. Would
   you look at him.
Kar.: No, I won't. Damn you, bitch!
Har.: Madame, don't carry on like this. Don't worry about your husband.
   Nothing is going to happen.

Karagiozena's jealousy is, nevertheless, justified. The Karagiozis
figure, after all, revives the classical mime fool, with whom he is
irretrievably associated, and is thus tied to a whole set of psychological
attributes that enhance his sexual appeal. His baldness is associated
with animal cunning, and his humpback with good fortune, as an
antidote to both the evil eye and abusive authority. Considered divinely
touched in their madness and immune to social criticism, fool-heroes
are permitted significant freedoms in the folk tradition on which
Karagiozis feeds. Their understood powers to perform miraculous
deeds and, most important, to serve as fertility figures make them a
powerful focus of male virility for their audience. A description of the
Turkish prototype, Karagoz, by Gustave Flaubert in 1858 in his *Voyage
en Orient* reaffirms this aspect of the hero's powers: "Quant au
Carragheuss, son pénis ressemblant plutot à une poutre; ca finissait
par n'être plus indecent. Il y en a plusieurs, Carragheuss, je crois le
type en décadence. Il s'agit seulement de montrer le plus possible de
phallus. Le plus grand avait un grelot qui, à chaque mouvement de
riens, sonnait cela faisant beaucoup de rire" (552). While the Greek

puppet figure does not wear the phallus he inherited, through Karagoz, from his classical predecessors—it was eliminated in the mid–nineteenth century—phallic humor still surfaces throughout the Greek comedies and histories. Karagiozis is, for example, characterized by a servant girl in Antonios Mollas's *Karagiozis Count* as possessing "such a nose" as never was seen on Praxiteles' statues. In modern performances, Karagiozis uses his leg as well to play on the lost organ; he shakes hands and attacks enemies with it in grand sexual salutes that reinforce the figure's primitive association with ancient fertility figures.

Karagiozena, in the end, is both denigrated and overwhelmed by Karagiozis. She proves not quite so immovable an object as he, in his archetypal fluidity, is an irresistible force. Karagiozis has, after all, been described by the master player Antonios Mollas (1963) as he who is everything and everywhere. The embodiment of the Greek people in all its varied phases, he is unsurpassable. It is unlikely in the male-dominated world of the comedies that so reality-bound a figure as the married nag could match him.

As long as Karagiozena is dependent upon Karagiozis for her family honor, the attributes she most deeply values—honesty, hospitality, and a sense of shame—remain inaccessible to her. She finds Karagiozis an unfortunate foil: lazy where she is tireless, spendthrift where she is economical, irrational where she is pragmatic. A brutal father, shameless husband, and, ultimately, a home wrecker to her homemaker, he insists tyrannically on his rights as a husband. In Ioannis Mustakas's *Karagiozis, the Seven Beasts, and Alexander the Great,* Karagiozis finds, nevertheless, that he is married to a woman who refuses the submissive role of wife:

Karagiozis: Wife, quickly, bring me the new old frock coat I grabbed off of Delapatridi.
Aglaia: Here, take it.
Kar.:   *(He takes it, unfolds it, and sees it's missing a piece from the lower part.)* Good. Hey, what's with the piece that's missing, over here; who tore it?
Agl.:   I did, my good man. I cut a piece to clean the frying pan.
Kar.:   The hell you say! Never mind, now you've ruined me; you'll pay for this. *(He takes the coat and wears it.)* Bring me the high hat I grabbed off of Dimopraterio.
Agl.:   Oh, no! I put the cat in it to give birth, Karagiozis; it's her time.

Kar.:   Goddamn it, you shrew! Run, throw her out, and bring me the hat so I
don't beat you black and blue. Can you believe it, she put the cat in it to give
birth because it's her time!

Karagiozena's domestic role in Basios's *Karagiozis Don Juan* takes
on a combative function, with Karagiozis as the enemy and their
children as her allies.

Karagiozena: You good-for-nothing, faceless, useless tramp, you're deter-
mined to destroy us! You worthless bum; I haven't had a decent day since I
married you! You used up my youth, lined me up with a lot of kids, and
now that you turned me into half a human, you ask for change. Bum,
whoremaster, parasite.

Kolitiris: She's right, you. You sleeps from morning to night. My guts are
rumbling from hunger, and I'm going to take a bite off your hump.

Karagiozis: Shaddup, you footstool for my feet, family joke! You'll bite my
hump!

Skorpios: Hey you, why don't you bring us food, Pops? I'm hungry, and I'm
gonna eat your eye.

Kar.:   Good God, what's happening to me, the poor wretch? Is this a family
or a tribe of cannibals? Eh, you, damn your hide. Didn't I bring you bread
and fifty drams of olives the day before yesterday? Did you eat it already?
Since you're nothing but a garbage dump, what can I do?

Kara.:   Listen, you, what are people going to say if they hear you?

Kar.:   They'll say I'm a terrific provider and take care of my family.

Kol.:   With one little piece of bread a week?

Skor.:   And fifty drams of olives?

Kar.:   Listen, you, it's science that's responsible for your maggot diet. Keep
your stomach light and your head cold, as the saying goes. What do you
want, to become liverish and your belly bloated like a balloon? Is that what
you want?

Kara.:   It's not food that makes you that way. It just serves your purpose to
say so. But here's a saying that doesn't serve your purpose. It goes like this:
Food makes big, strong kids.

Kar.:   Will you look at them how they go on about food! Get lost, the lot of
you. All of you go to the devil, you boors. Your brains are just slaves to your
stuffed bellies.

Skor.:   I don't want to go anywhere. I'm just hungry. I'm gonna go steal a
chicken from a neighbor, and say you did it, and they'll put you in the
cooler.

Kar.:   There you have it. Where there's a son, there's gold! And what will you do then, you mini-me, if they put your darling father in the pen? Who'll take care of you? Who's going to teach you to become socially useful?

Kara.: Now I've heard just about everything! You, the cultured one? And you want to teach your kids besides. Ach, my fine friend? So this is the house that Jack built, with words!

Kar.: I'm not interested in what Jack does. He might have money and enjoy building up and tearing down. Me, I'm not Jack. I'm just an honest worker who struggles for my family's bread.

Kol. Will you look at that. And he can keep a straight face besides.

Kara.: You two-faced snake!

Kar.: You goat!

Kara.: Ah, get lost, will you. You've got a lot of guts!

Kar.: Genovefa!⁵

Kol.: Speak for yourself, you. My mother's not an elephant. You are; you have the nose of a freighter.

Kar.: Will you look at the two of them, mother and son, declaring war on me! Shoo, the both of you. Let me stew in my darkness, and don't shake my circles.⁶ Damn it to hell! Git, go to hell, the both of you.

Skor.: You go to hell!

Kar.: What hell, you? You little scum. This is hell right here.

Kara.: And what have you done that's so good?

Kar.: Then live in your hell. I'm going to paradise, where I'll find a virgin and eat pilaf, as the Turk's Koran says.

Karagiozena's interaction with her husband is reduced to matters of purely primal concern—bitter quarrels over food, debts, and shelter. Refusing to obey her husband, she minimizes and demeans him, but she is herself demeaned, first by virtue of her class status (she comes from a poor family) and second by the inequality of her sex. Both factors contribute to her low property value in Xanthos's *Karagiozis Coal-Dealer:*

Kolitiris: Mom, leave this fool and take another old man, a handsome one.

Karagiozis: You see what your dear son says? Who knows what secrets he's hiding there?

Karagiozena: It's outrageous, I tell you, it's obscene to talk like that! You've used me up, scoundrel. Damn the day I met you.

Kar.: Oh yeah, it's really unjust, you the daughter of a lord.

Kara.: So I'm not the daughter of a lord. I'm poor, but honest. Now all of a sudden I'm not good enough for you. Now you want to go looking for others. You used up my dowry, and now you're trying to do away with me, you bastard, but your wish ain't going to come true.

Kar.:   Oh, shut up! As your husband, I forbid you to speak. When the husband speaks, the husbandess must listen, blindly. I ate your dowry! Get that now, friend, the smallest thing brings up the dowry, and all together what I got was two broken tripods, which I even had to fix, two backgammon boards, a soldier's blanket, a pillow and a sawdust mattress, three clay plates, a wooden spoon, two bent forks, and a pot. And then she wants to talk about my dowry!

Kara.:   Why don't you mention the cash? That doesn't serve your purpose.

Kar.:   By golly, you've got a point there, wife. I got a whole hundred drachmas, too.

Kara.:   You just don't have the face to admit it.

Kar.:   Wife, into your boudoir, quickly, strumpet, frumpet, humpit, apoplexy and cataplexy. Go in immediately, so I don't murder you. *(She goes in, muttering.)* Boy, does she get on my nerves. I'm going to be sick from all this. I might as well go in, too, since I made her feel bad, the poor thing.

Karagiozena's refusal to obey Karagiozis is the result of his failure as a provider. It is this failure that leads her to minimize and demean him in Xanthos's *Karagiozis Baker.*[7]

Karagiozis: *(Coming out.)* Goddamn it, damn it to hell. What kind of luck is this, my friend, that I can't even sleep peacefully like a man for an hour. From morning to night, all kinds of people are on me; no one will give me any peace, not even for five minutes an hour. All my creditors come—the baker, the grocer, the tavern keeper, the cobbler, the tailor, the barber— and what do they want, I ask you? And you'd think it'd be over once I gave them what I owe. And did I tell them I wouldn't give it to them? Certainly not! Gentlemen, I owe you it. Write it down. And if I don't pay up, leave it written down until it's erased. And so it takes three to four hours arguing with my creditors. Then, as soon as my droopy eyes begin to droop, the mosquitoes, the bedbugs begin, the fleas begin, and so with all this fuss, it takes two to three more hours. In short, all night! In the morning, then, I wake up, eh! Like the provider I am, I have to ask my wife what food we should cook. "Shall we get potatoes, wife?" Then you have to listen to her, "Oph! We had them yesterday, you wretch." "Shall we get beans, wife? Shall we get this, shall we get that?" "No, no, no, no!" As if it's a question, friend, of paying money. I'm not saying we would buy these things, certainly, but what can you do without money? Now listen, let me tell you a strange thing. Listen to a meal I told her to cook, and she didn't like it. My son and I went and gathered all the gasoline cans we could find so we could fill them up with thirty melon blossoms, and after we gathered them, I sent them to the house. The lady of the house didn't like that food. "So that's the way you're gonna be!" I say. And so I sit back and gobble up the blossoms and leave them hungry all day as punishment.

Karagiozena: (*Comes out with Kolitiris.*) Aren't you ashamed, you poor wretch, to sit here and talk for all the world to hear the secrets of your house? Aren't you ashamed?

Kolitiris: She's right, you tramp.

Kar.:   Shaddup, you son of a home owner.

Kol.:   Go to hell, you laundry thief.

Kar.:   Hey, you, if I get you in my hands, it'll take forty ranks of flies and ten divisions of sixty hand-picked fleas in each to unstick you.

Kara.:   Aren't you ashamed, Karagiozis, you wretch, to fight with a little kid? It's a little embarrassing.

Kol.:   She's right, you chicken thief.

Kar.:   (*Impulsively going to hit Kolitiris.*) Hey, shut up, you lazy bum!

Kara.:   (*Interfering.*) Don't hit him. Don't you lay a hand on him, or I'll gouge your eyes out with my nails.

Kar.:   You hag!

Kara.:   Just mind what I tell you.

Kar.:   (*With a serious air.*) Wife, I forbid you to speak from the moment you find yourself in the presence of your husband.

Kara.:   You know a lot about such things. But let me tell you, it won't do you any good.

Kar.:   (*Imperiously.*) Shut up and watch I don't balance things out this instant.

Kara.:   Come on, child, let's go inside.

Kar.:   (*Soliloquizes.*) And you have people telling you "Get married and have children to find happiness." Curse the hour I married and became a slave and wasted all my youth. (*Spits.*) Phtou! Goddamn it, boy did I get nervous? I'm not going to be sick from all of this.

A family of man-eaters, the members of the Karagiozis clan cannibalize each other, living off each other's emotional flesh. The dialogue's suggestion that this "hell" is self-created and its existential implication that from such a life there is "no exit" is not, however, supported by the performance as a whole. The domestic unit, rather, merely reflects a larger social collapse (that of a nation oppressed) that has resulted in the corruption of healthy values. The son Kolitiris, for example, finds in this conflict an opportunity to achieve his own ends: he wants to expel his father from the home and to take on himself the role of family head.

The state of disrepute into which the Karagiozis household has fallen is ultimately the result of the refusal of both husband and wife to perform their respective cultural roles, thereby obviating the complementarity necessary to support family reputation and exacerbating the asymmetry of their roles. As a result, having children does not redeem Karagiozena as a mother, and marriage does not serve as her salvation as a wife. Karagiozis himself is not a good *nikokiris,* either in his own home, where he does not pay his debts and finds it fashionable to get evicted; as a servant in the bey's house, where he tricks his master and beats his master's guests; or as vizier for a day in the serai, where he abuses palace hospitality and becomes a demagogue. He is not a good father in spite of the fact that his chief concern is for the future of his household, his children: he is concerned to fulfill his fatherly responsibility but trains his sons in the family trade, thievery; he is worried at his son's fate but plans to desert him.

As Hatziavatis, Karagiozis's sidekick, makes clear, Karagiozis is condemned to a life of disrepute since he has a wife who cheats on him, a wife, worse yet, who is a mother. Karagiozis worries that, since he killed his wife's Jewish lover, the people of the marketplace will insult him rather than redeem his honor. The critical lack of public recognition of his honor leaves him dishonored by his kin—Barba Giorgos sets his dogs on Karagiozis whenever he approaches the shepherd's hut—and not respected even by his wife, who, borrowing her status from Karagiozis, thereby has none, and his children, who, socialized by Karagiozena, borrow her inferior status in the domestic domain. Thus, Barba Giorgos assumes Karagiozis's guilt and hunts him down whenever a crime is committed, Karagiozena refuses to aid him in his schemes, and Kolitiris turns him in to the authorities whenever a reward is offered.

If Karagiozis's lack of status is made clear in the comedies, it is even clearer that the source of this lack of status is poverty. Like those who come to view the performance, Karagiozis has not received his share of life's rewards. Thus he eats up his daughter's dowry, cheats religious pilgrims, tricks officials, and deceives his fellow Greeks. He "dies" to get rich from funeral gifts so his friends and debt collectors cannot claim a share, asserting that the poor cannot afford honor. Even Hatziavatis, Karagiozis's alter ego, is drawn by his poverty into Karagiozis's schemes and is deprived of his honor by a faithless wife and daughter in Vasilaros's *Karagiozis in America.*

Outside the internal domestic circle of the poor Greek family represented by Karagiozis and Karagiozena, the female figure of greatest importance in the comedies is the Turkish daughter of the bey or vizier. In the comedies, where women are treated tangentially and only as they address the question of male honor and women's threat to that honor, the premarital courting of the bey's daughter has an importance second only to Karagiozena's postmarital keeping of the home. In both cases, women are represented as willful, disobedient, conniving, and sexually promiscuous, and their activities, like Eve's, appear disorderly and unstructured.

The bey's daughter represents the unmarried virgin who must be guarded from contact with the world outside her family lest she be sexually spoiled and thereby diminish both her own exchange value in marriage matchmaking and her family's honor. The irony of engaging the fox to guard the chicken coop—Karagiozis is inevitably hired as the house servant whose sole function is to keep suitors from gaining access to her—is matched by the ease with which the cunning daughter involves Karagiozis in her own schemes to set up a rendezvous with the suitor of her choice. In the figure of the bey's daughter, women are granted a limited subject status, but they must operate indirectly through the agency of men. Their actions are deviantly erotic; Turkish girls are perversely attracted to Karagiozis, who is described, even by them, as possessing the sexuality of an orangutan. They are fickle; their loyalty to their fathers is quickly transferred to their secret lovers, and they are notably promiscuous, leading on numbers of suitors. Moreover, they are untrustworthy; they inevitably deceive their co-conspirator Karagiozis, leaving him to take the blame in texts where the lover uses a trunk to smuggle himself into the bey's home or to trap or murder the bey.

The Greek daughters of Karagiozis and Hatziavatis adopt the same approach to family life as does the bey's daughter. When their fathers pretend to leave for Germany or the United States to find work, they invite a series of lovers to their beds. Unlike the bey, however, the Greek fathers have set a trap for their daughters to expose them in public. Avenging the female insult to family honor, the revenge of the fathers in the Greek household, rather than the deception by the children in the Turkish household, becomes the primary focus. In both instances, nevertheless, women are seen as polluted and in need of male control if the household is to remain orderly and family honor is to remain intact.

The ways in which Karagiozena and the bey's daughter are regarded
are not isolated events but indicate the light in which women in general
are held in the comedies. Admittedly, women are the objects of
idealized love in the songs of the young lover, the Turkish bey, and
Hatziavatis. This is the love of romantic convention against which the
comic performance as a whole mitigates, however, and not that of
the daily life of the common man, which constitutes the substance of
the comedies. We find the latter most directly expressed by Kara-
giozis, who takes songs of blighted love and turns them to mockery.
His love, he sings in Xanthos's texts, is crippled in the foot and deaf in
the ear; whoever looks upon her starves. She wrinkles her mug like an
old goat, and whoever kisses her must wash out his mouth. In a verse
from Mustakas's *Karagiozis and the Three Spani,* Karagiozis's song
turns erotic:

> The heat started again,
> the burning, the frying,
> and so the ladies began to shed their garments.
> Hey, you, what is this heat doing to us?
> My goodness, what lunacy drives us.
> Your sweet jokes, your crazy flirting,
> the pot's boiling,
> and the old woman's shouting.

Bringing the idealized woman of romantic song down to earth with
a thud, Karagiozis in Kareklas's *Gossip* and Vasilaros's *Karagiozis in
America* cries out to the cuckolded Hatziavatis in mock-heroic style:
"To arms, to arms . . . the American prick is in your bedroom." In
Mustakas's *Karagiozis Hostage in Haidari and Germany,* he accuses
God-crazed Greek girls of polluting their native sea while cavorting
with soldiers of the German occupation. In Ianaros's *Markos Botsaris,*
he speaks of their carrying the bastards of departing foreign tourist
hordes:

> In this sinful land
> where each race landed,
> came big Germans, Italians, Arabs,
> and English, Icelanders, and Canadians.
>
> Each line was graced by an evzone,[8]
> and instant destruction,

and one could see, openly, on the road,
and publicly,
open kissing without shame. . . .

This evening I'm going to talk to you about love,
and without me being embarrassed at all
that everyone plays tricks these days;
even telling you this, I'm in love.

When the Johnnies leave, boys,
all of you get married,
so the chicks won't be deserted,
and right off you'll find
yourselves with instant children.

Yippi aye aye yippi yippi yap,
to be unmarried and have children,
black ones, English ones, a variety of little bastards,
poor things, without fathers.

The pedestal still reverberating, Karagiozis extends his attack into obscenity in Panagiotis Mihopulos's *Captain Mavrodimos:*

Greetings, my old beanbag.
Hail, old corpulent one.
Whoever eats you
is heard in all of Greece.

More grossly realistic than even Karagiozis, Stavrakas, the drug addict and harbor tough of Piraeus, takes the comic view of women into the streets, playing on the violence of life lived along the docks, in the taverns and hashish dens of Piraeus. Women in Mustakas's *Karagiozis in the Jungle* are to be taken advantage of, not admired at a distance:

Two lovely things,
potted, poor things.
One morning, I took them
lying in the sand.

By the sea, in the sand,
I've got the hashish pipe.
I come there every day, my little one,
so we can feel the pain of love.

Chivalric conventions might still obtain, but only in defense of male, not female, honor in a song attributed by Mihopulos to Ayiomavritis (Petropulos 1976):

> Elli needs killing,
> she needs guillotining,
> for she left her husband
> and her children.
>
> Elli needs killing
> with a double-edged knife,
> for she left her husband
> and took up with a count.

Stavrakas's view, the direct product of the rebetika songs he sings, reflects the conscious sexuality of a male-dominated subculture. If in the songs of the bey men die for love, here they are poisoned by it.

Treatment of women in the Greek comedies borrows from the negative gender model that informed the Turkish Karagoz performance. The treatment of women in the Turkish performance is itself affected not only by the role of women in Turkish society but also by the way in which women were treated in Turkish literature and art.

Traditions in Turkish society that contribute to differences between Turkish and Greek texts in the treatment of women include the presence in Turkish society of the harem, polygamy, and the kabul. Harem life contributed to the treatment of women as slaves, for the harem itself comprised a multitude of female slaves chosen for the pleasure of the sultan. Sultans generally refused to take Turkish women into the harem, so that it tended to be made up of a large number of Christian women. Should a sultan or prince wish to separate from a harem wife—sultans did marry some of the women in the harem, particularly as the result of political alliances—he merely placed her out of favor and left her to a solitary, inactive life retired from the court. Nevertheless, harem life did empower women in some ways. Daughters of the sultans, wed to win over powerful subjects, were themselves permitted to put their husbands aside in favor of others (Alderson 1956). Mothers of sons who went on to become sultans exerted considerable influence over the court through their sons, rather than through their roles as chief wives of previous sultans

(Bates 1978). Like the harem, polygamy, more common among poorer Turks in agricultural communities of eastern Turkey, left Turkish women to live more completely within the world of women than did their Greek counterparts (Cosar 1978).

The world of women retained its own rules, social organization, and hierarchies and remained stable throughout the Ottoman period (Denglar 1978). The woman's world was held together by that form of organization called the kabul, a large network that emphasized the inequality of outsiders, established the status of insiders (Good 1978), and allowed women a role in political and economic functions through their assertion of informal social, political, and economic decision-making both within this circle and through the circle's influence on male kin (Aswad 1978).

As in Greek society, common Turkish women were empowered at several points in their lives, all associated with their relationships with men: upon engagement, when they were assigned their portion of the family estate through bridewealth; upon marriage, when the dowry was transferred to the bride's new home; upon the death of the bride's father and the formal division of family wealth; upon widowhood; and in old age, when a woman became dependent on her son or daughter (Starr 1984). Life among women was at all points more egalitarian than that among men, which retained a stricter set of hierarchical relationships (Good 1978). Men, in any case, were more completely exploited by the state than were women, who, at the period of their greatest strength, were preoccupied with child-rearing (Aswad 1978).

In urban areas, most marriages were traditionally arranged at an early age, and women in Turkey cannot, even in modern times, be conceived of as having emancipated themselves from marital power-lessness in spite of increased employment in the urban work force (Kuyas 1982). The urban male role was itself little affected by change, for socialization practices and ideology continued to support men's control over and subordination of women as well as women's limited access to the outside world (Kandiyoti 1982). Moreover, extended family relations remained as important in urban as in rural areas among all social classes, with little significant change in household types except in upper-income groups (Duben 1982).

In Turkish literature, repressed sexual tension led to the general avoidance of eroticism. Women characters were treated indirectly and remained insufficiently developed until late-nineteenth-century reforms in Islamic law led to greater independence in their treatment in both society and literature. Sex was regarded as a theme to be avoided, as the beloved was treated as an eternal virgin who, in this male-dominated world, was threatened by moral degeneration and disin-tegration. Women in Turkish society were regarded as desperate and dependent; they were seen as placing beauty above chastity and being led to ruin as fallen women. Change and Westernization were identi-fied with degeneration and were seen as opposed to centuries-old family values that demanded chaste and faithful women (Akatli 1981). Dense kinship networks kept women close to their natal families and under the strong control of their fathers and husbands, who sponsored a restricted ideology of honor and shame that led women to connive to take an active role in arranged marriages. If undesired, such arrange-ments led to elopements, abductions, and threatened suicides. Wo-men, held in Islamic law to the status of minors, were, in sum, unable to play a full, independent role in Turkish society.

The restriction of female figures in Turkish literature can be con-trasted with the greater freedoms taken by the Karagoz performance, which found acceptance as a satiric form that cultivated a broad popular audience. The most frequently appearing female figure in Turkish Karagoz is the free woman, a figure whose independence of male authority and values make her a target of abuse and the object of puns and sexual jokes (Hatzipandazis 1982). The impudent prostitute is the only female figure who frequents public places in the Turkish performance. A public property, the courtesan was permitted on the Turkish stage when women of the private world—wives, mothers, and daughters—were not. When the wife does appear in the Turkish performance, she is treated as a slave. Whereas family life and affection are not depicted, polygamy is implied both in the freedom of married Turkish males in the public domain and in the understood life of the harem, which is not itself depicted on the screen (Interview with Ilhan Basgoz, 1990; And 1975; Iliadis 1925).

Overall, the Turkish performance presents an intensely negative portrait of women. Through the free woman or the courtesan, women are humiliated and repudiated by men. Having lost her virginity outside the protected scope of the domestic domain, woman has lost her value in male society. Idealized as beloved partners only in conven-tional love songs that appear associated with certain characters (the bey and the young lover) in the performance, Turkish women are generally either despised for their independence or tolerated when silently submissive (Mystiakidou 1978). Under this world's double standards, men are free to entertain themselves without dishonor outside their homes, as long as their own wives are safely locked within.

Characteristic elements of Turkish Karagoz's treatment of women appear in the quarrel of lesbians who run rival women's baths *(The Public Bath)*, a courtesan who humiliates her lover *(The Bloody Nigar)*, lovers who take a trip to the seashore *(The Pleasure Trip to Yalova*, reprised in the Greek play *The Urn)*, witches who assist their children in a quarrel *(The Witches*, which appears as a secondary theme in the Greek play *The Haunted Tree)*, Karagoz's bride giving birth onstage to an obscene child *(The Big Wedding)*, and courtesans whom Karagoz sets up in a house for orgies *(The Raid)*. The use of Karagoz as a majordomo to watch over the bey's daughter (in *Tahir and Zuhre)* and the contest for a bride *(Ferhat and Sirene* and *The Purse)* are carried over into the Greek performance, whereas the themes involving courtesans are largely eliminated. Karagoz's quarrels with his wife in the Turkish texts *(The Dairy Farm* and *The Boat)* as well as his jealous guarding of her reputation are brought into the Greek performance through such plays as *Kutahya; or, The Fountain*, which resulted in the Greek text *Karagiozis in America*. Domestic relations between Karagoz and his wife, which appear in a text devoted to family affairs in a polygamous household *(The Partners)* are carried over as well into the Greek performance (And 1975).

In the Hellenic guise of the heroic texts of the Karagiozis performance, women are represented substantively differently than they are in either Turkish Karagoz or the Greek comedies. Sanctified in marriage, women in the heroic texts receive cultural recognition through their positive roles as wives and mothers. Their negative aspects and their potentially polluting sexuality are controlled within the household, and their subservience to men is viewed as sealed in the exchange of property from father to husband, both in the exchange of their own persons and in the exchange of dowry. Thus they do not connive to breach the authority of parent or husband. Less threatening to men, women in the heroic texts assume a gender role that is less asymmetrical than that imposed on women in the Romeic comedies.

Empowered by their newly endowed status, women are socially
sanctioned as active subjects, analogous to the freely acting male
subject, but limited.[9] In this context, women are like men in that they
function as actors with a set of goals who make conscious choices to
given ends that support their interests, which are tied to those of their
sons and husbands. Those interests might sometimes be opposed to
those of men, particularly of outsiders, for they operate on behalf of
families rather than kinship groups or the community at large (Collier
1974). Neither completely subservient to the social system nor fully
autonomous, women's behavior is channeled by cultural rules, avail-
able resources, and the choices of others. Women may independently
and individually generate strategies that are intrinsic to the processes
of social life and that help produce the social structures under which
they live, but they ultimately serve society, and their behavior is
moderated by it.

As active subjects both resisting and capitulating to forces of the
public domain, women in the heroic texts influence public life by
articulating the private-public opposition. They heal household mem-
bers wounded by outside economic interests and the claims of state
loyalty and then return them to that same public sphere (Dimen 1986).
The domestic sphere thus becomes a place of stability and change in
which women perform contradictory tasks that express their am-
bivalent feelings about themselves. Here the public domain invades
the private as women serve the needs of the state by reproducing its
social structure and its contradictions. Their choices are, however,
never free of the influence of male power and the larger structure of
their society. At the same time, they represent, in their insistence on
acting on behalf of sons and husbands, a form of social fragmentation
and social criticism that offsets that influence.

This complexity underlines the complementarity of role behaviors
that we find in the heroic texts of the Karagiozis performance, in which
women claim a legitimate authority within the domestic domain and
still exert power, if indirectly, in the public sphere (Strathern 1984a).
Insofar, as the two spheres work interdependently, women can act as
important agents of social integration and ideological continuity in
areas of universal human concern (Hirschon 1983b). Since the family
is regarded as the most significant social unit, domestic power can
even overshadow power in the public sphere (Friedl 1967). The hos-
tility of the public sphere is also well compensated for in the family, the

area of greatest stability, solidarity, and reassurance (du Boulay 1986; Dimen 1986).[10] Given the positive role attributed here to the domestic domain, lack of direct access to public life does not, as a result, affect women as deeply in the heroic texts as it does in the comic texts.

In the Hellenic view, women have thus been liberated from object status by indirect participation in productive aspects of the public sphere (Sacks 1974). The adult social status they are granted through such participation provides a form of sexual equality. Moreover, through the products of their labor, their ownership of dowry lands, and, above all, their preservation of such intangible property as honor and reputation (Hirschon 1984), women have generated a sense of their own inherent worth beyond their identity as property or property bearers and beyond their ties to family fortunes.

In the heroic texts, then, it is not a question of women liberating themselves from male control. Rather, it is through men and together with men that women achieve status and are able to fulfill the roles of wife and mother (du Boulay 1974, 1986). Women are thus able to transcend the evil nature of Eve associated with the Romeic perspective and redeem themselves through discipline and shame by bearing children, particularly male heirs, to enhance the family honor. In this role, women perform a divine function like that of the Virgin Mary (du Boulay 1976; Hirschon 1978; Dubisch 1983). The importance of marriage and deference to the husband rests in this redemptive power. Thus, in the heroic texts, women stand for Hellenic unity in the family context of their roles as wives and mothers (purity), in contrast to their function in the comedies as the sources of Romeic differences as individuals (pollution).

Overall, the Hellenic view of the heroic texts exhibits a balance of direct-indirect, overt-covert, formal-informal authority and power between men and women that capitalizes on a complementarity that is opposed to the oppositionality expressed in the comedies. At the same time, women allow men to preserve the outside appearance of an asymmetrical relationship that is necessary for maintaining male dominance in the community and thus preserving male prestige. In complementary, though still asymmetrical, roles of mutual dependency, men and women together protect family honor in the highest sense, women being responsible for chastity and men for fidelity in the pursuit of producing that which provides a family with its ultimate status—offspring.

Whereas the comic texts were heavily influenced by Turkish Karagoz, the heroic texts adopted a perspective more characteristically European. Influenced by the mix of eighteenth-century neoclassical drama, bourgeois drama, nineteenth-century melodrama, and opera that appeared in Athens during the period of the performance's nineteenth-century growth in post-1821 Greece (Myrsiades 1980b), the heroic texts sponsored more liberated heroines who not only ensured the domestic peace but also played on a stage of national, rather than strictly domestic or even merely public, values. Ironically, given the increasingly liberated posture of women in the heroic performances, the roles left open to women in these Hellenic texts were much more restricted in both range and number.

The active, if still restricted, female role of the heroic texts is exemplified by the hero Katsandonis's wife and the hero Athanasios Diakos's sister (sometimes his mother), and frequently by a vizier's or a bey's daughter. Eleni, sister of the hero Athanasios Diakos, goes in search of her brother when he is captured by the pasha. Seized to be placed in the pasha's harem, she resists and dies in defense of her honor. In *Karagiozis, the Seven Beasts, and Alexander the Great,* the vizier's daughter offers to convert to Orthodoxy, revolts against her grandmother, the ruling pashina, in defense of her lover, the Greek Alexander, and is assassinated. Katsandonis's wife is kidnapped by the Turks, defends her child, and takes up arms to do battle when the Greeks liberate them. In an expanded vision of the public nature of women in the Hellenic heroic texts, Mollas's *Katsandonis* presents Vasiliki, a Greek maiden impressed into Ali Pasha's harem, embracing a mission to aid the Greeks through influence over the pasha. She rejects his advances and refuses to convert to Islam, agreeing to marry Ali only if he frees Katsandonis from captivity. Finally, she contracts the assassination of the Greek monk who had betrayed the hero into Ali's hands.

In the heroic texts, the male hero expresses internal role conflicts that speak, as do those of the female, to the difficulty of achieving role complementarity in an essentially dichotomous relationship. Like his female counterpart, the Greek male plays a public role at the level of national awareness in the heroic texts. He is heralded as a paragon of cultural values. Larger than life and uniquely heroic, he symbolizes man's striving; at the same time, he shares essential characteristics with the common man, who thereby chooses to follow his leadership.

The hero thus allows his followers to achieve perfection, if only vicariously. The Greek hero represents the prepared mind ready to capitalize on an opportunity, a force for moral balance, for equilibrium, not an actively aggressive force like the brigand in the antiheroic *listi* text, a text type that developed in the performance, if not in reaction to the heroic text, at least as a Romeicly inspired counterbalance. The hero thus comes forward in times of disorder to exert an ordering force. He does not change himself but is unyielding, for his work is not the result of an active intelligence operating to understand its universe: it is, rather, an automatic rebalancing operation that functions without conscious thought. Intellect and imbalance are most fully expressed in the counterface to the Greek hero, the antiheroic Turk. Characterized as an embodiment of moral ugliness, irrationality, and cruelty, the Turk is seen as a predator of moral certainty, the deconstructing force of intellect that fosters confusion and defeats unity, qualities shared with Karagiozis.

In one respect, the Greek hero is best described as a case of stunted adolescent growth, forever frozen in a time slice of absolute certainty that refuses to acknowledge the possibility of moral ambivalence or ambiguity. In the idolatry accorded the Greek hero, we find the roots of the Greek male's own insecurity in the face of great change and environmental uncertainty. The Greek hero is a creation that enables the Greek male to see his own inadequacies as a superficial facade beneath which lies the truth of his own heroic self.

We find, as well, a certain ambivalence in the expression of the male-female dichotomy within the Greek hero himself. The hero functions both as protector of Greek womanhood and as the nemesis of the dominant Turkish authority (a female force). Moreover, just as the male allows females power only insofar as they are guided by men, so does he deny his own female nature recognition as the potential source of his greatness. In this ambivalent role, the Greek hero is psychologically vulnerable (Myrsiades 1988a), supported only by the protected status of family honor that has been assured by the domestic security afforded by Greek women. The false assertion of male power as real power and the male self as its true nature thus perpetuates in the heroic text the myth of the reality of male power dominating the appearance of female power.[11]

In the Hellenic perspective, the oppositional description of wo-

men's roles and functions in the public and private spheres of life
(Rosaldo 1980), as well as the gender distinctions that have been
described between culture and nature (Ortner 1974), both of which
are found clearly expressed in the comedies, are thus problematic
(Hirschon 1984; MacCormack and Strathern 1980; Strathern 1980;
Sciama 1981; Strathern 1984b). Oppositional descriptions stress dif-
ferences between men and women and the separateness of women
rather than role exchanges and shared characteristics. Moreover, the
closer we look at the perceived dichotomous relationship between
men and women, the more it becomes clear that in both the comic and
heroic texts the roles of men and women are, in may ways, interdepen-
dent and their cultural attributes interchangeable. Women, placed on
the nature end of the nature-culture continuum and, at the same time,
credited with converting nature into culture (Ortner 1974), are opposed
to men in certain contexts as cultivated and in others as savage. Indeed,
in some historical inversions women are identified with culture.
Culture itself is both a creative subject and a finished object, so that
man, as well, identified with culture, paradoxically flips from subject
to object (Strathern 1980). There is thus no consistent dichotomy, but
only a matrix of contrasts that result in ambiguities as the meanings of
nature and culture shift in relation to one another.[12] Boundaries, or
frames, thus blend, interchange, or even disappear entirely in this
invaginated process of analysis that began in binaries only to merge
into unities, demonstrating the lability of male-female labels, some-
thing we find in the listi, or brigand, texts as well as in the topical texts
of the Karagiozis performance. This very negotiability represents the
inner face of Greek political experience. But, whereas unofficial and
official ideologies are both necessary to the process, it is the dialectic
itself that takes the primary focus as it continually renegotiates the
cultural boundaries in an intermediary realm between the Romeic and
Hellenic forms of gender discourse.

The most truly active women in the Karagiozis performance are
found neither in the Karagiozis comedies nor in the histories, but in
the listi and topical texts. These popular culture products feed on
sensational tales in the media and on dime novels *(thrili)* that range
from the romantic to the macabre. While these texts borrow from and
are influenced by the impact of bourgeois literary forces on popular
culture that paralleled urbanization of the performance, they retain
closer ties to the Romeic world than do the heroic texts, which present

historical figures, largely from the 1821 war for independence, and which adopt bourgeois mores wholesale. Listi texts, by contrast, choose the less likely brigand or bandit population for their central figures, accepting their marginal status as characters who failed to find a place for themselves in Greece under both their old Turkish and their new Greek masters. In the context of the world of the socially peripheral listi, women are depicted as deviant, active, and independent, much like the male listi himself. The mixed and interchangeable natures of men and women are given expression here, blurring boundaries between private and public realms and male and female roles and easing the double standard maintained in society at large for male and female behavior.[13] In one sense, the rapidly proliferated but short-lived listi and topical texts express a lability that tolerates experimentation not only with new structural forms and new plots in the performance but also with new structural forms and expressions, including the treatment of gender roles. Few of them have survived as printed texts, and only a handful appear in player interviews, in spite of the fact that players' repertoires indicate that the listi texts make up as many as a third of the texts that were, at one time or another, performed. These texts create a liminal zone between official and unofficial cultures in which shared and interactive elements are free to deconstruct and reconstruct in a variety of new combinations.

In the listi texts, women adopt labile roles, taking on in the same text aspects of both Eve and the divine Mary. Men, too, are presented as mixed figures who carry attributes of both hero and antihero; they act in both the Romeic and the Hellenic guise and perform as both table-turners and defenders of the status quo. Thus, a brigand captain, as in Giorgos Haridimos's *Listi Bekiaris,* who raids the lands of Muslim and Christian, of rich and poor alike, travels among the people in disguise to discover their woes and right their wrongs.[14] Violence against a village woman by the listi's most trusted officer is met with the death of the violator; the brigand captain himself dies of heartbreak over his lost comrade. In these same texts, while witnesses testify about brigands who died helping the poor, the brigands themselves were decapitated, and their heads were placed on pikes or thrown into the audience to be torn apart. As Giorgos Haridimos explains, whatever good they might have done, they were still murderers and thieves and had to die. Their motive, unlike that of the klephtic heroes of 1821, was not to reverse an unjust order to liberate Greece, but to express the

egoism of the individual in texts that devolve into social anarchy on the
one hand and erotic idylls on the other.

Expressed by the klephts, that same egoism represented a social
stance of new beginnings in a hostile world. With the listi it served as
an enervating disunity that threatened social harmony. On the one
hand, it expressed the European individualism of official history
(personal heroism in defense of fledgling state interests), which one
finds again in the Karagiozis heroic texts. On the other hand, it
provided the motive force for the Oriental self-interestedness of local
experience, which one finds in both the listi texts and the Karagiozis
comic texts. Thus, while ego is fundamentally an ideology that
subverts order, it still represents a value of shared concern between
both official and unofficial cultures, a value that borrows elements
from both cultures only to use them differently as strategies in the
service of these differing ideologies.

The shared qualities of the official and unofficial aspects of egoism
is demonstrated in Giorgos Haridimos's *Listarhos Davelis,* in which
the listi Megas moves in a liminal zone between the dominant force of
an established Greek state and the residual force of the realm of
disenchanted klephts who find themselves marginal to the very power
they helped to enthrone. Pardoned by the queen, Megas hires out to
round up his old comrades, flushing them out of the hideouts he had
once shared with them. As he shoots his quarry Davelis, Megas is
himself killed, for, as the performer makes clear in a statement
characteristic of the shared Hellenic-Romeic nature of the listi text,
"Neither shall Megas be in the palace, nor Davelis in the mountains."
Megas's body is carried off to the palace as Davelis's head is skewered
on a pike. Karagiozis himself, as Haridimos describes, is ambivalent
in his relationship with the listi, sometimes taking on the role of a
pallikari, a hero type, to hunt them down, and sometimes standing by
as a servant who calls on the listi to intercede when an injustice is done.
In one Haridimos text, *Mavro Yaouri,* this combination figure, in
whom the culture's oppositional values are both expressed, takes on
the mythic, undying form of one who is repeatedly killed but does
not die.

In *Listi Pasadoros,* as in a number of similar texts, abduction of a
village girl becomes the focus, both as a way of breaking through
cultural traditions that make the listi marginal to such social arrange-
ments as marriage and as an expression of the residual object value of

women in the brigand world. The abducted is herself devalued by the abduction, so that prized goods, once possessed, become valueless. In this case, the listi text clarifies or supports the importance of traditional or conventional institutions and patterns of behavior, so that breaking the rule becomes another way of reinforcing it.

Nevertheless, women in the listi and topical texts, regarded by men as property to be ravaged, protected, or rescued, emerge from the sea of faceless ladies who inhabit Greek folklore to assert here their refusal to be moved about like helpless pawns. In Mihopulos's *Astrapoyiannis,* a mother not only kills a Turk but also volunteers to seek and deliver a liberator to reverse the failing fortunes of her people. Women make clear and adamant choices as active agents to guide their own destinies, frequently, however, outside the bounds of acceptable social conventions. In *Astrapoyiannis,* a khanum shoots her father, the bey, and rescues her lover. Fickle Helen in Mollas's *Orea Eleni* refuses an arranged marriage and elopes with a foreign officer, bombarding her own village to cover her escape. In text after text, women escape into the mountains to follow their brigand lovers. Descending further into the role of Eve, a woman in Giorgos Haridimos's *General Lafuzanis* blinds her son to protect her secret lover; in the same player's *The Heart of the Mother,* a bride orders the murder of her mother-in-law to assert unchallenged authority in her home.

The gender roles exhibited in these texts place men at the mercy of women through role reversals that challenge social expectations in a way that occurs in neither the comic nor the heroic texts. Going well beyond power in the domestic sphere or complementarity in the public, women in the listi texts have moved into a zone where anything becomes possible and the Wheel of Fortune is given a free turn. By this description, the liminal zone of the listi texts acts as the true middle ground between the official Hellenic world of the heroic texts and the unofficial Romeic world of the comic texts. These texts thus demonstrate that women are not easily restricted to a male gender model that describes them merely in domestic, local, familiar realities, just as men cannot be linked only to the realm of formal public or national identity (Dubisch 1983; Herzfeld 1986).

We find such a refusal of labels in Giorgos Haridimos's *Kargiozis and the Crazy House,* in which a female European jewel thief bears the dominant role. She carries off a heist in a store in which Karagiozis serves as jewel clerk; she lures him to the madhouse and tricks the chief of staff into committing him as a patient. Female activity is here represented as a liberated force that sets its own rules, borrowing from the newly won independence of the urban working woman in Greek cities. Increased participation of women in industry, better education, and diminished family solidarity in the city did not, nevertheless, provide urban women with role status similar to that of men (Spinellis, Vasiliu, and Vassiliu 1970). In addition, women's economic activity is negatively associated with the honor and reputation of the family, for it suggests that the male family head is unable to support his family (Cavounides 1983). Educated urban women represent a threat to male values, since pursuing careers represents pressure for change and exposes women to destabilizing outside contacts, enabling them to set up networks of relationships in areas distant from the domestic sphere (Vermeulen 1970; Hirschon 1983b). As a result, a figure like the jewel thief rather than the working woman becomes the representative figure used to exhibit the urban influence.

Women in the Karagiozis performance have not been liberated from the male model to a female model but have merely been displaced from one part of the male model in the comedies (the negative) to another part in the heroic texts (the positive). The two parts represent alternate faces of the same vision, so that women have not been granted equal status so much as they have been able to capitalize on their unequal status as far as possible. The next logical step (and one that lies outside the frame of the performance thus far) is to act within a female model, creating a true alterity that would make a nonproblematic dialectical discourse possible. In this regard, the prominence of Karagiozena takes on a new importance, one that puts her very much at center stage in the gender debate embodied by the Karagiozis performance.

In sum, three types of texts coexist in the Greek Karagiozis performance, representing three ideological positions: the Romeic comedy, the Hellenic heroic text, and the liminal listi and topical texts, in which the Romeic and the Hellenic perspectives blur boundaries to interface in the larger dialectical meaning of their opposition. The Karagiozis performance thus maintains a modified binary view of women that is analogous to the opposition posited between the unofficial Romeic and the official Hellenic models. In the comedies, it views women negatively as daughters of Eve and asserts their marginality in Greek social values. In the heroic texts, it views them positively as Mary-like figures and asserts their centrality in the constellation of Greek cultural values. In the listi and topical texts, it views them as interchangeable with men and denies the validity of male domination and the perspective of the male model. Taking its lead from the forceful presentation of Karagiozena in the comic texts, the liminal perspective breaks out of old forms and takes the performance to the edge of a new form that enables fulfillment of the true alterity of the "muted" female model. That it never passes beyond that edge is an acknowledgment of the fundamentally male world of the performance. This world, nevertheless, more than any other popular form in Greek folklore, experiments with interaction in the dialectic of gender values to produce the possibility of a vision that resists to the greatest possible extent the hegemony of male domination and through it the hegemony of official Hellenic culture.

CHAPTER FOUR

Text and Context

The study of folklore in the last several decades has radically altered a variety of notions that had been widely held, including traditional notions that stress the antiquity of folklore material, the collectivity of oral composition, and the simplicity of the folk (Ben-Amos 1972). This challenge has expanded the concept of folklore to include expressions that presently circulate in a culture and that assume new forms that can be transmitted in modes other than oral transmission. Here a distinction is drawn between residual and emergent cultures (Bauman 1972b), stressing the need to focus on the new meanings and practices of contemporary culture rather than on vestiges or survivals of residual culture. Folklore, in this view, is significant regardless of the amount of time it has been in circulation or whether it is oral or written. It is "not its life history that determines the folklore quality of a text but its present mode of existence" (Ben-Amos 1972: 14). In a further response to the challenge to traditional notions, folklore has come to represent a body of information stored in many individuals, often with varying interests and values and at different social and occupational levels, rather than being restricted to a peasant group identified as the "rural folk." The most significant change, however, might be the rejection of the idea of folklore as communally created and representative of the thought patterns of primitive peoples. Rather, folklore is described as the work of individual artists, expressing industrial and managerial culture as well as peasant societies (Dundes 1964; Dorson 1971).

One of these challenges to conventional theory is an approach to folklore that has come to be known as performance theory. Citing a commitment to the integration of form, function, and performance, proponents of the performance approach to folklore view "performance as an organizing principle that comprehends within a single conceptual framework artistic act, expressive form, and esthetic response [Abrahams's performance, item, and audience], and that does

so in terms of locally defined, culture-specific categories and con-
texts" (Bauman 1972b: xi). Subject to the same rules that govern all
human behavior (Bauman 1972a), the performative event is under-
stood as a communicative behavior with a focus on understanding
verbal art as doing, that is, as a performed way of speaking (Bauman
1977; Georges 1969; Hymes 1964, 1975). Following Hymes, perform-
ance is distinguished by its transcendence of the ordinary course of
events; it is seen as a speech act related to but essentially separate from
the everyday experience of speech.

The performative event is interactive. It requires the audience to
take responsibility for the competence of the performer even as it
depends on the performer to catch the audience up in the folklore
display (Bauman 1972a). The performer and the audience participate
in the same situational context and react as parts of the same reference
group to the same language, knowledge, and system of codes and
signals of social interaction (Ben-Amos 1972). In this review, the
performer overtly suggests activating an item while the audience
implicitly infers it (Fine 1984). Moreover, the performer is also simul-
taneously his own audience, while the audience actively contributes to
the performance through its paralinguistic participation—applause,
laughter, and interspersed commentary.[1]

The responsibility assumed by the audience extends to the very
meaning of the performative event, for both active carriers of a tradi-
tion (the performer who creates, preserves, and enacts the repertoire)
and passive carriers (those members of the community who are
familiar with and inform the performance by reacting and interacting
with it to complete it) are considered necessary to creating that
meaning. The interactive performative event itself designates bound-
aries of a context for action in which performance behavior is situated
and rendered meaningful by both active and passive participants
(Bauman 1977). The meaning of the performance event is thus socially
constructed and not preexistent, for meaning emerges across the
duration of the performance. The key to this transactional perspective
is the reciprocal functional relationship between art object and per-
ceiver. This relationship determines the priority of perceptual emer-
gent knowledge over analytical objective knowledge (Berleant 1970).
The unity of experience preserves the integrity of the situation without
isolating object and perceiver (Ben-Amos 1972).

Insofar as folklore is interactional, the performance assumes a common ground of certain social and cultural interests, almost as if the performance submitted itself to the wisdom of the group (Abrahams 1972). Nevertheless, the folklore performance does not require either that the item itself be a collective representation belonging equally to all participants or that all members have an equal stake in a common folklore. Rather, differences of identity not only between the performer and the audience but also within the audience may be differently perceived. Moreover, folklore may be differently distributed and performed by players (Bauman 1972a). Folklore can, as a result, be viewed as the province of a plurality of groups defined by age, occupation, region, or ethnic background. Nor do social groups have to be regarded as homogeneous, as long as they share a significant common factor. Folklore can thus be understood as occurring not only between people of shared identity but between those of differentiated identity as well. Through performance theory, we thus arrive at a more direct, empirical connection between a people and its folklore than is offered by the concept of collective art.

The performance approach has arrived at a notion of folklore that is historically specific and contextually bound. The cognitive, behavioral, and functional structure of folklore cannot, as a result, be always and everywhere the same (see Abrahams 1972; Finnegan 1977; Jason 1972). Universal classifications or functional schemes could not exist without regard for the ethnographic realities of particular cultures (Bauman 1972b). Context requires specification of time, place, and the company in which folklore actions happen to provide the temporal, spatial, and social dimensions that define folklore in a specific culture (Ben-Amos 1972).[2]

The performance approach has implications, finally, for our understanding of the function of folklore. Folklore is no longer seen as a mirror, a reflection, or a projection of culture, but as a dynamic factor, a sphere of interaction in its own right (Ben-Amos 1972). Influenced by Kenneth Burke's (1950) idea that poetry addresses situations by adopting various strategies, the performance approach describes folklore as embodying problem situations in a controlled context, addressing conflicts, and creating the illusion that such problems can be resolved in real life (Abrahams 1972). Folklore thus represents a symbolic action with a persuasive intent, both action and intent serving as guides to social action. It encompasses a combination of aesthetic and utilitarian purposes—a form of aesthetic patterning, which pleases and captures attention, used to rhetorical ends (Fine 1984)—that passes control from the formal expression to the situation itself.

The appropriateness of performance theory to local forms of folklore in the Greek context has been explored through proverbs, *mantinades* (rhyming couplets), *miroloyia* (laments), *glentia* (ritual celebrations), and folk songs. Scholars have addressed such issues as the continuous dialogue between aesthetic considerations and social functions, indigenous taxonomies, pluralism, and social context. Greek laments and folk songs, for example, have been studied through the aesthetic, historical, social, personal, and situational prisms of performance style, social usage, the individual personality of the performer, the community world view, local history, and tradition-shaping conventions.

In the study of laments, performance meanings, described as immediately apparent to participants in the culture but not apparent to outsiders, are studied "in a framework which interweaves form with the specific context of an actual community and treats ritual lamentation as a communicative event" (Caraveli 1980: 152). Context explains the apparent incompleteness of the lament text when it is separated from performance. The audience, familiar with the local repertoire and acting as a passive bearer of the tradition, itself supplies the means to recall the complete idea and to establish its contextual meaning. We find this process operating again in a situation in which, displaced from its specific ethnographic context, a metaphor loses its meaning (Herzfeld 1979). Here the text is regarded as a constituent element of context, in this case the internal context of comparison or opposition in a Greek folk song, rather than the external context of situation or event. Dependency on and interaction with the text's context thereby defines the communicative process of the lament and folk song, bringing together performer and audience, past and present, to complete incomplete songs through the meaning found in the context in which they are set (Caraveli 1982).[3]

Through the social, interactive process of folk aesthetics, both the past and the present complete the meaning of a text in performance, the first through traditional patterns and meanings and the second through the community's aesthetic and historical understanding (Caraveli 1982). Laments are thus made meaningful through social interaction that uses place, space, objects, and persons as the basis of metaphors for life. Through such interaction, laments act as windows to a larger world. It is, moreover, irrelevant whether the context by means of which the text is completed is residual or emergent, that is, whether it appears before, within, or after the performance or its creation, for the contextuality that informs the Greek lament serves to liberate performance meaning from both temporal and spatial boundaries through its expanded referents.[4]

The interactive performative context, which we find as well in Greek proverbs, folk songs, and glentia, is expressed in the lament tradition as lamenters monitor a complex network of messages from various addressers to various addressees with the focus shifting from one to the other in a multileveled communicative event rather than a static display of verbal artistry and structural balances (Caraveli 1980). Lament conventions, in this view, are not merely products of a textual tradition but are determined by the history of the deceased and the deceased's mourners. The deceased determines as well the meaning of the female roles involved in the lament, which intersect life and art and bridge the performance with everyday or informal conversation. Both before and after the lament, this conversation itself retells the deeds of the deceased and expresses suffering. Thematic units emulating speech and dynamic units of direct address maintain a steady focus on communication. In this sense, laments are not merely performed communicative events but, like glentia (Caraveli 1985), are coextensive with real-life communicative events with which they share meaning as well as content. Indeed, daily conversation is itself characterized by aesthetic sensibility and stylistic devices, differing from art only in the degree of metaphor it uses (Caraveli 1980).

The link between real-life and performative events in Greek folklore explains folklore's performative function. Greek laments serve the world of the participants and use the past not merely to draw comparisons but also to bear on the present as a survival strategy (Caraveli 1980). In this use, laments are not songs about or to the dead. Rather, they serve to invite the community to participate in mourning, turning a narrative relation of events into an actual interaction, thus servicing the identity of the living. The lamenter functions as both biographer and witness, as both addresser and addressee to the world of women she sings to and for whom she mediates between the realms of life and death. Indeed, performers can reinforce and renegotiate the social and moral order through manipulating the performance. Relationships between the mourner-audience and the dead subject of a lament thus serve as bridges across generations, sexes, and social roles. The performance acts as an active integrating agent, both expressing a cohesive social context and acting as a vehicle to create cohesiveness and expand boundaries. From the mourner's point of view, it complements ritual acts by offering control over the inevitability of death while it creates a heightened sense of identity. It addresses grievances against the community and appeals to it to share actively in the mourning. Laments thereby represent an enactment through poetic language of the social activity of the separate world of women and suggest not only appropriate behaviors and roles for survival strategies but ultimately remedies for death for the whole community.

Glentia perform a related function, as they forge relationships and meanings in which ordinary experiences are transformed into extraordinary ones. Through the increasing engrossment of participants involved in the social drama of performed mantinades, moral balances are negotiated, new cultural solutions to social conflicts are arrived at, and identities of community members are dissolved and reconstituted through dynamic interchanges, as a community is formed in performance. Moreover, glentia bridge the local world of the community of immigrants who moved to other parts of Greece or outside of Greece, to the United States and Australia, serving as a means of constructing and continuously negotiating ideology, communicating transcontinentally, symbolically constituting a global community, and linking local knowledge of the temporary performative event with larger historical processes and the meaning they create (Caraveli 1985). Following the work of Victor Turner (1974), we can see that the symbolic action of glentia forms a community in performance, interfacing everyday time and space with the extraordinary experience of mythic time and space of the ritual celebration.[5] Text and context become coextensive, allowing the creation of a symbolically extended community beyond the physical context of the original performance community to any location where the glentia come to be performed (Caraveli 1985).

Further examination of text and context, this time in Greek proverbs, suggests that distinctions between them are extremely labile (Herzfeld 1981a). Where one ends and the other begins is related to the needs of the participants themselves. Moreover, in the participants' own experienced world and in their own theoretical categories, such distinctions are not made. As a result, it is more profitable to consider how events are experienced by participants and how that experience is rendered in performative events than to isolate performative events as texts and social or even ritual conditions as contexts. Nor is performed folklore ever truly fixed or complete. New events surrounding the retelling of a folk song, for example, produce new information and new significance (Herzfeld 1981b). Meaning is thus created, re-created, and expanded in an open-ended process of continuous interaction rooted in a context in which performer and audience both participate.

Work on Greek folklore has thus announced itself in harmony with performance theory. Margaret Alexiou (1984), for example, outlines the theoretical basis for studying Greek folklore in a handful of precepts. Greek texts represent, first, an interaction of orality and literacy that implies that the folk can no longer be considered "simple." Moreover, Greek folklore exists in a constant state of becoming, such that its contemporary condition is not to be regarded as a fossil or a survival (Danforth 1984), but as a historically specific event (Lambropoulos 1985) that has survived because it has been sung and danced (Alexiou 1984). As a historically specific event, Greek folklore is treated as disconnected from its past rather than continuous, its importance lying in the moment in which it occurs. Folklore is seen as a social institution produced through the interplay of cultural forces, and attention is directed to its production as well as to cultural uses of the items, forms of its cultural constitution, and the politics of its interpretation. It becomes clear that the verbal text becomes indistinguishable from social conditions or context (Herzfeld 1981a; Lambropoulos 1985; Tziovas 1985) and that the item intersects with everyday discourse (Caraveli 1980; Herzfeld 1985).

It becomes clear as well that, given the paradoxical relationship between scholars, who, in some sense, deny the folk their own interpretation of folklore, and the folk, who become irrelevant to, if not victimized by, scholarly discourse (Danforth 1984), greater credence is being given in the study of Greek folklore to "local exegesis" (Herzfeld 1981a). Indeed, Michael Herzfeld (1987) argues that academic taxonomies should be criticized in light of folk taxonomies. Otherwise, folklorists run the risk of missing the total social context of the folklore items, of neglecting sociological data, and of assuming a unilinear model of textual evolution. Not only is the taken-for-granted data that appears in local commentary exactly what the scholar would consider the context against which to read text, but metatextually, local exegesis is as legitimate a text as the scholar's commentary (Herzfeld 1981a, 1985, 1987).[6] Indeed, the meaning the individual text in performance holds for its indigenous audience supersedes in importance a single analytical taxonomy of folklore variants. Indigenous theories of meaning, moreover, do not have to be conscious, coherent, or systematized by indigenous informants, but they may merely represent shared perceptions or indigenous assumptions. These indigenous classifications are interpreted through social and performative contexts that provide the basis for local theories of meaning (Herzfeld 1981a).

In our effort to be responsive to such local theories of meaning, it is important to be aware that the context out of which meaning is generated by a performative event preexists that event and creates the situational determinants that constrain participants and by means of which participants engage in drawing meaning from the event. Because the performance is a communication and because communication occurs within situations, participants in the situation act within a set of assumptions that informs the meaning of the event. As a social institution, folklore provides a situational context for understanding the performative event. Participants within that institution participate in its system for making sense; they become part of that discourse, their knowledge being an agreed-upon social construct (Fish 1980; Foucault 1975).

Thus performance is a behavior bounded by a relevant context, so that it is not an exclusive aesthetic effort but has a social and cultural base that requires that we see it as a dynamic subject rather than a reified object. A communication between participants (the player and the audience), the performance is characterized by a reciprocal integrative relationship that creates an emergent meaning at the moment, on the spot. The best sources for understanding that meaning, as a result, are the participants themselves. Valuing their reflexivity permits the emergence of local truths of practice and acknowledges the relevance of context. Equally, it replaces uniform definitions with a form of cultural anarchy (Herzfeld 1987).[7]

Just as the study of glentia, proverbs, folk songs, and laments is enhanced by the application of performance theory, so is study of the Karagiozis performance. Because Karagiozis spread across the whole of Greece—its islands as well as its mainland, its cities as well as its mountain villages, its economic centers as well as its trading routes—

the performance lends itself to geographic study (Myrsiades 1988a). Because it has been documented over a period of two hundred years in Greece—and four hundred in Turkey and the Middle East—it also lends itself to historical study (Myrsiades and Myrsiades 1988). Because close to two hundred names of Greek players alone have survived across that history, Karagiozis lends itself to examination by means of individual as well as interactive creation. It serves a plurality of groups whose interests and whose conflicts are not only represented in the characters of the performance and in the constitution of its audiences, but with which it has been interactive in the collection of its materials, in the context of the performative event itself, and in its effect as a socially constituted body of meaning that acts to address and mediate social conflicts. Karagiozis integrates both oral and written sources in this still largely oral performance as it negotiates the influences of both unofficial popular culture and official learned or elite forces. The product of a not-so-simple folk, it addresses both emergent urban and residual rural values as well as those of the dominant status quo. The Karagiozis performance, in sum, represents a process rather than a product, an interactive intertext that is contextually responsive economically, socially, politically, historically, and geographically to the Greek landscape.

The most immediate context in which the Karagiozis performance exists is the performative context, which consists of performance genesis, nature, and effect. Here, the interactive nature of the folk in the variety of its roles—everyday discourse, performer, performance content, and audience—is most apparent. Within the discourse community shared by the folk, its roles are experienced with a high degree of undifferentiated interactivity. In a 1986 meeting of Karagiozis players in Athens, Giorgos Haridimos's widely approved comment that Karagiozis is a creation of the Greek people, a people's spectacle identified with the people (*o idhios me to lao*), indicated that interactivity. In response, the player Manthos Athineos associated the performance itself in Haridimos's hands as *romeiko* (essentially Greek), claiming that its spectacle is so alive that it burns; a third, unidentified player referred to Karagiozis as "slices of life, food for life." It laughs at life, complains about it, and participates in it. As Haridimos comments elsewhere, the ideal player is one of the people. Indeed, asked in an interview in 1987 why he would not sell his used puppet figures to collectors, Haridimos expressed his identification with them and, through them, with the people: "Do you know what value these things have [for me]? Let me explain what I mean. I've lived, I speak from experience, that's the way it is, isn't it? I speak with these things. It's true they might be lifeless, but I bring them to life sometimes. I've spoken to an entire people. I played a role in their lives. I gave life to this lifeless form. I gave it life. For me it means something. How can I give it away?"

Haridimos clarifies the relationship between performer and reality, asserting that if you "depart from life, you will depart from the true function of the screen." It is not merely that the performance's sense of reality is rooted in the actuality of everyday experience, but, more directly, that the performance finds its materials in the life of the people. As Haridimos explains, you find the Karagiozis role on the road, and "you'll put it into the performance, whatever role it might be, depending on the situation." He refers to the early days when Karagiozis was a young performance, cities were sparsely populated, and there were few players. Players actively circulated throughout the neighborhoods to locate sources of performance material. Priding himself on having the ability to transform this material to the screen, Haridimos compares the process with hearing a story, a personal testimony, told by an old man at a café, and through the player's art turning this small piece into a performed or enacted event.

Ultimately, like Karagiozis and like the Karagiozis audience, the Karagiozis player lives the life of the folk with which he identifies his performance. The player Hristos Haridimos related in a conversation with his son Giorgos: "Do you know why I played good Karagiozis? Because I lived in the various classes of the community, I walked with the lowest bum up to the highest aristocrat. I went into the street to learn, and I learned many things." Beyond the simple rural peasant folk with which folklore has traditionally been identified, beyond the urban folk that became essential to the development of the Karagiozis performance, Haridimos speaks of a heterogeneous folk of pluralistic values covering all classes and social groups.

Giorgos Haridimos concludes that Karagiozis is a creation of this Greek people in an extended sense, for beyond serving as a source of performance content, they are active-receptive participants in the process of creation. They perform this function in both an aesthetic and a literal sense. They exert literal control through their reception of Karagiozis materials: "It's very difficult for a Karagiozis player to perform. Nowadays you can't hold the audience, as one might say, for two hours, and they really tire you out. . . . It kills you. And today the audience isn't like in the old days. . . . In those years, if you didn't perform well, you'd get beaten. While now, you won't get beaten, but they won't come back again." Aesthetically, the audience is even more immediate to the performance, which it perceives directly, without analysis, and as an involved party that refuses to be isolated. It supplies the content that completes the incomplete meaning of the text, constructing that meaning through its interaction across the duration of the performance as a surrogate performer. Haridimos said: "I think the audience themselves take the performance to heart and play Karagiozis. He lives, he lives in each one of them."

We find that the performer, having put a performance together from materials gathered "from here and there," depends on the audience to "tie it together." Thus it does not matter if the performance is sometimes "all mixed up," for the interactivity of performer and audience guarantees an appropriate context to complete the performance. The same role is described in other terms when the player discusses the need to recognize the point in performance at which a text has fulfilled or completed itself: "When your audience reaches the joy of laughter, there you hold it. It has reached the point that it should reach, and we have proof of it. We have as evidence the laughter of the audience. From that point on, you have a real hold on it . . . because immediately you have the criticism of your audience: what laughter comes from the right things and what value this kind of comedy contains."

However artistic a player is, however much he is accepted by critical sources, he still relies on his audience. Indeed, the player does not wait for critical acceptance from outside the world of the performative event, as Haridimos makes clear: "If my work is of value to you, and if they believe I am clever, I don't [need to] depend on [literary critics]. My audience is my witness." The player is thus careful to ensure a positive interaction with his audience: "Make sure the people like you. If the people like you, you have nothing to fear."

Immediacy is necessary for such interaction, and thus many players have rejected performing on television, according to Haridimos: "Karagiozis has to appear on his screen, on his little white sheet, in his shed. That's it! And all the mystery that's going to be performed must unfold on this screen. Then it becomes natural and acceptable." The audience is thus the ultimate standard of judgment for the performance, for, as the player reports, he himself always asks, "How can I manage to catch them? Because it's psychological, as we say. The town square plays a role." Indeed, the player himself, in a heightened expression of interchangeability, reflexively adopts an audience perspective for his performance: "I manage the Karagiozis player's exhaustion. This is important from the audience's point of view. Taka, taka, taka, taka, tak, adding the filling, adding the filling, adding the filling, and getting out quickly, players don't last. Deliver the jokes and bam! I wait for the audience to stop laughing, withdraw, jump into the next one or hold this one with the same words, hit it again, grab the laugh, and lock it up with a golden master key to get into the theme with gusto. . . . I try to be more brief, to go into the theme and right into the jokes, because today the audience expects laughs from me and not drama or [spectacle]."

The audience represents the final test of both improvisational ability and the fit to tradition as it validates or invalidates the player's efforts. Haridimos relates, "I use different jokes, or humor. You might say one joke, whatever it is, whether meant for young or old, and they don't laugh. You deliver others that lean toward love, and they don't like them either. Since they don't laugh with these things, they must like the literary. What can I do, so I gear at least half the work toward the literary. I watch and sneak up on them from behind by placing a phrase, a theft, a duel of frying pans; they like it. So now I prepare again. I pull out something else to create an episode they might laugh at. How about something else? I throw Karagiozis's watering can, the stairs trip up the donkey. That's how it's done with the classic pieces. I present something old with various good tricks of my own, various business, so we can laugh."

Not only has the player become his own audience to evaluate the performance reflexively, but he has also become a source of materials himself. Through his identification with the performance, he finds it is interchangeable with his own life. Haridimos relates how human Karagiozis's reactions are, how events from his own life appear in the performance as part of Karagiozis's life, and how that sometimes surprises him: "They catch me unawares, and I use them." In conversation, as well, the player frequently moves between the realms of his own personal life and those of the performance without any sense of boundedness, without using framing devices to clarify shifts in the nature of his discourse. In conversation, he sometimes speaks of himself as Karagiozis, in Karagiozis's words, and then congratulates himself at the end for a "beautiful dialogue: 'I'm not a thief; I'm hungry, and I take bread to eat. There's no other way. Since I'm hungry, I'm going to do whatever is necessary. I'll take it; I can't do otherwise. But I don't steal money, I don't rob banks and all these other things that you say.'"

The perceptual unity of perceiver, object, and creator displays the unity of experience that informs the Karagiozis performance. Not only do the Karagiozis performer and audience participate in the same situational context of the performative event, but they are coextensive of one another in much the same way that text and context are ultimately understood as so labile that clear distinctions between them become impossible to maintain. Moreover, the performer and audience intersect with the situational reality of the larger social context in such a way that they create a performance extending into the larger world. Such an understanding of contextuality liberates the performance in both its meaning and function from the boundaries imposed by time and space in the performance itself. As control passes from situational reality to the performance situation and back to reality again, symbolic action achieves a potency that ensures its persuasive intent as a guide to social action, relying on the interactive participation of the community in its everyday roles and its roles as performer and audience. The community's interactive role-playing permits the performance to negotiate physical reality and performative reality and act as a bridge between them, enabling the transformation of everyday experiences into extraordinary performative ones and the reduction of extraordinary experiences to real-life applications. As the performance negotiates different classes, occupations, ages, psychological types, national groups, and sexes, it expresses a pluralistic orientation that demonstrates the nature of the performance as a multileveled communicative event once again defined by the interaction of the folk in its everyday, performer, and audience roles. The performance is thus at the same time an integrating agent and an expander of boundaries.

The Karagiozis performance is not a closed but an open-ended dynamic process of creation, re-creation, and expansion in an emergent universe of new information, meanings, and significance that exists in a constant state of becoming as a multilinear and multileveled process of ongoing textual evolution. It is clear from player testimony, for example, that the Karagiozis text is not fixed but emerges in performance as a dynamic, ongoing process that strikes a balance between stability and instability, with instability acting as the driving force of the performative event. Whereas a set of textual restraints ensure continuity of the performance tradition and stability in both compositional form and transmission, the performance process is described by players as essentially a flexible, responsive force that emerges dynamically through the participation of audience and performer in the immediate context of the performative event (Myrsiades 1985a).

Within the interactive context of general environmental and immediate performative demands, Karagiozis players maintain a performance text that represents an internal context built up by generations of interaction between players and their masters. This dynamic text, transmitted from generation to generation, consists of a balance of physical playing techniques, spontaneous improvisation, and traditional ordering functions controlled by an inherent rhythm that pulls the performance together. The active performance is itself composed flexibly, that is, improvisationally. It responds to a range of forces both internal and external and is shaped by a negotiated order that emanates from the interactive balance of those forces.

Technique is the simplest level at which players discuss their performances. Technique includes a player's acrobatics (skill in manipulating the puppets) and strength (ability to maintain one's energy level across a performance), the use of sight gags, sound and scenic effects, as well as the general design and look of the stage, puppets, and properties (Myrsiades and Myrsiades 1988). Performance qualities are detailed by such terms as *lepto* (refined), *gliko* (sweet), and *ithopoia* (acting), as players emphasize their effort to refine their performance and develop *kathara* (clean) techniques, but above all to preserve their *mimesis* (mimicry), *fones* (voices), and *kalamburia* (jokes).

The second level is that of content, that is, the *kimena* (text) and *theama* (theme), which are controlled by the *skeleto* or *hypothesis* (the plot skeleton or outline), as the player Dinos Theodoropulos indicates: "A *hypothesis*, certainly. . . . I take the theme, and having taken the theme, I outline the general story. So that when I have a skeleton, I can remember what comes next; I write and I know. What shall I say, that's it." The skeleton is described as the overall outline of the received text, which each player fills in with his own improvisations, a general story outline that establishes the boundaries within which improvisation operates. If the skeleton is maintained in a performance, the performance is considered correct, but if the skeleton, in the player's words, is entered into, that is, if it is improvised upon, then it is given life.

The *sira* (order) is regarded as a secondary governing principle. As Haridimos puts it, each element has its own time, its own moment, for the elements, taken together and in turn, have an orderliness. New texts are said to have been given a beginning and an end and are arranged in an order from which future players should not depart. As described by Stamatis Generalis, the performance is made up of a player introducing many characters in order as he improvises jokes. Indeed, the very basis of an apprentice's training is the placement of figures backstage in their proper order, the introduction into the performances of the characters in their order, and knowledge of the text's order. The apprentice thus keeps the performance from becoming discontinuous. Even mistakes in dialogues and scenes are allowed to pass for fear of spoiling the order.

The third level is the art of the performance. This primary principle is instinctive; it depends on improvisation. It freshens, changes, and enriches, Haridimos claims, in the addition of new elements to the performance: "When I improvise, it gives me an opportunity to revitalize myself, my jokes, my dialogue, my movements, in all ways. . . . Freedom gives you the ability to enrich more things with jokes and to be always new and fresh. If we play *Karagiozis Cook* today, tomorrow we will perform the same skeleton, the same plot, but with other dialogue, with other jokes and improvisation. I will present new jokes, other dialogue, you see, and I will be different. . . . It emerges from the moment. . . . It occurs at that moment." Spontaneous improvisation embellishes the performance skeleton, while it is, at the same time, both allowed and shaped by the latter. Haridimos explains: "I know the skeletons of the performances and what's going on from one speech to the other and the improvisation that occurs around them, the jokes, you see. I ornament it. I search out how to perform it better."

Mimis Mollas describes the performance as the process by means of which skeleton and improvisation negotiate their mutual roles, contending that "my workbook is my guide . . . for the *hypothesis*. . . . Of course, the dialogue comes from experience and the performance locale. Again, the comedy I make in each individual performance is easily understood and is done with a sound pattern, a sound pattern. No matter where the spectator is, he will see only the action of the movement so he will be able to understand at what point the text cannot be followed and where I improvise."

Improvisations can themselves pass from immediate and momentary embellishments to stable forms that become part of the transmitted tradition. They thus pass into the collective memory of the performance, as Mimis Mollas explains: "I improvise and say some new jokes. The improvisation is imprinted in the memory to add to permanent jokes. . . . I take it up again and use it again in another performance so that the permanent jokes of Karagiozis are preserved at the same time that they are fed." Moreover, that new form is itself capable of generating an entirely new performance, so that the player "can immediately transform one improvisation, two words, or something that might occur in [his] work, in [his] improvisation, into an entire performance."

The art of improvisation is linked to *prosopikotita* (individuality) and *dimiuryia* (creativity), by means of which players ultimately rank themselves in comparison with their fellow players. These highly prized elements are considered essential to *alithino* (true) or *gnisio* (authentic) Karagiozis. Players use these terms to identify superior performances. As a result, players give considerable leeway to individual style in the performance. You cannot, Mimis Mollas claims, have "artistic expression without individuality." A player without such individuality or uniqueness may be regarded, as Savvas Gitsaris arbitrarily regards Haridimos, as being "seldom sufficient," of being incapable of creating his own works since "his mind doesn't create."

The three levels that constitute the internal context of the performance text—playing techniques, ordering functions, and improvisation—interact with other forces in the process of text creation. Just as the Karagiozis player interacts with his audience, so the process of text creation is an interactive collaboration between the performance tradition of the past and the contemporary reality of a new text. It is, as well, as intertext of items representing different discourses—literary, social, and performative. Improvising on the integrated material, the player enacts his text, embodying it in the actions of his characters, from whom emerge anecdotal scenes that merge into the skeletal construct of the original idea to enable a performance. Interaction with a performance audience shapes the newly constituted mass into a viable entity that is then taken up by other players who themselves make up

the present-day Karagiozis tradition. The performance is re-created
and expanded through repeated performances that set the new text in
the context of the contemporary scene.

The authority of the text is only truly established in the context of
the overall process, in spite of the fact that an individual initiated that
process and individual hands shaped it. On the other hand, the per-
formance is not truly an anonymously collective creation, for group
and individual responsibilities have been assumed and asserted. Still,
unique authorship cannot be claimed, given the intertextual and inter-
active nature of text creation. Giorgos Haridimos discusses the process
from the player's perspective: "Where was this written? We don't know
which player wrote it. We only know that the second one took it from
the one who gave it being, modified it, fixed it, performed it again and
again, gave it a beginning and an end, and now it has its *sira*."

The player may take up an idea from a novel or an event from real
life looking for Karagiozis in it. Once the text is in the player's hands,
he has responsibility for individual interaction with the text and
presentation of the text for audience interaction. He therefore must
possess considerable improvisational ability as well as a strong sense
of "fit" to the tradition, as Giorgos Haridimos reveals: "I can imme-
diately transform one improvisation, two words, or something that
might occur in my work, in my improvisation, into an entire perform-
ance. The whole performance that results will be correct, classical,
that is to say, that which I seek. You see? [The classical performance] is
so deeply rooted in me that it emerges by itself. My work gives it
birth."

The performer puts the performance together in a pragmatic way,
discovering his skeletal plot, putting Karagiozis first in the role he will
play, and then casting the other stock characters in the traditional
repertoire. The only material the player organizes before the perform-
ance is the skeleton of the plot and the order of introduction of the
characters. The dialogue itself, taken for granted, arises, according to
the player, at the moment of performance, which itself completes the
performance text. It is only in performance that all the textual ele-
ments—characters, plot, dialogue, improvisation—fall into place.
Haridimos relates, "I have all [the dialogue] in my brain, and at the
moment I'm performing, I'm looking for something else. At such a
time, let us say, I begin to pull out the good performance, to search it
out. . . . I bring it up to my screen. I play it the first night, and playing

it, I see what's going on. Then I play it again, and each time it opens up more. I keep replaying it and replaying it; it corrects itself, and it's never complete. Not in its reduced form or in its final form. Always a new performance."

This new performance can be built up from a short dialogue or scene that represents the core idea of the performance for the player. The piece need not be an abbreviated or skeletal plot but may merely be an idea onto which he will add freely in performance: "Now in this little piece, because it's small, here I put a vignette; here a little farther on I can throw up a little comedy, and I stretch it out. The vignette can come from whatever I want. This new piece is itself a vignette that I can use in some other performance that is short." Composition in performance is thus done in bits and pieces. It is aggregative and interactive with other texts and the tradition rather than fixed or made of a whole cloth.

In viewing the internal context of the performance, Karagiozis players distinguish a *palia* (old) style that stresses the manipulation of puppets, scenic effects, sight gags, and slapstick humor from modern performances that are characterized by *omilia* (speech) and *loyia* (words) rather than by *kinisi* (physical movement). The *tehni* (art of performing) of the old style is described as highly individual *peksimo* (playing) that is *elefthero* (free). Without a fixed model or limits, the old performance is characterized by its *brio* (high spirit) and its *dinamikotita* (dynamic quality).

Mimis Mollas, educated through secondary school, insists on the primacy of the old school and the need to maintain its *styl' icon* (visual style) of special effects and music rather than the language and themes on which modern players rely. He describes Karagiozis as essentially a "dynamic picture of conventional words" and objects to its having become a "conventional picture of dynamic words," that is, to the current preference for oral rather than visual values. But Haridimos considers the old style a living tradition that has changed and grown. Indeed, the fact that the tradition changes says something about its nature. It must be flexible, as Kostas Kareklas suggests when he claims that "players play differently. They cannot do otherwise." Such variation, nevertheless, itself denies the presence of a fixed performance text, even if, as Kareklas says, different players trained by different masters may very well perform a given figure in the same way.

The shift to a modern performance style was influenced by the increasing number of players who were educated past primary school. References to performers being illiterate but still good Karagiozis players suggest a defensiveness on the part of earlier players at being uneducated. Indeed, Vangos went back to secondary school when he was past thirty because he was ashamed of not being fully literate. Few players even attempted secondary school (among those known to have done so were Mimaros, Dinos Theodoropulos, and Mimis Mollas, each from a different generation of players); few reached the midpoint in grammar school (among them Mitsakis, Giorgos Haridimos, Evgenios Spatharis, Panagiotis Mihopulos, Vangos, Gitsaris, and Avraam, a group largely of now-mature players); and only a handful across the tradition had a clear reputation for having more than a grammar school education (largely lesser-known players, including Pandelis Melidis, Panagiotis Lambrinos, Giorgos Spanos, and Bobotinos, but also such well-known players as Haris Harilaos and Theodoropulos). It is fair to say that not only was the Karagiozis player associated in the common mind with the lower classes and the minimally educated, but a dichotomy had grown up between being educated and being a Karagiozis player, certainly until recent years. As Avraam testifies, a player did not need to be literate, for performing Karagiozis was a low and ridiculed profession. Moreover, players attributed to literacy a host of sins, as Giorgos Haridimos suggests: "Theodoropulos was never able to tie his themes to tradition. That is to say, he made his own performances. His work had an individuality. . . . In speech and mimicry he was creative. But there was something else. He had no connection with his tradition. . . . Dinos Theodoropulos was educated. And he did not have the humor and puns that my father [Hristos Haridimos] had. Because my father had a powerful voice. And he was powerful. A better mimic than Theodoropulos. . . . Because Haridimos had life and spirit. Dinos Theodoropulos began the playing of open Karagiozis. And the puns he spoke were clever, but they were heavy. The spectators didn't understand them, while Haridimos was one of the people."

Giorgos Haridimos explains that education interjects itself between a player and the inherited materials of his art, making it less likely that he will make himself their instrument. Rather, the player becomes critical and selective, separating himself from his audience as he distances himself from his tradition. For Haridimos, the choice is not always conscious, for having learned the written word, a player necessarily relies less and less on his ear, compromising oral composition: "Whatever the person, my ear imprints what I say at the very minute I'm speaking. There is no microphone. The ear imprints it. I work with the ear. Do you understand? . . . It's in the ear. I begin Karagiozis with the accent. From the beginning, I have him down with tones. Nothing at all is lost. Whatever character it is, the old man, the pasha, it's the same thing. From beginning to end you'll find me using the same motif. You'll find I'm the same from the time I start out to the end of the performance. I won't get higher or lower, I'll stay in the same place. Whereas [the other] Karagiozis players don't do this. For example, the way they work, everything becomes chaotic. They don't have the stamina. Their ear can't follow it."

Objecting to intellectualization of the performance or over-reliance on language, reflected in the moralizing humor found in educated players, Haridimos finds this kind of language closed in both its thought and manner of expression to "free treatment." Players frequently referred to as masters of mimicry are cited by other players for their ability to perform openly, freely, and clearly, qualities compromised by over-reliance on language in performance. Elevated language, by contrast, lends itself to static presentation in pseudo high Greek or Katharevusa, from which, players contend, neither tradition, experience, nor improvisation can rescue their performances. While some players can rely on language without compromising their ability for mimicry, the consensus is that the two are essentially incompatible. Mimis Mollas indicates this in his comparison of his father, the distinguished Athenian player Antonios Mollas, known for his *morfomenos,* or cultured Karagiozis, with Mitsos Manolopulos, an acknowledged master of the old style. He recalls the elder Mollas's own reduction of their differences: "I have performance texts and not mimicry. You have mimicry and not performance texts." Indeed, the cultured audience to which language values appeal is not regarded as the same audience reached by mimicry.

The most highly prized personal term used of a player is *nikokirosini* (a housekeeper of the art of the performance). Theodoropulos makes the point that only a truly good player of this sort would, for example, make a good teacher: "Karagiozis for me begins with the player being good. When the player is good, you will also find in him a teacher of the highest quality, you find in him a mentor, you find in him a satirist of the Turks, you find in him Aristophanes, you find in him a

bumpkin, you find in him a scientist, a doctor, you understand me."
Vangos explores the notion further: "For a boy to adapt himself to
become good in any kind of work whatever, you must give him
something of yourself so that he understands that you are a good man
and with that to show the way he must also become, let us say,
educated. You must become a second father, without tiring him so
much that following Karagiozis seems to him just another game. And
this is how Karagiozis is taught."

The first performance element transmitted by a master, according to
Avraam, is the simplest, the ability to construct a puppet booth and
figures. According to Gitsaris and Vangos, the apprentice next learns
to move the puppets, his first real responsibility behind the screen.
Learning the movements is not a difficult task, for it requires, as Git-
saris explains, no more than seeing the same manipulation done over
and over and then doing it oneself repeatedly. The first critical task,
then, is to learn the voices of the different characters, which are
themselves based in real life. As Mimis Mollas puts it, "And for
dialogue, of which I spoke, that depends on speech of common value
for our profession to fulfill itself." Both he and Gitsaris indicate that
their first objective vocally is to separate characters clearly from one
another, and the second is to create distinctive types. Haridimos
contends that the process requires not only imitating one's master in
manipulation and voices but also admitting the influence of natives of
various regions of the country, both for details of characterization and
for purity of dialect. The apprentice learns his voices, Haridimos
explains, as a singer learns his songs. He responds to sounds that rise
and fall like musical notes, loud and soft sounds, colors, shades,
pitches, tones, and dialect inflections. The sounds are memorized and
recalled just as one learns and recalls a musical score. They have for
the player the same exact placement and phrasing, the same tonality as
musical notes.

Relying on his ability to use his voice, the player must, Haridimos
reminds us, be able to play continuously without tiring and to keep his
tongue from getting twisted, his throat clear and unstuck, his sounds
clean and well distinguished, and his ability to mimic dialects un-
diminished. If he tires and the power of his voice lessens, he must be
able to maintain a strong laryngeal tone for each character and to play
without leaving a void, or empty space, in his performance, a trick
accomplished by a free use of the tongue. Always searching for new

vocal techniques, Haridimos describes his own development as moving in the direction of clearer tones, different and fresher sounds, greater experience and ease, more effective timing, greater intelligence, and a more refined "laying out" or patterning of his sounds. He does not need, he proudly asserts, to rely on a microphone, as do lesser players, whose sounds, as a result, are clouded and without color. Moreover, by developing good control and proper placement for each of his voices, he does not feel he runs the risk other players run of losing his voice in advancing years.

Voices are a significant element not merely in themselves but also for their embodiment of character, as Vangos discovered in his first solo trial before the public. His master, Yiannis Yatridis, warned him: "'If I myself don't hear you, you will not be moved to perform. . . .' He himself came out in front of the booth, naturally before the audience, and he says, 'Ladies and gentlemen, this evening a new player is baptized. It is my helper who is also known to give you what you are used to. For this reason, I'm doing this, so you'll give him your undivided attention so we can hear him and give him courage.' But the words I spoke had no effect. It was harmful to him that I spoke the first voices. . . . They had gotten used to the master, naturally. . . . But that master analyzed the model of a man, while I followed the scenario."

Antonios Mollas is reported to have advised Haridimos in his first appearance as a player that he would only truly understand what was behind the voices through the discipline provided by a master. Mollas's own experience was as an undisciplined player: "When I began, you wouldn't believe the stones they threw at me . . . because I spoke nonsense, while you, you won't speak nonsense because you stay close to the master, you understand, and you know what you'll say. We didn't know what we were saying then. . . . Afterward, naturally, they didn't call us masters, although you, you're inside our inner circle."

Beyond voices, movement, and style lies the text itself, which the apprentice learns as a *hypothesis* or story told to him by his master. Indeed, Theodoropulos, Giorgos Haridimos, Mitsakis, Kareklas, and Athanasios Spiropulos delight in telling the story of a performance text, much as a storyteller narrates a story. Having heard it told and then seen it performed over and over by his master, the apprentice learns the order in which he introduces the characters, thus nailing down the order of the text itself.

In general, the apprentice player does not appear to separate out unique elements to study. Alexopulos's response to studying with his master is typically generalized: "I liked the style, the performance, the quality of the voices, the manipulated figures, and all of it." Just as apprentices may find it difficult to distinguish the performance elements they were first taught as they grow into players themselves, they sometimes find it difficult to identify or separate the influences to which they have been subjected as a young player. Vangos struggled with this question:

I can give you a little picture. Eh, in my youth my greatest experience came from the style of the elder Haridimos. . . . I stayed for a long time, but it seemed very easy to me. And it was a very easy type. This was until I grew older and because [my] master Giatridis's style was missing. This made [Giatridis] sad, and he would always say to me, "In the name of God, I try to make a Karagiozis player of you, why do you take Haridimos's style? When did this happen?" Haridimos's style was easier and the dialogue simple, since the old one's, without wanting to put him down, was relatively illiterate. [Giatridis] was more cultured. As I grew, however, I could see that our art is more. Speech and masterfulness must be found in the tongue. For this reason, I abandoned Haridimos's style, the stereotype, and I create my own style in the footsteps of Giatridis so that more speech occurs . . . to embellish the scenario, let us say, not to leave behind any loose ends. Thus it began, then, that I put my own spirit into it more.

The process, in sum, from the apprentice's point of view, is one of progressively aggregating and later assimilating influences to arrive not at an imitative state but at one's uniquely individual style. The process of transmission, as we have seen, is informal and unstructured. Kareklas, in a revealing description, explains the relationship between master and apprentice as that of a teacher and his pupil: beaten, the pupil learns patience; by arguing, one teaches. Speaking out of his own experience as an apprentice, Avraam believes that ultimately a player learns by using his wits, that learning to be a player is like learning, as Giorgos Haridimos has said, a song that one merely picks up. Haridimos adds that not everyone is capable of picking up a performance as he does. Indeed, this inequality of players is, in Haridimos's view, one cause of the decline of the performance, accounting for the devolution of performance quality following the demise of the great artists of the 1930s: "They don't hold on to it well; [modern players] couldn't take from their masters, much less undertake the art." Vangos, speaking of an apprentice, decries this loss of understanding from one generation to another:

This Barba Giorgos [Uncle George puppet] said, "I'll give you *pletsana*." I say to [the apprentice], "What's *pletsana*? I'm saying *pleitsana*." And if I tell you I say to him, "What is *i pleitsana*," you'll hit your head. He asks me what it is. Simply, I'll tell you, milk and a crumb of bread. Something rustic as it's spoken, let us say in the villages. So. But I say to him, "You don't even have the curiosity to ask the meaning of the words I say." That's how the art changes from hand to hand. It's something like that with the patrons. They hear what's being mimicked but don't understand its meaning. This means that as soon as you understand the meaning, it's possible to give it back to the public better. There, this one understands the second time, and when I say to him "my *tzerdello*," afterward I'll find the means to say that my head hurts, because many don't understand what *tzerdello* means; he can't understand it. You have to speak in the common way.

The personal relationship that develops between a master and an apprentice is critical to the transmission process that preserves the art of the performance. The actual length of time a player apprentices, however, does not necessarily determine the depth of that relationship, for it varies. By 1930 a player generally began as an apprentice in his young teens and sometimes in his early twenties, an indication that schooling delayed the entry of later players into the profession. A second inhibiting factor was popular prejudice against the itinerant player. Throughout the history of the performance, families were reluctant to give their sons to the performance, preferring that they take up a trade. Some players did, in fact, prepare for trades to fall back on in lean years. Ianaros, for example, was a mechanic; Theodoros Bontzas, a junk dealer; and Vangos, a railroader. Of the older players, Theodoropulos, Vasilis Vasilaros, and Hristos Haridimos tell tales of being permitted by their families to become players only when it became apparent that they had no means or ability to go on with their education. In each case, the player was forbidden to perform under his family name. Thus Kalogeras became Theodoropulos, Andrikopulos became Vasilaros, and Haritos became Haridimos.

The length of time a player apprentices differs as well. Although Mimis Mollas claims that an apprenticeship of only five years is necessary, the fact that he began to play late in his life (after he served in the army) suggests a telescoped apprenticeship. A five-year apprenticeship is not, however, uncommon. Certainly, for Mitsakis, Nikolaos Lekkas, and Friksos, five years was sufficient. There are, however, differences between apprenticeships. Lekkas, in his early teens, studied under his first master, Theodoropulos, merely to get started in the profession. For other players, such as Gitsaris, who stayed twelve years with Stavrotheodoros, and for Antonis Antonaros, who followed Theodoropulos for eighteen years, apprenticeship came close to being a way of life. Alexopulos for example, having studied under Vasilis Agapitos for twenty-five years, went on to renew his subordinate status with a five-year stint with Theodoropulos.

Avraam exemplifies yet another approach. Having studied with three masters in as many years who provided him with only basic guidelines, he claims a beginner must move from master to master, observing the art of each and absorbing dialects and mannerisms from daily life. Avraam developed his own style dependent upon no single teacher, for he found masters reluctant to teach their secrets to a future competitor. But Giorgos Haridimos, himself trained by his player-father Hristos, explains of an apprentice who would learn his art without a master, "Whenever you involve yourself in a priest's work, you'll make a mess of things."

An alternative to apprenticing with a single master or series of masters was possible by merely attending the performances of other players, as Theodoropulos did: "Listen, it never interested me. I didn't distinguish between Karagiozis players. If I had the opportunity to see [Giannis] Moros or another player in my village, it was enough for me. If I saw another, I didn't distinguish even, let us say, to wait around to see more of the other. Nor did I ever pay much attention whether one was better than the other. . . . It didn't interest me to learn from them. What I can say is that either my mind operates or is impoverished for this work . . . or that for this work I'm not creative."

Moreover, Theodoropulos considered the audience itself as a mentor: "I understood what the village did to make me love it. Because I was still weak. I understood that I needed to be instructed more. I still needed practice. I needed to have the village so I could get better used to the way I presented myself, also to stand on my own feet. . . . And that's how I fell in love with the village, because in the village, if I was a little hurried, they wouldn't forgive me or condemn me." Theodoropulos's performance, highly reviewlike or vaudevillian in its structure, reflects the variety of influences the player encountered both in his village as a boy and on tour. By contrast, Vasilaros, whose performance also has a reviewlike structure, studied with a wide variety of older players—Thodoros Theodorellos, Dimitris Bekos, Manolopulos, Dimitris Pangalos, Bobotinos, and Thanasis Sotiropulos.

Among the largely illiterate early players, the system of loosely structured apprenticeship under a master prevailed as a means of preserving oral transmission. The system was itself esteemed among players, in spite of the authoritarianism to which it was prone. Vasilaros proudly claims to have trained ninety-five apprentices, although this would have left few players for other masters to train, even accounting for the movement of many players from one master to another. Vangos still keeps three to five apprentices at a time, while Giorgos Haridimos refers to the "uncountable" number of apprentices he and his father trained. It is Theodoropulos, however, in the course of his extensive travels and across a half century of performing, who must be credited with having left behind the largest body of new players. Certainly more players refer to periods of apprenticeship under him than under any other twentieth-century master. The preservation of tradition, it thus appears, was well served by a stable single master-student relationship, or at least by a student's apprenticeship with a limited number of masters. It is, in any case, that system of transmission that is most highly prized among conservative players.

The immediate and the internal performative contexts are not the only contexts in which the Karagiozis performance is set. Rather, the players and their performances are themselves part of a larger environmental context made up of uncontrolled historical, geographic, economic, and social forces explored best through diachronic study of the performance. Such study reveals the performance's difficult, itinerant history as a touring performance in Greece in the post-Turkish period (Myrsiades 1988a; see Myrsiades and Myrsiades 1988: 204, n. 159); the effect on the performance of the culture instability that resulted from years of insecure borders, wars, dictatorships, and invasions; and the conflicts that arose between different factions in the new state. In the nineteenth century the Karagiozis performance was caught in a power struggle between the Church and heterochthonous Greeks of the new government. Popular entertainments of a satiric nature found themselves with allies only among autochthonous Greeks, who, nevertheless, themselves maintained strong ties with the Church (Myrsiades and Myrsiades 1988). Moreover, the Karagiozis performance itself retained its Ottoman ties and was thus associated with Greece's old enemy—a charge the Church itself struggled against—and with Islam. The performance was also identified with indigenous Greeks, who had themselves become Orientalized during three centuries of Ottoman rule in Greece. Moreover, it rejected Hellenic notions sponsored by Greeks of the diaspora, who now represented the new Greek state, and resisted their preference for idealized values of the pagan classical past over modern realities of present-day Greek life.

The performance struggled in the late nineteenth century to naturalize itself in the new state and to resolve the dichotomy between Hellenic and Romeic ideologies as they informed the performance. It was caught in the development of a capitalist economy, the migration of population from the countryside to cities, and the growth of first the bourgeois and later the proletarian classes, all of which affected the performance economy by shifting locales and changing the composition of the performance's natural audience. More particularly, Karagiozis was caught in the theater wars of the mid- to late nineteenth century, in which such popular entertainments as Fasuli (a Punch and Judy type of puppet show) and Karagiozis were pitted against the European theater and opera troupes favored by the new rulers of Greece and the nascent Greek theatrical troupes preferred by autochthonous leaders and the lower and middle urban classes (Myrsiades and Myrsiades 1988).

Unlike folk performers of laments, songs, and proverbs in Greece, Karagiozis players were professionals rather than amateurs, itinerants rather than local performers, and thus economic context had a particular effect on the stability of the Karagiozis performance (Myrsiades 1988a). The Karagiozis player depended on his audience for his livelihood, intensifying the interactive nature of the performative event. A player's income differed widely from season to season, depending on whether he could play on a daily basis, as he did in the summer, or on weekends only, as occurred during economically or politically unstable years and during the winters. The size of his audience differed, depending again on the circumstances of his performance, and ensuring a more intimate interaction with audiences in outdoor cafés in the provinces, where one hundred patrons made up an average audience, than with audiences in enclosed city theaters, where players performed to a significantly larger number of patrons, sometimes as many as three thousand.

Payment patterns differed as well, from more informal bartering or payment in kind to passing a plate or, in larger urban theaters, selling tickets. A player's pay not only differed from year to year, but it was also dependent upon agricultural yield, access to currency, and urban employment. It was compromised by the number of members in a player's troupe, which could include several apprentices, a singer, and musicians, who sometimes made up a small orchestra and who often earned fixed pay. Indeed, the economics of operating such a troupe led players on tour to use local village singers and musicians. By the 1930s players eliminated live musicians altogether, either using recorded music or singing the songs themselves. Players who sang generally went without accompaniment, unless, like Antonaros, they used an apprentice to manipulate all the puppets. The result was a diminished responsiveness on the part of both performer and audience.

Touring has an aesthetic as well as an economic dimension. The peripatetic nature of the Karagiozis performance ensured that long-term residence in one location was an exceptional rather than a common practice until the development of a large repertoire in the 1920s and the establishment of a permanent urban performance base. Not only did players need to tour their performances when audiences dried up in one area, but they tried out innovations, polished new texts, and experimented with demanding audiences who not only represented a source of new themes, characters, and songs for the performance but were also vocally and physically engaged in the performative event. Moreover, apprentice players who wished to free themselves from their masters and set forth on their own found touring an inescapable necessity for developing their own performance style and expertise. As a result, a player's stay in one spot varied greatly when he was on tour. If he was moderately well received, he might stay thirty or sixty days, long enough to exhaust his basic repertoire. More often, however, a stay encompassed fifteen to twenty performances, although a stay of only one or two days was not uncommon, particularly when an audience was small or difficult to please. If a player was well known in a particular area, he might be invited by contract with a café owner to perform and could thereby ensure himself stable employment, protected by the good offices of his employer. Otherwise, itinerants merely appeared in a village, contacted the local constable, and made their own arrangements to set up in a *plateia* (a village square), an open space, or a café.

The social context in which the touring performance occurred thus held a variety of experiences that shaped the relationship of the player and the audience with which he interacted. Moving freely throughout the country and catering to the folk with audience-pleasing and often officially defiant material, the performances represented an open threat to organized authority. Players, as a result, were not always welcomed by provincial officials. Suffering the numerous inconveniences and the debased reputation of the itinerant, players had to trudge from village to village searching for one in which they would be permitted to perform. They were often subject to accusations of vagrancy by religious countryfolk who believed that puppeteering was a sinful profession. Because his fortunes rose and fell on local as well as regional political and economic tides, the player was forced to contend with moralizers who objected to the freedoms taken in his performances: Westernizers who found in his art an Oriental or backward influence; and police agents concerned with the camp followers that such a performance inevitably attracted—the impressionable runaways, the petty crooks—as well as the damage to property that often resulted from the hostility of a dissatisfied audience and the threat that some players—thieves, pederasts, and vagabonds themselves—posed. He had to contend with café owners who beat him when profits fell and bribed and cheated him when the audiences were large and pleased, the jealousies of competing players and of proprietors of rival houses, and the petty rivalries of his own helpers. The Karagiozis player had, in sum, to deal with bureaucrats in the cities and mayors and police chiefs in the villages, each of whom had the right to refuse him a license or permission to perform. Some, like Mihopulos, wary of long interrogations and persecution by local authorities, made it a point to procure permits from Athens before they embarked on a tour, in spite of the fact that such permits were generally disregarded in the countryside.

Heavily censored during periods of oppression—under German and Italian rule in World War II as well as under military dictatorships in the 1930s and the junta of 1967-74—burdened by a state tax he often could not pay, and plagued by a singular reluctance of government officials to allow him to perform at all, the Karagiozis player plied his tour routes throughout Greece, serving as the focal point of heightened feeling among the people. Divided into factions, village audiences often took sides in the evening's performance, argued with the puppet characters, protested against political jokes or unpopular endings, or simply took a dislike to the player himself, either for personal reasons, a lack of skill in the performance, or merely because he represented an urbanized interloper in their rural midst. It was not unknown for an audience to force the closing of a performance that had somehow offended local sentiments, as, indeed, occurred when Theodoropulos satirized the politician Papanastasis in Tripoli, unaware that Tripoli was his home city. Players who had cats, cans, and tomatoes thrown at them had to become inured, as did Andreas Spiliotopoulos, to audiences armed with great pumpkins and melons in case the performance soured and to café owners, protective of their property, who welcomed them with threats of breaking their heads and tearing down their booths if they did not perform well.

Audiences differed both regionally and by class. Working-class and peasant audiences familiar with the crude dialects and the earthy logic of the Karagiozis performance responded vocally to the performance, while sophisticated audiences, at home with theater, and later cinema and television, held themselves in reserve. To engage an audience, Kostas Manos informs us, a player had to watch each evening's group and note which of the different puppet types reached it. Salting Karagiozis's speech with examples of the dialect of the area, introducing local types, and judiciously selecting those pieces most conducive to attitudes of the local audience, players even went to the extreme of asking audiences which pieces they should perform. Responding to popular attitudes, values, themes, and speech without attempting to correct or regularize them to fit a learned standard, players nevertheless found themselves responding as well to the learning and elite values of literary and written texts, which were inevitably demanded by literate urban audiences that fed on the products of official mass culture.

Players, in sum, had to reach a range of audiences. In the north, a player learned to perform heroic pieces, which, the player Kostas Manos explains, were preferred there. In the south, he had to demonstrate greater facility and provide more variety, particularly, says the player Avraam, in Salamina, Patras, and Kalamata, where followers of the performance would close out a player after only a few days if his performances did not meet their artistic standards. Those in Macedonia were intolerant of all players, regardless of their skills. By contrast, audiences in villages around Tripoli, says the player Dimitris Manos, and throughout Evia, according to the player Lekkas, were particularly helpful to starting players.

Established circuits did not exist to facilitate touring, although certain patterns did emerge. In the late nineteenth and early twentieth centuries, the Peloponnisos formed the central location for Karagiozis performances, including such cities as Patras, Tripoli, Kalamata, Pyrgos, and Argos. Performances in the Athens-Piraeus area remained the province of players in their prime, masters of the art from the period of 1920 and thereafter, and educated players; less-practiced players were forced to perform outside of Athens or in the provinces until they proved themselves. A nearby route covered the environs of Athens, including the Athenian suburbs of Kallithéa, Néa Ionía, Galátsion, Kaisarianí, and Kifisiá and central Attica. Another well-traveled route passed through western Thessaly along the road from Larissa to Lamia, while another encompassed eastern Thessaly from Larissa to Volos. The least-frequented areas were northeastern Greece and Macedonia; many parts of these areas were never introduced to the performance. By contrast, performances were so widely toured on the island of Crete that it maintained its own school of players.

The modern Karagiozis performance has changed in many ways from the conditions described here, declining in contemporary times to a despairing state. Players have largely abandoned hope of owning, or even operating out of, a permanent theater based in an urban center or, in summers, in seaside towns. Land values are such that the pressure on small theaters has become intense. Moreover, audiences have dwindled to the point that a player might perform for one or two dozen patrons on any given weekday evening. Players thus perform at schools, in cinemas, at municipal parks, and even at summer camps for foreigners, held intermittently in such places as Corfu and Thessaly.

Each of the two major television stations has offered weekly fifteen-minute Karagiozis skits, for which players receive a salary that is less than a third of what they earn for an evening performance. The television performances are aimed at children, as are most modern performances that play at parks and schools. A number of players have fit up small trucks to transport easily assembled puppet booths to any of a variety of locations. A player may, in fact, perform in different neighborhoods from the back of such a truck.

Younger Karagiozis players hold other part- or full-time jobs and, as a result, perform irregularly, while some players in their prime have simply gone over entirely to other professions so they can more easily support growing families. A number of older players have retired to live on their pensions from the Karagiozis Players Association, rather than struggle on in such difficult circumstances, in spite of the fact that their performances are still competitive and viable. By contrast, several players have turned into rather good businessmen and are actually able to make money from the performance by catering to those audiences that do exist—largely children and foreign tourists. Their performances, more than those of other players, exploit the performance at the expense of its traditional artistic values.

The Karagiozis performance has, of course, changed in modern times to reflect changing tastes. The familiar prologue has been retained, but it is likely to be followed by a popular adventure plot or a love story in which the Karagiozis figure may be the only traditional stock character that appears. In another attempt to hold modern audiences, one player has resorted to continuous live guitar background music, turning the performance into something of a musical. Many players have replaced the leather puppets with plastic figures that are brighter and have better definition, but that lack sophistication of design and the texture of the leather originals. Shop windows in Athens offer up leather puppets, signed and sold by the players to merchants, at exorbitant prices running as high as four or five hundred dollars apiece.

The future of the performance depends on the number and kind of apprentice players it is able to attract. By the late 1980s players were finding it impossible to get able helpers, much less a team of them such as the developed performances require. Helpers have to be recruited from among groups of boys who hang around the theater, many of whom are rowdy and few of whom can be depended upon as even semiregular apprentices. Virtually none of these apprentices see their future in the performance. Some players turn for help to family members and neighbors, who treat their summers backstage as something of a hobby. In any case, the Karagiozis Players Association does report the application of several young players who have given test performances before an association committee to earn membership.

Membership in the association is important not only because it carries
social security and pension benefits with it but also because it identi-
fies players who tour to local police.

The environmental context thus represents the incorporative larger
circle within which the interactive performance process takes place.
Some might argue that such historical, social, geographic, and eco-
nomic constraints exist outside the creative process and that their
dysfunctional consequences for the development of a folklore tradition
have no effect on the performance. Such a view assumes that the
developmental process is essentially an orderly, text-based process
(Lord 1971; Propp 1968).[8] On the contrary, however, the develop-
mental process presented by players themselves is essentially erratic
and even disorderly, both in its necessary interaction with uncontrolla-
ble external forces (the performance's external context) as well as in its
responsiveness to irrational or disorderly tendencies from within the
process of text generation itself (the performance's internal context).[9]

It thus appears that the various contexts of the Karagiozis perform-
ance act as disequilibrating rather than stabilizing forces. The perform-
ance arises out of a sense by both community and performers of a
plurality of interests that coexist within the culture, and thus within the
text, without being resolved (Abrahams 1972).[10] Environmental con-
tingencies, such as the influence of topical events and popular novels,
new tastes and fashions, and even economic and social pressures, can
be seen to operate as forces that change the Karagiozis performance in
unknown and unanticipated new directions. As such change replaces
old patterns to create new enriched ones, erratic environmental influ-
ences lead to a performative process driven by irrationality that places
emphasis on the emergent nature of the performance. Transformations
that occur in a performance—the inspiration for new texts—are thus
associated with an unstable environmnt that subscribes to no formal
order.[11] From this perspective, rationality and irrationality, as an
interplay of contradictory forces, result in irregular patterns of change
pushing the form into erratic lunges forward in the development of the
performance. Since the growth of the form does not move purposefully
forward, organizing controls cannot ensure consistent goals and con-
gruent interests across a tradition, but rather must continue to negotiate
a plurality of interests.[12] Given these differentiated pressures on the
performance and the necessarily emergent nature of the performance,

the form is pushed forward spontaneously and multilinearly toward transformations responsive to creation and re-creation of new and existing forms rather than preservation of original authentic forms. Expressing impermanence (from the perspective of maintaining the status quo) and multiplicity, it accepts destabilizing consequences as a necessary aspect of the process of change and as a necessary corollary of survival.

To a significant extent, then, chance and randomness emanating from both external environmental and internal performative contexts guide performance development, informing the performance through the interaction of performer, performative event, and performance audience. Under the impact of uncertainty in an environment tending to change, the tradition, seen as manifesting itself through never-ceasing transformations in an effort to maintain itself, adds a dynamic historical dimension to our understanding of how folklore exists in a constant state of becoming (Abrahams 1968; Dundes 1964; Georges 1969).

This examination of folklore performance theory leads us to a new understanding of the process of the folk performance. The differentiated interests exhibited in the general cultural environment and in the Greek folk audience can no longer be said to represent a collective understanding of shared assumptions commonly held, but rather, they represent the individual interests of the varied addressees to whom the performer speaks as well as the interests of the performer himself. The approach presented here displaces the emphasis from past residual forms to present emergent forms and acknowledges that folklore resides in more than one class, in more than one kind of society, and in more than one setting. Consequently, the notions of class consciousness and collectivity are diffused as this approach acknowledges a plurality of interests among folk groups, as well as between folk groups and the larger social order, differentiated sensibilities, and specific ways of life in contrast to abstract cultural universalism.

In addition, emphasis is clearly placed on the autonomy of folk expression to the extent that indigenous testimony is preferred to the critical terminology and taxonomies of the literary establishment, which are distinguished by their attempts at social dominance and control. The aesthetic act of performance functions as an ideological force, for folklore is active. This active nature is most completely expressed in the folklore performance in which the performer, audience, and social context interact through the performative event as part of a communicative process that, while it is extensive of everyday life, transcends the ordinary course of events. A holistic transaction, the performance functions as a socially based unity of experience that is distinguishable from everyday life by its interpretive framing of the performance event. This framing requires an acceptance of the performative event, emerges out of the interaction of participants in a performance situation, and thus remains essentially performed verbal art.

CHAPTER FIVE

Giorgos Haridimos, Karagiozis Player

The lives of the Karagiozis player Giorgos Hardimos and his player-father, Hristos Haridimos, offer a study in contrasts that reveals the differences between two ways of becoming a Karagiozis performer. Moreover, to truly understand the son, it becomes useful to understand the father, whose work the son inherited and continues. Since both Hristos and Giorgos Haridimos have spoken and written about their lives, it becomes possible to trace the connections between them through their own words.[1]

Hristos Haridimos was born in the St. Paul area near Larissa Station in Athens, of Athenian parents. His father, Giorgos Haritos, worked as a chimney sweep at the palace of George I, now the parliament building. The only son of five children, Hristos lost his father at the age of five and was left to the care of his sisters when his mother took up a position she was to hold for twenty-eight years as washerwoman to the queen. He refused to attend school in spite of beatings by his mother. Instead, from the time he was thirteen, he began attending Karagiozis performances in the park in St. Nikolaos, Pefkakia, where Hristos Leventis was playing. From there, he began to follow Karagiozis players in Athens in the different places they performed, particularly in Dexameni in Kolonaki, where he followed Bekos, the apprentice of the master player Mimaros of Patras. Later, he was to follow Yiannis Moros, Antonios Poriotis, and, most important, Dinos Theodoropulos. Having taken up the design of puppets, young Haritos attracted Theodoropulos's attention and was taken on as an apprentice. When an owner of a theater in Methana asked Theodoropulos to recommend a player, Haritos's master advised him to hire the boy, giving his word that his young protégé could perform. Hristos auditioned with several voices, and the reluctant employer hired him for his first independent season of performances at a salary of one hundred drachmas. At this time, players had small repertoires of ten to fifteen performances and thus had to perform one piece over and over if they were to remain in a single spot; Theodoropulos, for example, stayed in one place a year or more. Thus, after two months, having run out of repertoire, Haritos moved on, playing at cafés, plateias, and theaters in the environs of Athens over the next seven years, until he went to serve in the army in 1920. The reputation of the Karagiozis performance was then so debased that a first cousin who had a high position at the palace visited Hristos's performance and requested that the Karagiozis player change his name to avoid embarrassing the family by linking it with such a low profession. It was at this time that Haritos became Haridimos.

Having performed for the troops in the army, Haridimos returned to performances in the environs of Athens, where he hired Miltiadis Lambros, who served as his backstage assistant for twenty-five years, until he died in Haridimos's arms. Performing in Kifisiá, Haridimos met a young girl from a well-to-do family and eloped. In 1924 his son Giorgos was born and almost immediately was introduced to the performance, playing at six months the voice of the newborn in *The Birth of Kolitiris*. A two-year stay at the theater near Platano in Kifisiá was followed by performances in Patras and a tour of its surrounding towns. Here Hristos discovered the singer Sotirios Kaproulias, who was to remain with him for fifteen years. From the Peloponnisos, he traveled throughout Boetia and the nearby island of Evia before returning permanently to the Athens-Piraeus area. He located himself in Pasalimani, Piraeus, eventually setting up his own theater, the Ermis, where he performed until 1949, when he went on pension. His player-son, Giorgos, continued to perform at the Ermis until it was destroyed in 1957.

Only during World War II, when Piraeus was bombarded, did Hristos and Giorgos Haridimos leave their theater for Athens. At the Cinema Ellas, the master Athenian player Antonios Mollas had offered to share his theater with his Piraean counterpart. Here one evening Mollas and Hristos Haridimos conspired to launch the younger Haridimos's solo career. Mollas told Giorgos that his father was unable to go on and that he would have to take his place. At intermission, recognizing his father in a corner of the theater and aware then of his father's hand behind his debut, Giorgos ran out without completing the performance. Mollas, catching him in flight, embraced him, telling him, "You have it in you" to become a true Karagiozis player. Following that episode, Giorgos performed regularly both on his own and while sharing a theater with his father. He operated a small theater in Pasalimani in the winter while his father played in a larger theater in Moshato. In the summer, they shared the theater in Pasalimani, performing twice a day; Giorgos played the afternoon performance, and his father played the evening one. The younger player never had to travel, as did his father, on a tour of villages, nor did he study with players other than his father, the man he regarded as a university in himself.

Following the demolition of the Ermis Theater in 1957, Giorgos played at his own theaters at the end of the railroad line in Piraeus and then in Tamburia, Piraeus, where he sold some four hundred tickets a night during the week and eight hundred for weekend performances. He was later reduced to performing short pieces in an amusement park and, until 1969, in a cinema in Tamburia, as land values shot up and theaters became more difficult to come by. Approached by a property owner in Plaka, Athens, he ultimately opened a 150-seat theater in Lysicrates Square, which he operated daily in the summer, performing on weekends in his winter quarters at the Theater Avlea in Pasalimani.

The only one of six brothers to become a Karagiozis player, Giorgos Haridimos has two young daughters by his second wife, from whom he recently separated. His first wife, who remained childless ran the business end of the theater for her husband, leaving him free to focus on his performance, until her death in the midseventies. Nine times president of the Karagiozis Players Association, Giorgos Haridimos is noted for a family tradition that has worked to preserve the laic nature of the performance in balance with a pure or classic style. It is a tradition that he and his father maintained over three quarters of a century, even as they became the preferred players of Piraeus in an area noted for the openness of its black market, the pervasive influence of the Greek underworld, and the absence of a police presence. Indeed, Hristos Haridimos himself was noted as a *mangas aristocratos* (an aristocratic hood) in his dandified white suit and jewelry, his love of the *zembekiko* dance, and his generosity with the poor. At the same time, he carried the nickname *kefalos,* an acknowledgment of the intelligence of his performance as well as a comment on the shape of

his head. Giorgos Haridimos has steered his own work between the
puritanical and the commercial, the vulgar and the child-oriented,
maintaining a political and satiric edge missing in the work of others
of his generation. He has reduced his once-inflated repertoire of four
hundred performances to sixty-five classic pieces, which he preserves
in an attempt to revitalize this much corrupted art. The last great mas-
ter player of the Karagiozis performance, Giorgos Haridimos retired
in 1989. His apprentice, Kostas Athanassios, has set up as a travel-
ing player and presently performs by invitation in different parts of
Greece.

We first met Giorgos Haridimos one evening in 1965 at his Shadow
Theater in the Plaka district of Athens. Having already spent several
months gathering Karagiozis scripts and attending performances
wherever we could find them, we discovered during an evening stroll
around the Pillars of Olympian Zeus a well-kept, whitewashed build-
ing with Karagiozis figures painted on it. The sign in front of the door
informed us that performances were given nightly at 7:30 and that the
program changed every two days. The following evening we arrived
for the performance. The woman at the window who sold us two
fifteen-drachma tickets eyed us suspiciously. We entered a doorway
covered with a curtain and were met by a middle-aged man, stout and
exceptionally thick-necked; he wore an old gray sweater, although it
was already June and hot. He smiled and greeted us as he took our
tickets, and we were told to sit in any of the hundred or so chairs
available. The puppet booth itself was no more than a small stage
under a white sheet set in an outdoor yard, which was covered with
pebbles and surrounded by a high wall. The stage acted both as a
screen and as a storage space to house the performer's tools and
puppets. It was the only part of the theater with a ceiling. A little office
built into the right side of the stage served as a ticket booth; a small
window in the wall was used to dispense the tickets.

Just as the performance was to begin—some twenty-five to thirty
people were seated in the audience—the woman who had sold us our
tickets came rushing to our seats in the front row, screaming and
pointing at Kostas's hand, in which he held a small recorder. "No, No,"
she said in Greek. "It is not allowed." On hearing the commotion, the
stout, jovial man who had earlier greeted us came from behind the
stage to see what was happening. The woman was still shouting at

Kostas, pointing to the recorder, while the man tried to calm her down. Interceding, he introduced himself as Giorgos Haridimos, the Karagiozis performer; the screaming woman was his wife. We introduced ourselves as students interested in studying Karagiozis; the recorder, we tried to explain, would help us remember the performance. Haridimos informed us that cameras and recorders were not allowed in his theater. His wife referred to a bad experience with an Englishman who a few years earlier had come to "steal" Karagiozis from them. That was our first encounter with Haridimos.

We returned to Plaka in 1969-70 and 1973-74 and continued to attend Haridimos's performances, without cameras or recorders. We would often talk with Haridimos before the performance, and on a few occasions we were invited behind the stage to watch him perform. By now his wife recognized us and would smile a hello whenever we arrived. We were becoming regular customers. Nevertheless, it was obvious that both still felt uncomfortable with us, and they volunteered little about the Karagiozis form. Haridimos preferred to address his remarks to Kostas rather than to Linda. Although he was polite, he treated women other than his wife with a certain amount of indifference, an indifference that turned to disregard when the conversation involved the male-dominated performance itself. We decided that in order to learn about Karagiozis from Haridimos, we had to play by his rules. Henceforth, Kostas would talk with and interview him and Linda would remain in the background, playing the role of a dutiful Greek wife.

It had become apparent that we could only study the Karagiozis performance effectively if we could develop an intimate, long-term relationship with Haridimos. Not only was he, in our view, the best surviving player in the tradition, but his knowledge of the present state of the performance as president of the Karagiozis Players Association would prove invaluable. Such a relationship would require two commitments on our part. First, we had to disassociate ourselves from a variety of previous collectors, including the "Englishman," Mario Rinovolucri, whose visits had caused Haridimos and his wife much concern. Kostas's childhood in a peasant village on the island of Samos provided the right class and national background to convey this commitment, as did the informal conduct of the interviews and our decision not to collect texts until late in our relationship (when, in fact, the player himself brought up the issue and offered to open his performances to taping). Second, Haridimos had made it clear that he felt he had no equal in the art of the Karagiozis performance. Questions about other players were met with impatience and mistrust. He felt slighted when he was compared with other players, and he let us know that drawing such comparisons suggested that we did not appreciate the quality of his performances. In the small world of Karagiozis performances in Greece, he would easily have discovered it if we had gone off to interview and study other players. His wounded pride led us to the decision that we would work exclusively with him, knowing that, in any case, we had access in the United States to Rinovolucri's taped interviews with twenty-one players.

At this point, in 1973, Kostas was teaching at the American College (Deree) at Athens. He persuaded the school to have Haridimos stage a classic Karagiozis performance. After some negotiating, the school allotted five hundred dollars for such a performance. Both Haridimos and his wife were excited. He admitted that this was the most he had received or earned for a single performance. Determined to show himself at his best, he decided to perform the complete version of *Karagiozis, Alexander the Great, and the Cursed Snake* with live music (four musicians and a singer). The audience of Greek and American students and professors received it as the best Karagiozis any of them had seen. The performance over, we shook hands with both Haridimos and his wife, who invited us to their home in Piraeus. We were now friends. Our children, aged seven and three, were to accompany us. From that moment on, we were to see Haridimos and his wife often, both at the Plaka theater and at their home. He spoke on a variety of topics concerning Karagiozis but only offered material that we could easily find in articles written about the form. Moreover, he was not telling us anything more than he had already told Rinovolucri. Nevertheless, by the time we left Athens in June, our friendship was sealed, and we had agreed to correspond.

Kostas had learned from the venture at Deree that not merely the player's relative poverty but also the proprietary nature of his role as a "keeper of the performance" isolated the exchange of money as a sign of respect due not so much to his eminence as to the art of Karagiozis itself. He was assured at last that we were not there to steal his art, but to preserve it. We kept faith with this understanding on each future visit by sharing with him whatever rewards our research brought us. On one visit, it was the proceeds of an article Linda had sold to a

Left, the Alexander the Great figure, designed in the nineteenth-century style with cut-out holes and executed in cardboard by Giorgos Haridimos. Right, the original Barba Giorgos (Uncle George) puppet designed by Hristos Haridimos and used by both him and his son Giorgos Haridimos in Karagiozis performances throughout their careers.

popular Greek magazine; on a second, it was part of a grant given by Kostas's university; on a third, it was a share of an honorarium for a book we had published together.

By the time we saw Haridimos again in 1979, his wife had died and he had married a young woman from the neighborhood who gave him his first children, twin daughters. He was not only open to the most intimate interviews about the performance, but he also began to display his *arheio,* or personal archives of Karagiozika. He unpacked the trunk of puppets he kept under his bed, brought out his two small notebooks in which he kept his "ideas," although he could hardly write, and resurrected important materials from storage at his brother's house. By now we were seeing him both socially and professionally every time we were in Athens. The most intensive and revealing work we did together, however, did not come until 1987, when, recorder in hand, Kostas spent two weeks alone with him obtaining eighteen hours of interviews on all facets of his work and life. Haridimos even asked on several occasions why Linda had not come along.

In 1989 Haridimos retired as a performer, separated from his young wife, and moved into a one-bedroom apartment in Piraeus surrounded by what he has always considered his true family, his Karagiozis puppets. When Kostas arrived in Athens in August, he called Haridimos from the Herodion Hotel where we often stayed. Haridimos's self-enforced exile had made him anxious. Why had we taken two years to return? Was the recorder in good working order so that what he had to say would not be lost? Before Kostas left, and without his asking, Haridimos gave him his two notebooks, which Kostas had always wanted to photocopy. "I'll copy them and return them to you tomorrow," Kostas said. "No hurry," he replied. "Take them with you to America, and bring them back next time you're in Greece. We're friends, aren't we?"

On several occasions over the years Kostas had asked Haridimos to sell him a puppet or a poster to bring back to the States. Each time Haridimos gave us figures he had made for tourists as gifts, or he would create new ones for us. He never sold or gave away the large figures he used for his performances, even when he had three and even four copies of the same puppet. His method was to make his performance puppets, each about two feet high, from lambskin and use them for a number of years; he would then retire them to the trunk under his bed and create new ones to replace the retired puppets. In some cases, as with those puppets most often used (Karagiozis, Barba Giorgos, Hatziavatis), he would retain several in use at the same time so as not to overwork a particular puppet. He used those puppets he had inherited from his father only on special occasions. He kept these at the bottom of his trunk and was reluctant to allow anyone to see or photograph them. These were his inheritance, as he told Kostas on many occasions, "his real family." His favorite among these was the tallest puppet in his repertoire, his father's Barba Giorgos, the old man from the mountains of Rumeli. Not only was this puppet, according to Haridimos, one of the best ever made, but it had been used throughout his father's career and throughout most of his own. Furthermore, Barba Giorgos held a particular place in Haridimos's heart, because it was the puppet that had required of him the greatest concentration and study, and it was the puppet that for him more than any other stood for the Greek spirit, the unbending, stubborn, driving force of the common

Greek peasant, *o laos,* the people. During Kostas's last interview in August 1989, Haridimos pulled his trunk from under his bed and reverently placed each figure on a white sheet on the floor. While Kostas photographed each figure, Haridimos spoke about them and reminisced about the performances in which each had appeared. Finally, at the bottom of the trunk, he came upon Barba Giorgos, somewhat bent and chipped from the long years of service it had rendered for his father and himself. Tears came to his eyes as he held it up in the light for Kostas to photograph. "This is my favorite," he said. "It's part of me. This is my true family. Many have asked me for these puppets. They want to put them in the museum, but I can't let them go. How can I put a price on these things? You've asked me for a performance puppet. Take Barba Giorgos. I know you'll take good care of him."

While Haridimos was an active performer, his entire life centered around Karagiozis. Early in the morning he would spend his time cutting Karagiozis figures from cardboard and plastic or drawing posters of various sizes depicting scenes from his favorite perform- ances, which he would then display in his theater for tourists. He also placed a number of these puppets in tourist shops, and from this he made a little money. For himself, he painted Karagiozis figures on his lamps, dishes, chairs, and walls. We ourselves had brought him a polished stone paperweight from the seashore of Kostas's home island, Samos. When we visited him at his home that Easter, he presented us with a heavy object wrapped in newspaper. We waited to return to our apartment before we unwrapped it; it was our Samian stone, on which he had drawn a scene from Linda's favorite Karagiozis heroic perform- ance, *Katsandonis,* with the words *Kalo Pasha* (Happy Easter) below it. A generous, if poor, man, Haridimos was never aggressive about marketing these various forms of his art. He was perfectly happy to hang them in his own apartment, whose walls were covered with Karagiozis paraphernalia.

Haridimos's early morning of puppet-making was followed by a simple lunch, consisting almost exclusively of greens cooked in olive oil, and then a nap, which he took in preparation for his evening performance. At around four in the afternoon, he boarded a trolley for Athens and the Plaka theater. There he swept the stage, cleaned the theater of debris left from the night before, watered the pebble floor to cool it down, dusted the chairs, and set out the puppets in the order in which they were to appear in the evening's performance. His first wife had accompanied him to the theater each night to put the house in order and prepare the tickets. His second wife, by contrast, stayed home with the twins. Haridimos complained that she did not have the passion for Karagiozis, nor did she understand his love for the performance. His art was, for her, merely a means of securing a livelihood.

After the performance, around ten, Haridimos put his important puppets (usually his father's) in an old suitcase he carried with him and took the bus home. Lesser puppets he locked in a trunk behind the stage at the Plaka theater; several break-ins resulted in the theft of many of these figures. By eleven he was home for a light supper. He spent a little time entering new ideas into the two notebooks he carried in his suitcase and then went to bed to dream of new tricks for Karagiozis, tricks that awoke him in the middle of the night to be entered in the notebooks beside his bed.

Opposite: Front cover from a script for *Karagiozis Baker*, one of many thirty-two-page booklets for Karagiozis performance that were common in the 1940s and 1950s. In the background, holding a cane, is Uncle George; at center is Karagiozis, while one of his children eats in the foreground.

PART TWO
Karagiozis Baker

Karagiozis Baker

Transcribed and translated from
the modern Greek oral performance of
Giorgos Haridimos

Characters

Uncle George	Karagiozis's uncle, a rustic shepherd from Rumeli
Karagiozis	The humpbacked fool-hero of the performance who plays the role of baker
Kolitiris	Karagiozis's eldest son
Skorpios	Karagiozis's second son
Pitsikokos	Karagiozis's youngest son
Veligekas	Veziris's first officer
Hatziavatis	Karagiozis's sidekick, an acquiescent Greek
Sembanaga	An old Turk, owner of the bakery
Veziris	The local Turkish official
Mouhtar Bey	A young rich Turk from Egypt
Arab Boy	Servant to Mouhtar Bey
Nionios	Omorfonios of Corfu, a friend of Karagiozis

Information in brackets indicates audience reaction, while commentary on the aural and visual elements of the performance is enclosed in parentheses. Words in full capitals are spoken loudly. Words in small type are whispered. Terms such as " . . . [2]" indicate pauses; the number in brackets is the length of the pause in seconds. Hyphens separating words signify rapid speech, and a ◠ sign at the end of a line means that the following line is spoken with almost no pause.

Uncle George: Aha
   I'm me.
   Giorgos Vlatsaras, they calls me.
   Honorable gentlemen,
   good evenings to you from here to there.
   Our theater t'night has a good performance . . . [7]
   (*A voice behind the screen says, "It's time for Karagiozis."*)
Karagiozis: Uncle, Uncle.
Unc.:   Ya here, ya crook. ◯
Kar.:   Now, wait a second, Uncle. What did I do to you that you call
   me a robber?
   (*Music begins and plays for three seconds. A bell rings for three
   seconds, after which the music continues alone for five seconds.
   Whistling is heard over the music for seven seconds. Music
   plays for another thirty-eight seconds, during which Karagiozis
   dances. At the end of this period a voice is heard over the music,
   "Eeee," for four seconds, ending with "Op, op, opa," as Ka-
   ragiozis continues to dance.*)
Kolitiris: Attaboy, Pops, opa, opa, opa, opa. (*Music for twelve
   seconds.*)
Kar.:   (*His voice is heard over the music.*) This is living. (*Music for
   two seconds.*)
Skorpios: Opa, opa, opa, Pops, you ol' windbag. (*Music for two
   seconds.*)
Pitsikokos: Opa, opa, opa, opa, Daddy (*Music for twelve seconds
   more before it dies out.*) . . . [3]
Kar.:   Merci, maestro.
   I'll pay you tomorrow because I don't have any loose or tight
   change.
   Good-a-night . . . [8] [*Children's voices heard in the audience.*]
Unc.:   Aha
   I'm me.
   Giorgos Vlatsaras, they calls me.
   Honorable gentlemen,
   good evenings to you from here to there.
   Our theater t'night has a good performance.
   Ya just all sits tight and have a good time.
   It's goin' to be a good one likes I tells ya.
   Hey, boy, ya with the pipes and drums, where are ya?

Let's haves a tsamiko so we can shuffle about a bit.

Come now, m'boy, let's hear 't, let's hear 't.

(*Music begins. Tsamiko music is normally played here, which is associated with Uncle George, followed by six whistles in thirteen seconds. Singing and music for another twenty-four seconds.*)

(*Over the music.*) Po, po, po, po, po,

Well, shiver my timbers, I'm gonna lose m'mind t'night.

(*Music continues for thirty seconds, then there is one whistle followed a second later by three more in quick succession and ending with a fifth, which is held. Music continues for thirty-three seconds. Throughout the music Uncle George dances and does somersaults; at times he holds his handkerchief in one hand and dances on one foot.*)

(*Over music.*) Aha ha haaa ah

God bless me! (*Music continues for twenty-nine seconds.*)

(*Music stops.*) A haa haa, come on now, toot yore pipe, toots it.

Hey ya, I almost gots giddy as I was whirling around.

Whirl again, whiiiirrrrl.

(*A long four-second whistle is heard with Kleftiko music playing in the background, the music associated with Veligekas and the sign for Veligekas's entrance. Music and singing continues for forty-seven seconds, and then a shout is heard from behind the screen followed by three claps of a board over the music. Music continues for eight more seconds.*)

Veligekas: (*Over music.*) It's me, the Albanian Vergenangas, me, the gallant one.

Unc.:   I'll rips yore tongue out. (*Music continues for thirty-one seconds.*)

Attaboy lads, but holds yore piping a bit.

Come over heres, closer, ya Turk.

Now tell me, m'boy,

why dids ya come here singin' and dancin'?

Did ya do it to breaks off m'song?

Vel.:   Ahhhhm.

Po, you talk to me, you?

Unc.:   To ya to ya,

I'm talkin' to ya, m'boy.

Ya see anyone else 'round heres?

Vel.:   I'm number one Vergenangas, number one guy.

Unc.: Well dear me! (*Laughs.*) Did ya hears that? [*Laughter.*]
Hey Turk, where ya at?
Don't crowds me,
because I'm Giorgos Vlatsaras,
and one plus one makes 1851.
Comes any closer and I'll puts my fist through yore mouth and pulls
out yore nose.

Vel.: I'll kick you like this and this and this, just like a cat.

Unc.: Ya, ya, ya, ya gonna hoofs me like a cat, m'boy?

Vel.: Po ya, ya Greek.

Unc.: Watch it or I'll gives ya a free flying lesson.
Watch ya don't crowds me.
What, ya still here, ya Turk?
Why don't ya goes pray for yore departed so they don't goes without
prayer t'night.

Vel.: Get cracking, git, git.

Unc.: Good heavens, woulds ya looks at the wretch.
Looks at him, he's ready for a scuffle.

Kar.: For goodness sakes.
It seems our two great powers want to lock horns. (*Laughs.*)
Uncle?
Uncle?

Unc.: Ya heres, nephew Karagioz?

Kar.: It's me, Uncle.
Let him through, will you, Uncle.
You've upset the entire neighborhood.
What's the matter with you? Why are you shouting like that?

Unc.: Careful, Karagioz.
I, m'boy, beens milling about down at the market.

Kar.: So you were down by the market,
and what happened, Uncle? [*Audience talking.*]

Unc.: As I was twirling about here, Karagioz,
this here Turk comes and makes out like a big shot.

Kar.: You didn't do anything to him, Uncle?

Unc.: Listen, ya, I didn't do nothing, m'boy.

Kar.: Hey you, you big oaf, aren't you ashamed of yourself,
picking on my Uncle George?
HEY YOU, WHAT DID MY UNCLE GEORGE DO TO YOU?

Vel.: Po, ya pipe down, numskull. ◯

Kar.:   Nuts to you, nitwit, [*Some laughter.*]
     calling me a numskull.
     Take a look at your own mug; it looks like a lobster puss. [*Laughter.*]
Vel.:   Ya talking to me, ya?
Kar.:   D'YOU SEE ANYONE ELSE AROUND?
     YOU THINK I'M SCARED OF YOU?
     IF YOU'RE SUCH A BIG SHOT,
     GET OVER HERE, YOU (*Hits him.*) so I can get out of here.
     GET OVER HERE, YOU. YOU GOT MY BLOOD BOILING.
Vel.:   Po, why, ya Greek, ya.
Kar.:   Grab-him-Uncle-so-I-can-let-him-have-it.-Grab-him.
     [*Laughter.*]
Vel.:   Park yore ass.
Kar.:   Grab him, Uncle, so I can let him have it.
     Hold him tight; don't let him get away. (*Laughs.*)
Unc.:   Hey, don't hits m'boy.
     The boy gots an uncle.
Kar.:   Finally, he stands up for me.
     That's my Uncle.
     (*Turns to Veligekas.*) You don't think I'm going to come right up
        and let you have it so you can blacken my eye tonight, do you?
        [*Laughter.*]
Vel.:   Where ya at, you?
Kar.:   Grab him so I can get at him, Uncle, grab him. [*Sounds and
     laughter.*]
Unc.:   Hey, sits, ya. Don't touch th' boy.
Kar.:   Get over here, Uncle,
     get over here.
Unc.:   What's the squeeze, Karagioz?
Kar.:   Listen to me closely, nunky,
     Its just doesn't sit right with me
     that you should stoop to fighting in the middle of the street like a
        pair of children with this (*Hesitates.*)
     Veligekas.
     Uncle, people like and respect you
     because you're a good man.
     Uncle,
     I'm going to take it upon myself as your nephew
     to get in front

and catch this Veligekas
and pound him
and pound him
and pound him
until, nunky, he makes my face black and blue. [*Laughter.*]

Unc.: Ya thinks ya can handle him, Karagioz?

Kar.: Can I handle him, you ask?
I haven't gotten in a fight for fifteen days.
I assure you, nunky,
I'm going to bite him, and in three seconds he'll have rabies.

Unc.: What are ya, a dog, to bites, m'boy? [*Some laughter.*]

Kar.: Come on now, Uncle, stop joking around; you know our
family comes from a long line of dogs. (*Laughs.*) [*Laughter.*]

Unc.: And ya thinks ya can takes him, m'boy.

Kar.: Yes, Uncle.
You don't believe me?
You can't imagine the pounding I'm going to give him.
Watch out, let me get up front
so I can get at him,
but listen, don't go away.

Unc.: I won'ts, Karagioz.
Come now, m'boy,
gets in front so ya can pounds'm.

Kar.: Yes,
I'll get in front, but don't leave me now.

Unc.: I won'ts, Karagioz.

Kar.: Gooood.
Aren't you ashamed, you dirt bag,
just because you found a good, innocent man like my Uncle George,
you want to make out like a big shot.

Vel.: Where ya at, you numskull?

Kar.: WHY, YOU NITWIT. [*Sounds and laughter.*]
YOU'RE GONNA CALL ME A NUMSKULL?
YOU THINK I'M SCARED OF YOU?
Uncle, don't leave me now.

Unc.: I won'ts, Karagioz, let 'm haves it, m'boy.

Kar.: I'm gonna pound him.
YOU-KNOW-ME-WHEN-I-GET-NERVOUS.
Uncle, don't leave me now, nunky.

Unc.: I won'ts, Karagioz; pounds him.

Vel.: Why ya ◌

Kar.: SHUT YOUR FACE.

DO YOU SEE THIS? (*Shows his fist.*)

Vel.: Po, what's it, ya . . .

Kar.: It's a hand grenade.

Vel.: Phew, yipes, yipes, yipes, yipes, yipes, yipes. [*Laughter.*]
Really, ya? A hand grenade?

Kar.: Yes, it's a hand grenade.

Unc.: Karagioz?

Kar.: What, Uncle?

Unc.: Ya haves such things on ya, m'boy?

Kar.: Yes, I have one hand grenade.

Unc.: Watch outs, m'boy, ya don't shakes too much an' we alls goes
up in a puff.

Kar.: We'll get to the moon before the astronauts, Uncle. (*Laughs.*)
WHAT? YOU THINK I'M SCARED OF YOU?
Uncle, don't leave me.
HEY-YOU-STAND-STILL. (*Hits him.*)

Vel.: Ouch, poor me. ◌

Kar.: SHUT YOUR FACE.
I'm going to throw my hand grenade.
Uncle, don't leave me.

Unc.: Bravo, Nephew, bravo, m'boy.

Kar.: SO . . .
JUST BECAUSE YOU FOUND AN INNOCENT MAN, YOU
THINK YOU'RE A BIG SHOT
WHAT-YOU-LOOKING-AT-ME-LIKE-THAT-FOR-YOU? (*Hits
him.*)
WHAT-YOU-LOOKING-AT? ◌

Vel.: Po, why ya . . .

Kar.: SHUT YOUR FACE.
I'M HOLDING A HAND GRENADE, I SAID.
Hold on there now.
I gotta search you.

Vel.: Oh me, the poor devil.

Kar.: SHUT YOUR FACE. (*Hits him.*)
Don't talk. [*Laughter.*]
When a search is in progress there's no talking.

Wowwww.

What's this, you?

Vel.:   That's m'watch.

Kar.:   Your watch?

And you allow yourself to circulate at this hour with a watch?

It's forbidden, so I'm confiscating your watch. [*Laughter.*]

Would you believe it?

Vel.:   Oh me, the poor devil.

Kar.:   SHUT YOUR FACE.

Uncle, don't leave me.

Unc.:   I won'ts, Karagioz.

Kar.:   So there.

All this time you thought you're a big shot.

You think I'm scared of you.

Where you gonna go before I get ahold of you? (*Uncle George leaves.*)

I'll lift you over my head.

Say,

oh, oh,

the clodhopper's gone.

Hey, Uncle?

Vel.:   Why, ya dirty Greek.

Kar.:   I got you now; there's no escaping.

Vel.:   Ya get ahold of soldier like me?

Po, all this time ya make out like big hero.

Kar.:   Hey, Uncle, where are you? (*Laughs nervously.*)

I was just kidding around

to make this old hick Uncle George laugh.

Here, take your watch back.

Go ahead, pound me some too, so we'll be even.

Vel.:   Po, ya see now, ya, I'll get ya.

Kar.:   STOP IT. (*He's hit over and over again.*)

For the sake of your sweet little mother (*Hitting continues.*)

HEY, UNCLE. (*Hitting continues.*)

Ouch, ouch, ouch, ouch. (*To the rhythm of the beating he's getting.*) Ouch, ouch, ouch, ouch, ouch.

Vel.:   Hey ya, what ya scream for?

Kar.:   OK, you can stop now; I got the message. [*Some laughter.*]

Vel.:   Hey ya, what ya scream for?

Kar.:   (*Hitting continues again.*) STOP IT
for the sake of your sweet little mother. (*Hitting continues.*)
Stop it.
Ouch. (*Hitting continues, and Karagiozis begins to sing to the rhythm of the beating he's getting.*) Singing in the rain . . . (*Hitting stops.*)

Vel.:   Po, wait ya now, ya numskull.

Kar.:   What?

Vel.:   How d'ya like that?

Kar.:   Eh,
God be praised; not so bad.

Vel.:   Po, come a bit closer.

Kar.:   What?

Vel.:   Po, come a bit closer.

Kar.:   I'm not drawing near because it smells like another clip on the ear. [*Laughter.*]

Vel.:   Come close, ya.

Kar.:   Aaaaah.
Just wait 'til I get ahold of you.
You won't get away.
Aaaaah.
Someday you'll come through my neighborhood.

Vel.:   Come close, ya dirty Greek, come close.

Kar.:   HEY, SPIROS, GRAB HIM.

Vel.:   Where this Spiros? ◯

Kar.:   (*Hits him.*) Here's Spiros. [*Loud laughter.*]

Vel.:   Why that smart-ass Greek,
that smart-ass Greek clever.

Kar.:   (*Laughs.*) Did you see Spiros, huh? Did you see him?

Vel.:   Hey ya, ya always hit.

Kar.:   You just wait and see now; I'm going to destroy you.
Just and wait and see what I have in store for you.
I'm going to get my big cannon.
ANDREAS, APOSTOLIS, ANDONIS, over here.
SPIROS, come quickly.
Push
the big cannon.
Everybody-get-behind-Veligekas.

(*Hits him.*) Ohhhh. [*Laughter.*]

Quickly, lads, over here; I'll show you. (*Laughs.*)

Good God. (*Laughs.*) (*Veligekas leaves.*)

When did Uncle George go without my noticing it? (*Laughs again.*)

But a little beating never hurt anybody.

If I go too long without it, I get a high fever. [*Some laughter.*]

Now that Veligekas beat me black and blue,

I feel I just came out of a bathhouse; I'm drained. (*Laughs.*)

I'd better call my kids now. (*Laughs.*)

Company,

Attention! (*Two clapping sounds are heard.*)

About face!

Kolitiris: Move over a bit, will ya, move.

Kar.:   (*Hits him.*) Kolitiris, shut up.

Hey you, the middle one, Skorpe (*Mispronounces the name, corrects himself, and continues.*) Skorpios, sound off.

Skorpios: Listen, you hunchback, I'm all sounded out. (*Karagiozis hits him.*) [*Laughter and shouts from the audience.*]

Kar.:   . . . [3] Ready,

forward

march. (*Karagiozis's sons begin to march in place while Karagiozis counts in rhythm to the beat of their marching.*)

One, two; one, two; ha, ha; ha, ha; one,

one, two; one, two; ha, ha; ha, hal ibe.

. . . [4] Kolitiris, slow down; come closer.

One, two; one, two; ha, ha; ha, ha; one.

Kolitiris, get back in line.

You, the middle one, lift your head higher.

. . . [4] Lower your head, you.

Lift your head, you namby-pamby.

Get-your-head-down-you-namby-pamby.

I'm going to let you have it, Skorpios, you're gonna go hungry.

Skor.:   And when was the last time we ate, you liar?

Kar.:   Quiet, keep that under your hat, you nitwit.

One, two; one, two; ha, ha; one.

About face, march. (*Karagiozis's three sons continue marching in place.*)

Left face, march; one, two; one, two; ha, ha; one. (*They continue*

marching for five seconds; Karagiozis blows a whistle to the
rhythm of the marching for nine seconds.)
One, two; ha, ha; one.
Companyyyy . . . [3]
division.
Kol.:   What division? We can hardly move anymore.
Kar.:   Keep still, you nitwit (*Karagiozis's sons continue marching.*)
   . . . [4]
Company,
division,
ready
and
halt. (*Karagiozis's sons start marching faster in place.*)
What? (*Marching speed accelerates.*)
   . . . [5] I said halt. (*Speed accelerates.*)
Haaaallllt.
HALT, I SAID. (*Marching speed accelerates.*)
Listen, you, HALT.
HAAAALLLLT, I SAID. (*They still continue marching.*)
Whooooa, steady there, fella.
Kol.:   Do you think we're donkeys, Father, and you tell us to whoa?
Skor.:   Do you think we're mules, Dad, and you tell us to whoa?
Pitsikokos: Do you think we're ponies, and you tell us to whoa?
Kar.:   (*Hits Pitsikokos.*) Pipe down, you.
   Just because the other two talk back, this little pip-squeak thinks he
      can talk back too.
   You good-for-nothings,
   can't you see I'm an officer
   and have the authority to discipline you
   when you're not up on your training?
Kol.:   Excuse me, Officer, sir!
Skor.:   Excuse me, Mr. Big Cheese, sir!
Pit.:   Excuse me, Mr. Kingpin, sir!
Kar.:   (*Hits Pitsikokos.*) Pipe down! I said.
   Now look here, boys, soon you'll grow up
   and become young lads.
   You'll be called to serve in the army;
   you'll have to know how to drill.
   Here, let's have a little practice

to see whether you know anything about drilling.
OK. Sound off.

Kol.: One.

Skor.: Two.

Pit.: Nine.

Kar.: (*Hits Pitsikokos*) What do you mean, one, two, nine? You go to school, don't you, Pitsikokos?

Pit.: You knows I do.

Kar.: Don't you do math in class?

Pit.: You knows damn well I do, Pops.

Kar.: So, one and two make nine?
Can't you count?

Pit.: I can counts.

Kar.: Yeah?

Pit.: From one to . . .

Kar.: Yeah?

Pit.: to . . .

Kar.: Yeah?

Pit.: To what?

Kar.: What's he babbling about?
Up to what, do you know?

Pit.: From one . . .

Kar.: Yeah?

Pit.: To . . .

Kar.: Yeah?

Pit.: What?

Kar.: Damn it, boy, you're asking me up to what?
How would I know?

Pit.: I knows how to counts from one to one hundred.

Kar.: I don't want you to count from one to one hundred.
Like the good little boy you are
and the good student you are,
without rushing and making mistakes,
I want you to count for me from one to ten.
Can you do that?

Pit.: I knows, Pops.

Kar.: Begin counting, then.

Pit.: Oooo . . .

Kar.: Yeah?

Pit.: Oooo . . . oooo . . . oooo . . . oooo . . . one.

Kar.: Bravoooo.

Pit.: Ooo . . . ooo . . . one.

Kar.: Good for youuuu.

Pit.: Oo . . . oo . . . one.

Kar.: (*Hits him.*) There's nothing but one, you dummy?
One, two, then what follows?
Let's go, from the beginning again.

Pit.: One.

Kar.: Bravo.

Pit.: Two.

Kar.: Bravo.

Pit.: Two.

Kar.: Here we go again.
Look here, you, one, two, then what follows?

Pit.: One, two, tie.*

Kar.: (*Hits him.*) Why, the good-for-nothing's playing soccer now.
Did you hear that, one, two, tie?
Say, Kolitiris, tell me.

Kol.: In the flesh, Pops.

Kar.: When you enlist in the army,
the captain might call you,
and right off you'll (*Performer gets mixed up here and completes his thought in the next line.*) and he'll say, "Step forward, comrade."
You'll report and say, "Awaiting your orders, Captain, sir!"

Kol.: Yes.

Kar.: If, my boy, the captain asks you,
"Tell me soldier,
what weapon makes the loudest noise?"
What weapon will you tell your captain?

Kol.: I'll tell him it's the cannon.

Kar.: Bravo.
If your captain were to ask you too, you, the middle one Skorpios . . .

Skor.: About what?

---

*In the popular soccer lottery Pro-Po, one can bet on one's favorite teams in any of three ways: to win (1), to lose (2), or to tie (X).

Kar.:   What's the loudest weapon, what weapon would you point out?
Skor.:   What weapon makes the loudest noise?
Kar.:   Yeah.
Skor.:   Baked beans.
Kar.:   You just had to come up with your rot, didn't you?
    You, Pitsikokos, tell me.
Pit.:   Uh-huh.
Kar.:   You, m'boy, give us an antiaircraft weapon.
Pit.:   Aerosol.
Kar.:   Brilliant, these kids, aren't they?
    Tell me, Skorpios.
Skor.:   In the flesh.
Kar.:   When you enlist in the army, where will you go?
Skor.:   I'll go, I'll go to the army.
Kar.:   Of course, you'll go to the army.
    But where will you be staying?
Skor.:   So, where am I going to stay, in the street? I'll stay with the army.
Kar.:   Look here, m'boy, you'll stay in a company.
Skor.:   Oh yeah, I'll have company.*
Kar.:   What's he talking about?
    What comes after a company?
Skor.:   We have the army and plenty of company.
Kar.:   Listen, m'boy, the division comes next.
Skor.:   Oh yeah! I know.
Kar.:   What follows the division?
Skor.:   The multiplication.
Kar.:   Pitsikokos, tell me.
Pit.:   Uh-huh.
Kar.:   What can we do to avoid a sea battle in the Mediterranean?
Pit.:   Empty the sea.
Kar.:   How, m'boy?
Pit.:   With an ink blotter.
Kar.:   Why, these kids are brilliant.
    Kolitiris, tell me, are you a good student in school?

---

*Company is a play on words. Company (*lohos*) is mistaken by Skorpios for the name of a person. Regiment (*syntagma*) is the name of a famous square in Athens, which leads Skorpios to name *Omonia*, another square in Athens near *Syntagma*.

Kol.: An excellent student.

Kar.: Bravo.

See that you all get an education so you can all become good men and useful citizens.

Like the good student you are, tell me, what's your favorite subject?

Kol.: Mine is history.

Kar.: Bravo.

And yours, Skorpios?

Skor.: Mine is anarchy.

Kar.: (*Hits him.*) Tell me, Pitsikokos.

Pit.: Yeah.

Kar.: Of all the subjects in your class . . .

Pit.: Yes?

Kar.: which is your favorite?

Pit.: Recess.

Kar.: Bravo.

Since you're good in history, Kolitiris,
perhaps you could tell us, if you remember from your
classical studies . . .

Kol.: Yes?

Kar.: what ancient Greek did the most for mankind?

Kol.: The one who did the most for mankind is . . .

Skor.: Aristides, the corner shoemaker.

Kar.: You numskull!

Kol.: It's . . . It's . . . Plato.

Kar.: Bravo.

Tell me, Kolitiris . . .

Kol.: In person.

Kar.: Skorpios. (*Here the performer corrects his mistake; he meant to call Skorpios, not Kolitiris.*)

Skor.: In the flesh.

Kar.: Kolitiris told us that Plato illuminated the world.

Skor.: So, what else is new; didn't I know that already?

Kar.: Look here, you, nobody said you didn't know it.

Tell us, then, who was Plato?

Skor.: Plato was an electrician. (*Karagiozis hits him.*)
What-d'you-hit-me-for-every-time-I-open-my-mouth-you? ◯
Always-hitting-hitting-hitting-hitting-hitting. ◯
What-d'you-hit-me-for? ◯

Kar.: SHUT UP, YOU.

Skor.: Always-hitting-hitting-hitting-hitting. ◡
What-d'you-hit-me-for? ◡

Kar.: PIPE DOWN, I SAID.

Skor.: Always-hitting-hitting-hitting. ◡
What-d'you-hit-me-for? ◡

Kar.: PIPE DOWN, I SAID.
All this kidding around comes from hunger.
Tell me, Kolitiris,
do you know a two-footed animal?

Kol.: A two-footed animal?

Kar.: Answer quickly now.
if you're a good student.

Kol.: A chicken.

Kar.: Bravo.
You, Skorpios, give me
a four-footed animal.

Skor.: A four-footed animal?
Two chickens.

Kar.: (*Hits him.*) Pitsikokos, can you tell us. ◡

Pit.: Yeah?

Kar.: What animal can survive in water for years at a time?

Pit.: Kool-Aid.*

Kar.: Why, they're pure geniuses.
Let's see now. Which of my three children is the smartest?

Skor.: Hey you! I'm the smartest.

Kar.: Shut up, numskull. I didn't ask you.
OK. First I'll ask Kolitiris.
Tell me, Kolitiris, if you're a smart boy,
can you explain to me
how we can tell the difference between a piece of iron and a piece of
steel?

Kol.: Sure I can, Father.
I'll take the iron and the steel ◡

Kar.: And then what?

---

*Literally, *vanilla*, a popular dessert in Greece in which a spoonful of a white
gumlike substance is served in a glass of water.

Kol.: I'll take them to the flea market to sell, and the junk dealers
will know what they are and separate them.

Kar.: You don't earn any points for that answer.

Skor.: I'll tell you.

Kar.: You'll tell me what?

Skor.: Why not, you? Aren't I allowed to talk? Aren't I also your son,
you, huh?

Kar.: Why, the numskull.

Fine.

What d'you want?

Skor.: Hey you, you want to separate a piece of iron and a piece of
steel, right?

Kar.: Yeah.

Skor.: So, you know what we'll do?

Kar.: What will we do?

Skor.: We'll catch a pig.

Kar.: A pig?

Skor.: Yeah.

Kar.: OK.

Skor.: We'll get some lamb's wool too.

Kar.: OK.

Skor.: Well, then we'll have pig iron and steel wool.

Kar.: (*Hits him.*) Why, the bum
will drive us crazy tonight.

I'm going to put one more question to each of you
in order to discover
who's the brightest.

And in order to help you out, Kolitiris, so that you can answer
correctly, I give you the following hint:
In the morning, when a person wakes up and gets out of bed
and doesn't want to walk barefoot on the tiles,
he puts what on his feet?

Kol.: He puts on his slippers.

Kar.: Bravo.

Careful now with the question I'm going to put to you.
There's an empty object under the bed. What is it?

Kol.: I don't know.

Kar.: What else could it be, m'boy? It's an empty slipper.
When we don't wear our slippers, they're empty.

When we wear them, they're not empty.

Be careful now.

There are two empty objects under the bed. What are they?

Kol.: Two slippers.

Kar.: At last. It took you long enough.

Tell me, Pitsikokos.

Pit.: Yeah.

Kar.: Four empty objects are under the bed. What are they?

Pit.: Four slippers.

Kar.: Bravo, m'boy. Bravo. Bravo.

Skor.: HEY-YOU-ASK-ME-TOO-ASK-ME-TOO. ○

Kar.: LISTEN HERE, YOU, WHAT ARE YOU SCREAMING LIKE THAT FOR?

Skor.: Why-aren't-you-asking-me-huh?

Kar.: Ask you what? You always make a mess of things.

You're always monkeying around.

Skor.: Ask-me-damn-it-and-you'll-see-what-a-smart-kid-I-am.

Kar.: OK.

I'll ask you.

Now then, Skorpios.

It's something ○

Skor.: Yes.

Kar.: With four legs.

Skor.: Fine.

Kar.: It has green eyes.

Skor.: Yes.

Kar.: It climbs up on the roof.

Skor.: Fine.

Kar.: It eats fish.

Skor.: Yes.

Kar.: It's called a cat.

Skor.: Yes.

Kar.: What is it, m'boy?

Skor.: I GOT IT!

Kar.: What?

Skor.: It's . . . it's . . . FIVE SLIPPERS.

Kar.: (*Hits him.*) Why, the good-for-nothing!

YOU NUMSKULL, WHERE DID YOU GET FIVE SLIPPERS?

Skor.:   Listen, you, we have four to begin with.
So four slippers plus one cat make five slippers.
Kar.:   Why, you numskull.
GET LOST!
All right now, boys,
let's welcome our distinguished public
and let everyone know the performance our theater will present
    tonight.
Kolitiris, I'm asking you
so that you can set an example for your brothers.
Let's hear you now.
Kol.:   Honorable ladies, honorable gentlemen, mademoiselles, and
our beloved children, good evening to all of you.
This evening our theater will present the old, classic comedy of the
    shadow theater,
My Father, the Baker.
Kar.:   Bravo, m'boy.
Kol.:   Tomorrow we have a change in our program.
Tomorrow we will present the old, classic comedy of the shadow
    theater,
My Father and Captain Gris.
Kar.:   Bravo.
Kol.:   Our theater changes its program every two days.
Our theater is open nightly, and on Sunday we have two perform-
    ances.
Kar.:   Bravo, m'boy.
Now you, the second one.
Skor.:   I, I, I,
I, I'm . . . here, I am.
Kar.:   I'm glad you got that out.
What do you mean, I'm here?
I want you to say exactly what yor brother said. Come on now.
Skor.:   Listen-you-what-d'you-want-that-I-say-all-that-at-once-
so-that-my-mouth-gets-stuffed-up-and-I-choke-tonight?
[*Laughter.*]
Kar.:   Is it too much for you to say "honorable gentlemen"?
Skor.:   Abominable gentlemen ͻ
Kar.:   (*Interrupts.*) WHAT ARE YOU SAYING, DUMMY?
[*Laughter.*]

Just because we can't stand each other, you think everyone is that way?

Honorable gentlemen.

Skor.: All right then, people.

Kar.: What the hell is he talking about?

Skor.: Once upon a time there was a dragon.

Kar.: He's telling them fairy tales.

Skor.: The dragon ate two little kids.

Kar.: (*Hits him.*) Stand up, you.

Skor.: Hey, you, lay off me, so I can tell how many little kids the dragon ate.

Kar.: Get lost, you dummy.

Pitsikokos.

Pit.: Yeah.

Kar.: Greet the audience, m'boy.

Pit.: Devourable gentlemen, I'm hungry.

Kar.: (*Hits him.*) Take that.

Pit.: Ohhhh.

Kar.: What's the matter?

Kol.: Oh Holy Mother,

he killed my little brother.

I'm going for the police.

Skor.: And me for my congressman.

Kar.: Oh, come on now, you kids,

come on now.

Aeiiii.

Oh, dear Mother,

could it be that the punch I gave him

got him in the brain and left him dead?

(*Begins to cry.*) Eiiii Pitsikoko,

oh my darling little boy.

Aeiiii Psikoko,

oh, my little boy,

oh, my adoring little boy.

Skor.: (*Sings.*) Irene good night. Good night Irene, good night Irene ○

Kar.: (*Interrupts.*) Get out of here, you.

Get out of here, Skorpios, crying like that.

Oh, I killed my most precious little boy.

Skor.: Wait 'til my mother finds out about this.

Boy, oh boy ◯

Kar.: (*Hits him.*) Get out of here, you.

Get out of here.

Oh, only a little while ago the poor little dear

was asking me for some melon,

but I didn't have money to buy him any.

Only this noon was I able to grab one from the grocer who was napping. (*He breaks into a cry.*)

Now that I killed you, my little boy,

who's going to eat the melon?

Pit.: Where's the melon? Where's the melon?

Kar.: (*Hits him over and over again.*) [*Laughter.*] Why, the good-for-nothing.

As soon as he heard about the melon

he was resurrected like Lazarus.

All these tricks of theirs are inherited from my wife,

because whenever I lay a hand on them,

she hollers at me, "Karagiozis, don't hit the children. They're too young to understand."

But I'll tell you, if my wife takes their side

I'll be forced to get a divorce. What kind of life is this after all? ◯

Honorable ladies,

honorable gentlemen, mademoiselles, and beloved children, good evening to all of you.

We thank you very much for honoring us here at our small theater.

Our theater is open nightly,

and every two days we change programs.

Tomorrow night we will present *Captain Gris and Myself.*

(*While Karagiozis is talking, his three sons are fighting.*) I don't think these brats are going to make it home alive tonight.

I'm going to kill them. (*Hits his sons.*)

Watch out, you dimwits. (*Karagiozis's sons leave.*)

(*High noise.*) Oooo. (*Hits his head as he comes out of the hut.*)

Now look what you did. You made me break all my head springs,

and I don't mind, except that I don't have any rubber bands to change them, do you get my drift?

But it won't happen twice, I know how to handle things. (*Karagiozis now enters sitting down and moving backward.*)

Going under, glug, glug, glug.

(*Ringing of bell is heard for eight seconds, signifying that the performance proper is beginning. Silence follows for twenty-eight seconds. Recorded music is heard for four seconds before it is interrupted. The wrong record was used. Seven seconds later the bell is rung again for eleven seconds, and a few seconds later the correct music begins, which plays for one minute and eighteen seconds before Hatziavatis begins to speak. The music used here is the Mane, associated with this character.*)

Hatziavatis: A good day to you, reverend sir, good morning, elder Sembanaga.

Tell me, how are you doing?

Sembanaga: (*Speaks in slow measured tone.*) Wellll, welcome, my friend Hatziavatis.

How are you, friend, are you well?

Hat.:   As far as health goes, I can say I'm well, my elder.

As I have told you on other occasions, elder Sembanaga,

I am a man with a large family.

Unfortunately, I am not well educated, because as a youngster, I was an undisciplined child.

Although I was counseled by my parents, both by my mother and father,

to go to school and learn to read and write

and more so to learn a trade,

I was too undisciplined as a child,

and as a result I remained illiterate and unlucky,

and today, my elder,

having brought children into the world and having raised a large family,

I have neither the work nor the energy to raise them properly,

to send them to school, to educate them to become good human beings so they will not suffer in life as I do.

Sem.:   So

what can I tell you, Hatziavatis?

All of us, whatever type of men we might be, as children,

what can I say,

we were mischievous.

Of course,

those children who were better behaved

were educated
or better yet learned a trade,
and today as adults lead somewhat better lives.
You're right, Hatziavatis.
Education is a necessity.

Hat.: Yes, master,
isn't that the truth.
So, my elder, please forgive me.
I made you dizzy with all my talking.
But I noticed, master,
I noticed that you were walking and singing to yourself.

Sem.: Yes,
that's true, Hatziavatis.

Hat.: Master,
you don't know how glad I am to see you so happy.
You're in good health,
and when you stroll you sing to yourself.
Well, it seems to me that you must be very happy, master, very
exuberant.

Sem.: What can I say, my poor Hatziavatis?
You're right to assume I sing to myself out of happiness and joy.

Hat.: Why, master, there are tears in your eyes.
What's the matter?

Sem.: Hatziavatis,
listen to me.
Although for the moment you see me walking and singing to
myself,
it doesn't mean I do it out of happiness,
but rather as a release from great sorrow.

Hat.: For God's sake, my elder,
what happened?

Sem.: Tell me, do you live far from here?

Hat.: Just a little ways from here, master, in this quarter.

Sem.: You're a neighbor then.

Hat.: Yes, master.

Sem.: Have you lived here many years? [*Children's voices heard in
the audience.*]

Hat.: Many years, master, right here in this quarter.
Why do you ask?

Sem.:   Please, tell me,
do you see this bakery right here?
Hat.:   Yes, master.
Sem.:   Did you by any chance know the baker?
Hat.:   Why certainly, master.
How is it possible not to know John?
He was a very young man, a tall, handsome lad,
and a good man with a good heart.
Sem.:   So, I see you knew the baker well who owned this bakery.
Hat.:   Indeed, master.
Sem.:   Did you know that this baker had a heart attack?
Hat.:   Yes, master, why, it was all over the neighborhood.
You don't know how bad we all felt for the poor baker.
He was a handsome lad and a good man.
It all happened so suddenly, and he was so young
to die from a heart attack.
I'm not sure, but it must be about a year ago.
Sem.:   It's been exactly a year, Hatziavatis.
But you should know, my child,
that John the baker,
that lad you remember,
was my brother.
Hat.:   What did you say, elder Sembanaga,
the baker was your brother?
Sem.:   Yes, yes, yes, yes,
very young, my child,
much younger than me.
Hatziavatis,
this brother was the only thing I had in the world; I have no one
else.
You see, I was foolish enough not to marry, and now I am a lonely
recluse.
I loved my brother a lot,
but I lost him much too early,
and whenever I pass by this bakery,
(*Sad, almost in tears.*) I am reminded of my poor brother.
That's why I sing to myself, Hatziavatis.
Hat.:   I understand, master, I understand.
I don't blame you, master.

Sem.:   Why couldn't Allah, Hatziavatis,
    take me instead?
    I'm already old.
    I've had my years.
    But instead he took my brother, a young man.
Hat.:   Don't talk that way, master; may you live a thousand years.
    What can I say? Allah chose to take your brother to his side.
    That's life. Some die young while others die old, my elder.
    There is nothing we can do, have patience.
Sem.:   You're right, Hatziavatis.
Hat.:   Tell me, master . . .
Sem.:   Yes?
Hat.:   You see,
    from the day your deceased brother died,
    I noticed the bakery hasn't opened,
    nor has any other business opened here.
    That's why I'm curious,
    for in this quarter
    we don't have a closer bakery other than this one here on the square,
    and as a result the entire neighborhood
    is forced to go all the way to the upper quarter, master,
    in order to buy bread or to have our food baked.
    What can I say, it's inconvenient.
    Why don't you reopen the bakery, master.
    I remember that business was good here, and there were many
        customers.
Sem.:   Hatziavatis,
    thanks to Allah
    I have no need of work or money.
    I have a large fortune.
    Although I am well acquainted with the baker's art,
    from the day my brother died,
    I've had no interest in reopening the bakery.
Hat.:   It seems a pity.
Sem.:   What are you saying, Hatziavatis?
    I lost such a brother, tall as a tree,
    a young man,
    and you talk about the bakery? I could care less if it fell apart.
    I lost my brother.

Hat.:   I know how you must feel, master.
  You don't ever intend to open it, then?
Sem.:   Never.
  Never, Hatziavatis.
Hat.:   Master,
  (*Crying.*) let me cry before your feet.
  You know how I suffer; you know my wretched circumstances.
  I don't have bread to give my unfortunate little children.
  Do me a kindness, master.
  Since you don't intend to reopen the bakery,
  won't you rent it to me?
  Let's agree on some rent
  so I can begin to work this bakery, master,
  so I can give my poor little children bread.
  Do me this kindness, master,
  please. (*Kneels before Sembanaga's feet.*)
Sem.:   Come now, Hatziavatis, get up.
  What are you doing,
  falling before my feet?
  For shame, for shame, my child.
Hat.:   Master, I beg you.
Sem.:   Now hold on, child,
  there's no need for such begging.
  Your idea's a good one; I like it, and I agree with you.
  Yes, Hatziavatis,
  either way you look at it, my child, the bakery is closed.
  Why not give it to you to work for a few years
  so you can make a living for yourself and your little children?
Hat.:   I thank you, master.
  So, what should we set the rent at, master?
Sem.:   Hatziavatis,
  I don't want even a penny's rent from you.
  Only, only
  once in a while
  (*Welling up with tears.*) perhaps you can pray for my brother's soul.
Hat.:   Blessed be your brother's bones, master.
  May Allah receive his soul in his right hand.
  Master, you don't need to worry.
  I'll pray for your younger brother every day.

Sem.:   Thank you.

But I want to ask you just one thing.

Hatziavatis, do you know how to bake?

Hat.:   Well, master, since I don't like lying, and since I've told the truth from childhood,

I don't have the slightest idea about baking.

Sem.:   What can I tell you, Hatziavatis.

Many think the baker's trade a simple, easy job.

Unfortunately, however,

a baker's job is demanding.

A baker must be able to knead good dough.

He must know how to bake it well.

Moreover, he must know how to bake various foods

and various pastries.

It's not an easy thing to do.

How will you be able to run the bakery?

If you don't know how to bake, you'll lose all your customers.

Hat.:   I don't believe this is going to be a problem, master.

I'll look for a good baker

who will work for me in the bakery,

and in time I too will learn the baker's art.

Sem.:   Bravo.

I agree,

it's important to find a good baker

so you can learn the trade.

However, you must keep one thing in mind.

Hat.:   Yes, master.

Sem.:   I want the bakery

to be run honorably.

Hat.:   Indeed, master.

Sem.:   And don't be guilty of what other bakers do

when we send our foods

for baking.

Some bakers try to steal our meat, our macaroni, our potatoes.

Bakers are used to never baking for themselves

but to eating others' foods.

Hat.:   Yes, master.

Sem.:   Furthermore,

be careful how you weigh the bread.

Keep it honest.

Hat.:   Yes, master.

You'll see once I take over.

Sem.:   Good.

Come then, dear Hatziavatis,

come, in memory of my brother

enter the bakery,

and I'll hand it over to you right now with everything in it.

Come in.

Hat.:   Thank you, master, thank you.

Your kindness is great. (*Both enter the bakery.*)

Sem.:   Here you are.

Here, Hatziavatis, is the wood for the oven.

Hat.:   I see it, master.

Sem.:   Here, Hatziavatis, is the pot for boiling water.

Hat.:   Yes, master.

Sem.:   Here, here, my child,

here is the kneading trough.

Hat.:   I see it, master.

Sem: Here also are all the pots and pans.

Hat.:   Yes.

Sem.:   Well, look here, you're lucky; here are four sacks of flour.

Hat.:   Will you take them with you, master?

Sem.:   No, no,

what would I do with them? I'll just check to make sure they're still
   usable. (*Checks the flour in the sacks.*)

They're fine.

You'll be able to use them.

Hat.:   Yes, master.

Sem.:   Here's the storage place where we put the wood to light the
   oven.

Hat.:   Aren't we going to list all these things?

Sem.:   Listen, I have faith in you,

Hatziavatis.

Go on, take the store

and work it for five full years.

In five years if I'm still alive, I'll return to claim it with everything in
   it.

Hat.:   Yes, master.

Sem.:   If, on the other hand, for argument's sake, since I have no one,
   I'm dying, and I can't make it back here in time, you and your
      children will be lucky,
   for I'll come and turn the bakery over to you.
Hat.:   No, master,
   I pray you'll live a thousand years and return someday to claim your
      store.
Sem.:   Well, bravo, then.
   I'm leaving.
Hat.:   Master,
   I should go to my relatives
   or friends to borrow money
   so I can order flour from the mill to make dough for the bakery.
Sem.:   It's not necessary for you to be in debt to friends or relatives.
   Come here.
   I'm going to help you.
   Here,
   take these five gold pieces.
Hat.:   Yes, master.
Sem.:   That should be enough to order flour from the mill for your
      work.
   I'll come by regularly to see you
   and advise you, since I know the baker's trade well.
Hat.:   Go in peace, master.
Sem.:   So long,
   and I wish you good luck in your work.
   Just make sure you find a good baker.
Hat.:   Rest assured, master.
Sem.:   So long. (*Leaves the screen.*)
Hat.:   God bless you, master.
   May your brother's bones be blessed, master.
   I just can't believe it.
   Not in my wildest dreams did I imagine
   that I'd have this bakery for my own.
   My babies are saved.
   I can finally say good-bye to poverty,
   but I don't have time to lose.
   Let me get going then.
   I must find a good baker

for my bakery.
I should open up today already,
and I should let the neighborhood know
that from today the bakery is once again
open here in the square. (*Hatziavatis leaves the screen from the right and enters again from the left at Karagiozis's hut.*)
Karagiozis: (*Crying aloud.*) OHOOOO.
Hat.: What the hell is *his* problem, crying like that?
Kar.: (*Speaking through his crying slowly, emphasizing each word.*)
OH, WHAT MISFORTUNE HAS BEFALLEN ME. (*Crying aloud and howling.*)
Hat.: Why the hell is he crying like that?
Kar.: (*Crying and howling.*) Ohoooo.
Hat.: Hey you.
Kar.: (*Crying.*) Eh?
Hat.: Why are you crying like that?
Kar.: (*Crying.*) Because I don't know any other way. [*Audience laughs.*]
Hat.: Put a cap on it, you faker. Have you lost your marbles? What's the matter?
Kar.: (*Crying.*) A great disaster, Hatzatzari;
a great misfortune has befallen me.
Death is in the midst of it all.
Death, I say.
Don't ask me anything else.
Hat.: Death, Karagiozis?
Could it be that some car ran over one of your kids?
Kar.: No.
If only it were an injury, but it wasn't any such thing.
Hat.: Could it be, Karagiozis, that your wife died?
Kar.: (*Crying.*) That'd be a blessing; I'd get a rest from her mouth, from her daily curses.
Hat.: What's the matter then?
Kar.: (*Crying.*) A great disaster, Hatzatzari.
Hat.: Who died, Karagiozis?
Kar.: (*Crying.*) My little dog conked out, Hatzatzari. [*Laughter.*]
Hat.: Goddamn it, man.
Did you say your dog conked out?
Kar.: (*Crying.*) It was a good little dog, Hatzatzari.

It took after my side of the family.

Hat.:   You don't say, Karagiozis.

Kar.:   (*Crying.*) Yes.

It was waiting since morning, the poor little thing.

I went over to pet it lying there.

"What's the matter," I said,

and it answered me, "Bow wow, bow wow, bow wow."

(*Crying heavily.*) Then suddenly it closed its eyes. (*Crying heavily again.*) Oh my God.

Hat.:   And you, you're crying for the dog?

Kar.:   (*Crying.*) Listen, you, I loved that dog a lot, Hatzatzari.

Hat.:   So you loved it that much, Karagiozis?

Kar.:   (*Crying.*) I loved my doggie a lot

because it had the eyes of my dead (*Crying aloud.*) FATHER. (*Crying aloud.*) OH MY GOD.

Hat.:   Goddamn it, man.

Listen here, you, get over here, you nitwit.

Stand up and quit crawling crying for a dog.

Kar.:   Why, for the love of God, (*Hits him.*) you nitwit,

you uncivilized ignoramus,

can't you see there's a funeral going on in my home, and all you can do is make fun of me?

Hat.:   You're not in your right mind, Karagiozis.

Listen, you, get ahold of yourself.

Kar.:   Why, when did I get loose?

Hat.:   Come on now, listen up, it's only a dog, Karagiozis, not the end of the world.

Stop acting this way.

Kar.:   It was a kind dog.

(*Crying.*) I used to go to the market to beg the butchers

for bones for my doggie, and it kept me company,

and we provided for each other.

Hat.:   What did it provide for you?

Kar.:   Bones.

Hat.:   Bones?

Kar.:   Yes.

(*Still sobbing.*) And I used to eat them with my dog, Hatzatzari.

Hat.:   You mean it, Karagiozis,

bones?

Kar.: I used to chew them over the second time around.
Do you follow me?
Hat.: Goddamn it, man,
don't waste my time; I have work to do.
Kar.: Oh yeah, and what kind of work is that, Hatzatzari?
Hat.: Karagiozis,
I'm in need of a good baker.
Kar.: What's that you say?
Hat.: I said, I'm in need of a good baker.
Kar.: And what would you do with a baker, Hatzatzari?
Hat.: Karagiozis,
I want a good baker
to work in my store.
Kar.: Your what store?
Hat.: In my bakery.
Kar.: In your bakery?
Hat.: Yes.
Kar.: (*Hits him.*) Get the hell out of here.
Hat.: Goddamn it, man, what are you hitting me for?
Kar.: Come on, get out of here.
Come on, get going, you liar.
Listen, Hatzatzari, I'm hungry too,
but I'm not crazy enough yet to go around
telling everyone I see that I need a baker
to work in my bakery.
What's the matter with you? Are you nuts?
Hat.: Listen, you, you think I'm crazy?
Kar.: No, just nuts.
Hat.: Listen, I'm serious.
I'm in need of a good baker
to work in my bakery.
Kar.: Hatzatzari, listen close, I'm going to give you a black eye
tonight.
Hat.: Why?
Kar.: BECAUSE YOU'RE DRIVING ME CRAZY TONIGHT.
Say?
Where did you find this bakery?
Hat.: Listen, Karagiozis,
do you see this bakery here?

Kar.:   Yeah,
    I see it.
Hat.:   Well then, you should knoooow
    that as of today this bakery
    is mine.
Kar.:   (*Threateningly.*) Hatzatzari,
    I'm going to beat the shit out of you.
Hat.:   Why?
Kar.:   Listen, you, I know this baker.
    We even hold a grudge against each other.
Hat.:   With the baker?
Kar.:   Yeah.
    It was about a year ago
    when I snuck into his bakery unnoticed
    and stole a basket of bread.
    The next day
    I came again to steal some more bread,
    but he was waiting for me.
    He was hiding behind the door
    holding a huge wooden paddle up to here.
    And as soon as I poked my head in the door,
    he raised the wooden paddle and let me have one just like this (*Hits*
        Hatziavatis.) POW.
Hat.:   Goddamn it, man,
    you made me dizzy.
Kar.:   And I only used my hand, but what about me, who got it with
    the wooden paddle? [*Laughter.*]
    He gave me such a welt, Hatzatzari, big as an orange.
    I tell you,
    I felt ti . . . (*Performer gets tangled up in his words.*) tipsy; it
        swelled up so that it reached all the way up here.
Hat.:   Really, Karagiozis?
Kar.:   Yeah.
    And from that day I put a curse on him; I said,
    "I hope to God you don't last the year," that's what I told him,
    "you who did me in."
Hat.:   Well then, Karagiozis, you should know
    that the baker
    who a year ago beat you with the wooden paddle

Kar.: Yeah?

Hat.: died.

Kar.: Died?

Hat.: Yes.

Kar.: Is it a year ago he died?

Hat.: Exactly.

Kar.: Oh my God,
my curse worked, Hatzatzari.

Hat.: What?

Kar.: You know, I cursed him.
Are you sure about this?

Hat.: Of course, I'm sure, Karagiozis,
and it was my good fortune to meet the dead baker's brother,
and I begged him, and he turned over the bakery to me, Karagiozis.
I don't have to pay a penny for it.
I can operate it for five years.
So the bakery is mine now, Karagiozis,
and I need a good baker.
Do you know any good bakers?

Kar.: Hatzatzari, are you on the level?

Hat.: Why would I lie to you?

Kar.: So
the baker died?

Hat.: Yes.

Kar.: And the bakery is yours?

Hat.: Yes.

Kar.: What are we waiting for? Let's call the junk dealers and get rid
of everything once and for all.

Hat.: Listen, you, your mind is always on selling.
I want to work this business, Karagiozis.
Do you know any good bakers?

Kar.: So, tell me now . . .

Hat.: OK.

Kar.: Who told you
I was a good baker?

Hat.: Get off it. You, a baker?

Kar.: Hey,
I swear it.
If I'm lying may

a man-seeking bomb fall on me
made of cork, and I should be behind a mountain so it doesn't touch
   me at all. [*Laughter.*]
What d'you think, I'd lie to you?
Hat.:   So you're a good baker?
Kar.:   You nitwit,
let me explain to you
how well I know the baker's trade.
All my ancestors were bakers.
Hat.:   All your ancestors?
Kar.:   Yeah.
My grandmother's grandmother's grandmother's grandmother's
   grandmother . . .
Hat.:   Yeah?
Kar.:   was a baker.
Hat.:   No kidding?
Kar.:   What—you think I'm fibbing? [*Laughter.*]
My grandfather's grandfather's grandfather's grandfather's grand-
   father was a baker.
Hat.:   You don't say, Karagiozis.
Kar.:   Yeah.
Listen, you, Hatzatzari,
I was even born in a baker's kneading trough. [*Laughter.*]
That's how good I know the baker's trade.
Hat.:   Bravo, Karagiozis,
it seems you must be a good baker.
You must know how to knead dough.
Kar.:   How can I not know that?
Hat.:   And to bake it well.
Kar.:   And to steal it too.
Hat.:   Say, you must know how to bake all kinds of food.
Kar.:   And how to eat it too. (*Karagiozis laughs.*) [*Laughter.*]
Hat.:   You must also know how to bake good pastries.
Kar.:   Listen here, you, don't worry about it. (*Small chuckle.*)
I'm the man you're looking for. Hire me and I'll steal you blind; I
   won't let you slip by me. (*Small laugh.*) [*Laughter.*]
Hat.:   Wonderful.
There's no need for me to find another baker, then.
I'll hire you, Karagiozis.

Kar.: Yeah,
  hire me and you'll see how hard I'll work. (*Small chuckle.*)
  Your customers will show up once and then never again. [*Talking in
    audience.*]
Hat.: Bravo, Karagiozis.
  Say, tell me . . .
Kar.: What?
Hat.: Since we've been friends from childhood, Karagiozis, and
  raised in the same neighborhood . . .
Kar.: Yeah.
Hat.: Now that we'll be working together,
  I don't want us to lose that friendship.
  I don't want any hard feelings.
Kar.: Wonderful.
Hat.: Tell me, Karagiozis,
  what conditions do you want to work under at the bakery?
Kar.: Hey, I'll let you take care of the details, Hatzatzari.
  It depends on the food I steal, and on the beatings we get at the
    police station.
  We'll figure it all out.
Hat.: Would you mind, Karagiozis, since the bakery is mine,
  if I should earn a little more than you?
  Isn't that my right?
Kar.: Of course.
Hat.: So,
  Karagiozis, you'll work on commission, then.
Kar.: What's commission?
Hat.: You'll work for 40 percent out of one hundred,
  and I for one hundred (*Performer stutters slightly at the mistake.*)
    and I for 60 percent out of one hundred.
Kar.: Sixty for you and forty for me?
Hat.: Yeah.
Kar.: These calculations are too much for me.
  Explain it to me simply so I can get it into my empty noodle. [*Some
    laughter.*]
Hat.: OK.
  Say
  that our business
  made

ten drachma.

Kar.: Sure.

Hat.: You'll receive
four.

Kar.: I'll receive four?

Hat.: Yeah.

Kar.: And you?

Hat.: I'll receive six.

Kar.: Six for you.

Hat.: Yeah.

Kar.: Bravo, not bad.

Hat.: Why?

Kar.: Listen, you, what d'you take me for, a nitwit?
That's not how to calculate.
We earned
ten drachma.

Hat.: Yeah.

Kar.: I'll receive ten drachma.

Hat.: And I?

Kar.: You'll wait until we earn ten more for you, do you follow me?
[*Laughter.*]

Hat.: Goddamn it, man,
you're looking for a partner.

Kar.: What's a partner?

Hat.: We earned ten drachma.

Kar.: Sure.

Hat.: Five for you and five for me.

Kar.: No, no, no, no, no.
I'm the only one earning; you shouldn't earn anything.

Hat.: All right, Karagiozis, let's not spoil everything.

Kar.: Wait until we earn some money, and then you'll see some
prizefighting. (*Chuckles.*) [*Laughter.*]

Hat.: Come on, Karagiozis,
I'll show you around the bakery,
and since you know the baker's trade so well,
see to it that everything is made ready for our grand opening.
Light the fire, knead the dough;
you'll even find that I have five sacks of flour in the store.

Kar.: Five sacks of flour?

Hat.:   Yeah.

Kar.:   Good God. (*Laughs greedily.*)

(*Laughing to himself.*) I'll make five sacks . . . (*Catches his mistake and begins again.*)

I'll make me a huge pancake using all five sacks. (*Laughs.*)

(*Gleefully and warbling.*) You can't imagine what's going to happen around here.

Hat.:   Come on.

Kar.:   Reporting.

Hat.:   Enter.

Kar.:   The bakery?

Hat.:   Yeah.

What you looking at?

Kar.:   You simp,

it just dawned on me.

Did the baker put you up to this—

to lie to me that he died—

so when I entered he could break another wooden paddle over my head?

Hat.:   Listen, you, enough with this nonsense; the man is dead, I tell you.

Enter and don't be afraid.

The store is mine.

Kar.:   Yeah.

(*Hatziavatis pushes inside.*) Hey you, stop pushing.

Confound it!

Doggone!

Hat.:   Look, you, don't be afraid.

Kar.:   Mr. Baker?

No monkey business now, do you here?

Hey, baker, I wish you and Mrs. Baker a lot of happiness.

Watch out, you, I see his feet. [*Some laughter.*]

Hat.:   How can you see his feet, you? The man is dead.

Kar.:   He's behind the door.

Hat.:   Listen, you, how can you see him behind the door?

The man is dead.

How can a dead man come to the bakery?

Kar.:   Maybe he got permission from the gravedigger to come to his store.

Hat.: Hey, have you gone nuts?
Enter.
Kar.: Hatzatzari, listen, you, if I get a licking, you'll get a black eye.
Hat.: Hey, Karagiozis, this way,
Come this way.
Kar.: THERE.
THERE, Hatzatzari.
Hat.: What is it?
Kar.: There, look, the wooden paddle.
Hey, you, there's the broken wooden paddle the baker used to break
my head. [*Some laughter.*]
Hat.: Come on, get over here, Karagiozis.
Come over here so I can show you where everything is.
Kar.: Yeah.
Hat.: Right over here, Karagiozis, as you can see,
is the cauldron where we boil water.
Kar.: Boil water?
Hat.: Yeah.
Kar.: I'll be able to bathe my feet.
Hat.: Here, Karagiozis, is the kneading trough.
Kar.: Oh, my wife will be able to do her wash in this.
Hat.: Over here are the pans and the cooking trays, Karagiozis.
Kar.: I'll sell all of these to the junk dealers.
(*Gleefully.*) I won't leave a thing.
Hat.: Here we store the wood to light the oven.
Kar.: Yeah.
Hat.: Attaboy now, Karagiozis.
Kar.: What?
Hat.: Go on,
put on your baker's hat.
Kar.: Yeah?
Hat.: And
let's cross ourselves
for good luck.
Kar.: Yeah. (*They cross themselves.*)
Hat.: All right, Karagiozis,
I'm now going
to let the neighborhood know
that from this day onward

the bakery here in the square is once again open.
Kar.: Yeah.
Hat.: We're going to have a lot of customers, Karagiozis.
Take care of the ones who come.
Kar.: I'll grab as much as I can from them.
Don't you worry about it. [*Laughter and talking.*]
Hat.: I'm off, then.
Afterward I'll go order the flour.
Kar.: Yeah,
go quickly.
Hat.: Get the store ready.
Light the fire.
Kar.: What is it I should do?
Hat.: Light the fire.
Kar.: From which end?
Hat.: Which end?
Kar.: In order to burn the bakery.
Hat. Goddamn it, man, what are you talking about? You're going to
burn the bakery?
Kar.: Why not? It could be insured, and we'll collect, you nitwit.
Hat.: Listen, you, we don't want any of that stuff.
Kar.: Some people burn entire ships to collect insurance, and you're
worried about a bakery, you nitwit?
Hat.: No, Karagiozis. Light a fire so we can bake food aaaand bread.
Kar.: Oh, all right. I know how.
Hat.: Good-bye, then.
Kar.: Bye.
Hat.: The best of luck to us. (*Leaves the screen.*)
Kar.: Let's hope for a fast buck, you should say. [*Laughter.*]
Good God, never in my wildest dreams did I think I'd be a baker.
I'M THE NEW BAKER HERE NOW.
LISTEN UP, EVERYBODY.
BRING ON THE FOODS, I'M HUNGRY.
Wait a minute.
Let's get things ready.
Let me dust
and mop the floor.
The store should be clean. (*Laughs heartily.*)
Good.

I'll be OK here.
I've been everything in my time,
but this is my first as baker. (*Laughs.*)
Good God, this store needs a lot of cleaning . . . [5]
Attaboy. [*Talking in audience.*]
Let me dust all over the place.
Will you look at all the dust?
The baker died, and the store filled with dust.
Attaboy
Attaboy [*Children's voices talking in audience.*]
Attaboy.
(*In a high-pitched voice.*) Aeiiii!
Wow, look at the dust on these tiles; I don't believe it. [*Laughter.*]
(*A loud exclamation followed by a loud clap; Karagiozis is hit.*)
OUCH. (*Exasperated and somewhat out of breath. He speaks in a
　　subdued voice.*) Good God!
Oh God, I'm done for.
I thought a whole village square fell on me, damn it.
OK.
There goes my hump by express mail; it's straight again.
　　[*Laughter.*]
Wait a minute.
Let me light the fire
and-pick-up-this-wooden-paddle-to-practice-so-I-can-see-
　　whether-I-can-shovel-the-bread-in-and-out-because-I'm-
　　going-to-eat-all-this-food.
You just wait and see what's gonna happen tonight . . . [6]
Attaboy.
Just a minute now, and I'll start the fire (*Strikes the matches.*) . . .
　　[6]
Damn it, would you believe it. These matches won't light . . . [2]
(*Strikes again.*) It won't light.
Missed again. (*Laughs.*)
(*Strikes again.*) Damn, just a second now; let me take out my
　　lighter and light this thing.
Attaboyyyy.
There we go, it's lit. (*Laughs.*)
THERE'S A GOOD BAKER HERE . . . . [9]

Just a second now, let me get ahold of the wooden paddle also
   (*Laughs.*) . . . [9]
Good God.
(*Laughingly.*) I'll grab ahold of the largest wooden paddle.
Boy, oh boy, the time I'm going to have.
(*Tries to figure out how to use the wooden paddle.*) How the hell is
   it done, now?
This way? this way? this way? this way? this way?
Oh well, I'll learn.
I'll steal about five hundred meals, and we'll see what happens.
Attaboy. (*Laughs.*)
It's not at all bad here.
THERE'S A GOOD BAKER HERE.
COME ONE, COME ALL, I'M HUNGRY.
Maybe I should lie down a bit
in case a customer comes.
I'll lie right here; he's bound to wake me.
Let me take a little nap . . . [12]
Veziris: Vergenika, come over here, come closer.
Veligekas: Po, at your orders, effendi.
Vez.:   It's a strange thing, Vergenika.
   What kind of smoke is this?
   It's all over the serai,
   and my eyes sting from this smoke.
   I can't even sit in my office to work.
   Where do you suppose all this smoke is coming from?
   Wait a minute.
   Look there, Vergenika.
   There's your answer to the whereabouts of this smoke.
   All this smoke in the serai
   is from that bakery.
   Come and take a look how it's smoking.
Vel.:   Po, yes sir, effendi.
Vez.:   I must call the baker
   to demolish this bakery right away.
   How dare he build a bakery
   right outside the serai. (*Enters the bakery.*)
   Faker,

faker,
hey, you, faker,
faker,
you have to be around here someplace.
Vel.:   Pagan down here, master, lying down.
Vez.:   Whyyyy, the poor soul.
It's well known, Vergenika,
that these poor bakers work all night long.
He must be tired, and that's why he's lying down.
Step out of the way, Vergenika.
Let me see him . . . [4]
Faker.
Kar.:   (*Snores.*) Khawwww.
Vez.:   Faker.
Kar.:   Khawwww. [*Laughter.*]
Vez.:   The poor devil is snoring.
Faker.
Kar.:   (*Snores and spits.*) Khawwww. Phtou! [*Laughter.*]
Vez.:   He's having a bad dream.
He's spitting in his sleep.
Baker. (*Here performer forgets and pronounces the word correctly.*)
Kar.:   (*Snores and spits.*) Khawwww. Phtou! [*Laughter.*]
Vez.:   This is some dream he's having.
Faker.
Kar.:   (*Waking.*) Ehhhh?
(*Stretches.*) Ahhhh.
(*Makes noise as he wakes.*) Aeeee. (*Hits Veziris.*) ◯
Vez.:   Oh, by Allah! ◯
Be careful, faker.
You hit me with your wooden paddle.
Vel.:   You-want-I-should-work-him-over?
Vez.:   No, the poor devil didn't mean it.
He's having a bad dream.
Kar.:   (*Snores.*) Khawwww.
Vez.:   Faker.
Kar.:   (*Snores and spits.*) Khawwww. Phtou! (*Karagiozis makes this sound throughout the scene with Veziris.*) [*Laughter.*]
Vez.:   I'm bewildered how he can spit in his sleep.
Faker.

Kar.:   Volah. (*Hits Veziris.*)
Vez.:   HEY, WATCH IT NOW. YOU'RE MAKING ME MAD.
Listen, faker,
get up now and put the baking paddle down.
Kar.:   (*Sing-song.*) Present, present, present, present.
Vez.:   Put the wooden paddle down.
Kar.:   Scared of it, are you? (*Laughs.*)
OK, pasha, sir,
you can relax now.
Vez.:   Tell me, are you the baker?
Kar.:   Indeed I am, pasha, sir.
Vez.:   Is this your bakery?
Kar.:   Sure, it's mine, pasha, sir.
Vez.:   Tell me, will you please,
are you aware that all the smoke from your bakery
goes into the serai and smokes us out?
You've blinded us with smoke.
The serai's employees can't work in their offices.
I can't even sit
in my own quarters, baker,
from all the smoke.
You've ruined the serai's curtains,
the furniture.
Everything is full of smoke.
Tell me who gave you permission
to build the bakery right outside the serai?
Kar.:   Well, eh, eh, master.
What can I say? The bakery was already built.
It's not my fault; it's the weather that blows the smoke in your
   direction.
What can I do about it?
If the wind blew the other way, there wouldn't be any smoke.
Vez.:   I'm not interested in the wind.
What I'm interested in, baker,
and I'm ordering you,
in twenty-four hours
to have workers here
to tear down this bakery.
Kar.:   (*To the audience.*) Oh boy, heeeere we goooo.

We've just hit the jackpot. (*Chuckles.*)

Hatzatzari, wherever you are, know that I'm about to tear down
    your bakery.

(*To Veziris.*) Master,

I'm a poor man,

a family man.

If you tear down my bakery,

how will I feed myself and my children?

Vez.:   That's not my concern.

I want peace and quiet

and clean air

here where I live.

Besides, it's not permitted to have a bakery blowing smoke
right in front of the serai.

Now then,

I don't want to hear any more about it.

In twenty-four hours you will have workers

tear down this bakery.

If the bakery is not torn down,

I will order my own soldiers from the serai

to take shovels and pickaxes

and tear down the bakery,

and you'll

be taken to prison

and punished.

Kar.:   Yes, master.

Vez.:   How did this bakery get here, anyway?

Kar.:   It's a long story, master.

    I'll tell it to you, but you won't believe it.

Vez.:   How did it get here?

Kar.:   Let me tell you, pasha, sir.

It was about two years ago.

Vez.:   Two years ago?

Kar.:   Yes.

I was sitting right here in this old shack.

Vez.:   You live in this old shack?

Kar.:   Yes.

Vez.:   Do you have children?

Kar.:   What else, rabbits? Naturally, I have children.

Vez.:   How many children?
Kar.:   I have
three little boys.
Vez.:   Bravo,
the best of health to them.
Kar.:   Thank you, and by next year I hope you kick the bucket.
Vez.:   Thank you.
Kar.:   (*To the audience.*) The dummy said thank you,
get that. [*Laughter.*]
Vez.:   Do your boys go to school?
Kar.:   Yes.
My oldest son is a good student.
A very good student, my oldest son.
He always passes with straight A's.
Vez.:   Your oldest son?
Kar.:   Yes, my oldest son.
Vez.:   What grade is he in?
Kar.:   He's a sophomore in high school.
Vez.:   Bravo.
Congratulations.
Your oldest son is a sophomore in high school.
Kar.:   Yes.
Vez.:   How is (*Performer gets mixed up here.*) old is he?
Kar.:   What?
Vez.:   How old is he?
Kar.:   My son?
Vez.:   Yes.
Kar.:   Six months.
Vez.:   But that's unbelievable.
Six months old, and he's in high school?
Kar.:   Yeah, he finished grade school before he was born, do you
follow me? (*Chuckles.*) [*Laughter.*]
Vez.:   Hey, hold on here, now; let's have the truth.
Kar.:   Well,
as I was coming out of my shack . . .
Vez.:   Wait just a minute, baker.
Kar.:   What?
Vez.:   Half of your shack's roof
is missing.

Kar.: I know it.

Vel.: But when it rains, there's no roof.

Kar.: Yes.

Vez.: So where do you take your family when it rains?

Kar.: When it rains?

Vez.: Yes.

Kar.: I take them outside.

Vez.: Why would you all go outside?

Kar.: Because inside we get wetter. Do you follow me?

Vez.: Oh well, let's drop it.
  How did this bakery get here?
  Am I going to find out?

Kar.: Yes.
  It was this way: as I was coming out one morning, pasha, sir,
  right here on this spot where the bakery now is,
  I stumbled and fell.

Vez.: You stumbled?

Kar.: Yes.
  I say to myself, "What the heck was this thing that tripped me and
    messed up my face?"
  I turned a bit, and what do I see?
  A tiny little brick, just so big.

Vez.: You're not serious?

Kar.: Would I kid you?
  I felt sorry for stepping on it, pasha, sir,
  so I went home, got a pail of water
  and dumped some on it to water it.

Vez.: The brick?

Kar.: Yes.
  The next day when I passed by I saw that
  with my watering
  it had grown twice as big.

Vez.: It had grown with your watering?

Kar.: Yes.
  I continued to water it, it kept growing, I watered it, it grew.
  Finally it got to be as big a brick as you are, yeeees. [*Laughter.*]

Vez.: Like me?

Kar.: In height, I mean.

Vez.: Yes.

Kar.: So
  I gave it water, it grew.
  Finally we had a bakery.
Vez.: Listen, baker,
  all these stories you're telling me are stupid nonsense,
  and all your nonsense
  is not going
  to save the bakery from being wrecked.
  The bakery
  will be torn down in twenty-four hours.
  That's final.
  I have nothing more to tell you.
Kar.: Yes sir.
Vez.: Good-bye.
Kar.: Good-bye . . . [2]
Vez.: Come on, Vergenika, I'm leaving.
Vel.: Po, yes sir, effendi. (*Veziris and Veligekas exit the screen.*)
Kar.: Now what?
  Hey you, take that. (*Makes an obscene gesture.*) [*Laughter.*]
  Take that. (*Another obscene gesture.*)
  I haven't even gotten to eat, and they're going to take the bakery.
  You think you're so smart.
  Would you believe it? (*Chuckles.*)
  Wait until Hatzatzari finds out the bakery will be torn down.
    (*Laughs.*)
  Oooooh,
  if only I was lucky enough
  for somebody to bring some kind of food.
  I'd even eat it raw; I don't mind. (*Chuckles.*)
  If only I could get a chance to eat, and then they can tear down the
    bakery; I could care less.
  I might as well take a little nap . . . [14]
Mukhtar Bey: Wonderful.
  This is really nice,
  to learn
  that the bakery
  on this square will once again be working.
  As it is now, we are obliged
  to go to the upper quarter

to buy a loaf of bread or to have our food baked.
But now this bakery is very close to our quarter.
How I would like
to meet the baker.
(*Calls out in a sing-song voice.*) Hey there, baaaa-keeeer.

Kar.:   Eeeeeh?

Bey: Hey there, baa-keer.

Kar.:   (*Sing-song.*) Present, present, present, present, preeee-
seeeent.
Ah,
it has to be a customer.
It's a customer. (*Laughs.*)
Let me see now.
Here I am, sir.
Here I am.

Bey: Good day to you, baker.

Kar.:   Welcome, (*Chuckles.*)

Bey: Are you
the baker?

Kar.:   Eh?
What's the matter; you blind or something, you nitwit?
Can't you see this huge wooden paddle, symbol of my trade?
Can't you see it?

Bey: So you're the baker.

Kar.:   Yes.

Bey: I'm glad to know you.

Kar.:   I'd be glad to throw you. [*Laughter.*]

Bey: You know, baker,
I'm a neighbor, and I'd like to be a customer of yours.

Kar.:   Oh, thanks a lot.

Bey: Say, baker . . .

Kar.:   Yes sir.

Bey: You should know that I've been here
in your country for only a few years,
since I
was born and reared
in Egypt.

Kar.:   No kidding?

Bey: No, I'm not.

It's been exactly three years
since I arrived here in your city.
Kar.: Well then, welcome to our city, Mister . . . (*Chuckles.*)
And your name?
Bey: I'm called Master Kemil.
Kar.: Well, welcome to you, Master Cameeeel [*Laughter.*] . . . [4]
Bey: Listen, baker, today
relatives of mine
arrived from Egypt,
and I'll be hosting them at my home.
That's why I'm in a hurry.
I have them at home, and I want to give them a dinner.
Kar.: What's that you say?
Bey: I'm going to give my relatives from Egypt a dinner.
Kar.: Are you a philanthropist.
Bey: What philanthropist?
Kar.: You're going to give them a diner.
Bey: No, my good man.
I said I'm going to have them at my home, and we're all eating
together.
Kar.: Oh, now I got you.
Bey: And you know, in order to please my relatives,
I decided to serve them
the goose I had at home.
Kar.: Goose?
Bey: Yes,
baker, and
I killed it,
plucked it,
and stuffed it with a variety of spices.
Kar.: The goose?
Bey: Yes.
With nutmeg . . .
Kar.: You don't say?
Bey: Yes.
With chestnuts, ground meat, rice, and a variety of other things.
Kar.: Really?
Bey: Yes.
It's an exceptional meal, baker.

That's why I came to explain it to you first before I bring you the
  goose for baking.
You must be careful
not to burn it.
Kar.:   (*To the audience.*) No way I'm going to burn it, but I can't
  promise anything about not eating it.
It won't get away from me. [*Laughter.*]
(*To Mukhtar Bey.*) Certainly, Master Camel, sir.
Yes, yes, bring the goose.
Bey: Thank you.
I want you to take good care of it.
If you do, I'll
become your best customer.
Kar.:   Yes, Master Camel, sir, certainly.
Bey: Keep in mind
  that the goose will be delivered by a young Arab boy.
Kar.:   An Arab boy?
Bey: Indeed.
You see, when I left Egypt
I brought with me a young Arab orphan
who now lives
in my home as my own child
and serves me in various ways.
Kar.:   So-you'll-send-the-goose-with-a-young-Arab-boy.
Bey: Indeed.
Well then,
baker,
you'll permit me
to make you a small gift.
Kar.:   OK.
Bey: Here, take this gold coin.
Kar.:   A gold coin?
Bey: Yes.
Kar.:   (*Scream of amazement.*) Eiiii.
Why is it yellow?
Bey: Gold is yellow, isn't it?
Kar.:   Could it have come down with jaundice?
Bey: You must be pulling my leg, right?
Kar.:   Good.

Thank you.

You're paying me for the baking job.

Bey: No.

I'm giving this gold co . . . (*Performer gets mixed up here.*) as a gift,

as a good luck charm for your store.

Kar.: And for baking?

Bey: You'll receive more money.

Kar.: That sounds good.

Sure.

Thank you very much.

Bey: In a little while

the young Arab boy will come with the goose.

Kar.: Yes, quickly though, since I have a good fire going, do you follow me?

Bey: Yes, yes.

Good-bye.

Kar.: So long, so long.

Bey: Au revoir.

Kar.: Drop dead, wherever you are.

Bey: What did you say?

Kar.: Drop in whenever you want. [*Laughter.*]

Bey: Yes, yes, good-bye. (*Leaves the screen.*)

Kar.: Adieu, adieu.

WOW, WHAT A TERRIFIC GUY, THAT MASTER CAMEL.

AND SENSIBLE, I CAN'T TELL YOU.

YES SIR, A SENSIBLE MAN.

He says to himself,

"I'm going to give him a high-class hors d'oeuvre, a goose stuffed with a variety of spices.

It's a superior hors d'oeuvre.

Karagiozis is a poor man.

Since he's going to eat the goose, a superior hors d'oeuvre, shouldn't the man have some beer to drink with it?

Let me give him a gold coin for some beer, the better to enjoy the hors d'oeuvre he's going to have." Do you follow me? [*Laughter.*]

What a good man. (*Laughs.*)

Boy, oh boy, a goose. (*Laughs.*)

You just all wait and see the kind of Thanksgiving I'm going to have tonight with this
  goose . . . [16]

Arab Boy: E, e, esma,

  e, e, esma,

  endole, esma,

  a, yahalohe, esma,

  esma, endole, e, bakeman, bakeman,

  e, esma,

  endole,

  e, esma,

  e, bakeman, bakeman,

  e, bakeman, e, esma, endole, bakeman. (*The performer here invents
    a variety of sounds to approximate the speech of the Arab boy.*)

Kar.:   Whose needle got stuck? [*Laughter.*]

Boy: Endole, esma,

  esma, e, bakeman, yiahalanha.

Kar.:   What he say?

  What-is-this?

  Let-me-take-a-look.

  (*Lets out a scream.*) Eiiii.

  Hey you, it's a little Arab kid.

Boy: E, e, bakeman bakeman, esma,

  esma.

Kar.:   What the hell is *esma?*

Boy: E, endole, yiahalanha, esma.

Kar.:   (*Snorts like a pig.*) Oink, oink. [*Laughter.*] Why's this good-
  for-nothing snorting like a pig? [*Laughter.*]

  What d'you want?

Boy: E, esma, bakeman, master, master, esma.

Kar.:   What's that? What did the master say?

Boy: E, master, bake, moose, moose.

Kar.:   What he say?

Boy: Master, bake, moose.

Kar.:   I don't have any moose; you'll have to go to the zoo, m'boy.
  [*Some laughter.*]

Boy: E, moose, moose, master, e, yiahalanha, esma.

Kar.:   (*Snorts like a pig.*) Oink, oink [*Laughter.*] He comes from a
  long line of pigs.

  NOW I GOT IT. Boy, am I thick.

(*Screams.*) Eiiii.

He's carrying a huge tray on his head with a goose in it, and I didn't even see it.

Wait a minute.

Bring it over here, you.

This must be from Master Camel; there's no other explanation.

Boy: Esma, esma, yiahalanha, esma, eh, bakeman, bakeman.

Kar.: Shut up, you.

Get-the-hell-out-of-here-you-and-your-esma-esma.

My head is reeling.

All right, now. (*Takes the tray with the goose.*)

Come here, my lovely; in you go.

Attaboy.

Boy: Eh, esma, endole, esma, eh, bakeman, bakeman.

Kar.: WHAT IS IT, YOU?

Boy: Eh, yiahalanha, esma. (*Loud clap as Arab boy throws a pinecone at Karagiozis.*)

Kar.: OUCH, DAMN YOU.

GODDAMN IT. (*Loud clap again along with warbling commotion followed by a series of claps, as Arab boy continues to pelt Karagiozis with pinecones.*) GET THE HELL OUT OF HERE. [*Laughter.*]

Why, that little alley cat.

He took me by storm with those pinecones, do you follow me?

Boy: Esma, esma. (*Loud clap as Arab boy throws another pinecone at Karagiozis.*)

Kar.: Ouch.

Boy: Endole, esma. (*Loud claps as Arab boy continues to pelt Karagiozis.*)

Kar.: Ouch.

LISTEN, YOU. (*Loud clap as another pinecone hits Karagiozis.*) OUCH, OH, MY GOODNESS,

why, that little good-for-nothing alley cat.

Boy: Esma, (*The clap of another pinecone hitting Karagiozis.*) ESMA.

Kar.: Come over here, I'll . . .

(*Loud clap as Karagiozis hits Arab boy.*) Come over here, I'll show you.

Why, the little alley cat; look what he's done to me tonight . . . [5]

Boy: Esma,
   eh, bakeman, bakeman, eh, yiahalanha,
   eh, bakeman, bakeman, eh, yiahalanha,
   esma.
Kar.:   (*Chants to the melody of a hymn sung in the Greek Orthodox
   Church during Holy Week.*) And to your Memory, Life . . . now shove
   off. [*Laughter.*] (*A series of claps as Karagiozis hits the Arab boy.*)
Boy: Eh, ESMA,
   eh, ESMA. (*Clapping sounds of Karagiozis hitting Arab boy
      continue.*)
   ENDOLE, ESMA. (*Series of clapping sounds as Karagiozis con-
      tinues to hit Arab boy.*)
   EHHHHESMAAAA. (*Leaves the screen.*)
Kar.:   EHHHHESMAAAA. (*Chuckles.*)
   I'll show you.
   Did you catch some of those pinecones he was throwing my way?
   Come around here again and I'll show you.
   Why, the dadblasted one,
   he bombarded me with pinecones, do you follow me?
   I'd better take a little nap.
   Attaboy . . . [21]
Veziris: (*Addressing the audience.*) This is all very puzzling.
   What a beautiful fragrance.
   This smell
   is everywhere.
   Does it come from our neighborhood? . . . [3]
   I'm curious.
   Let me check and see where this beautiful fragrance
   comes from . . . [5]
   (*Turning to Karagiozis.*) Put the wooden paddle down, please,
   and come over here.
   I want to talk to you.
Kar.:   Yes . . . [2]
   Here I am, my pasha.
Vez.:   Do you know why I'm here, baker?
Kar.:   (*Sheepishly.*) I have no idea.
Vez.:   This fragrance
   has filled
   the entire quarter.

Kar.: You don't say, my pasha.
Vez.: Yes.
  I believe
  that it must be some nice pastry
  you're baking in your bakery
  whose fragrance has overrun
  our entire quarter.
Kar.: No, my pasha,
  let me explain.
  I'm not baking pastry,
  but I can tell you
  that in my oven
  I have a customer's
  goose
  stuffed with a variety
  of spices.
Vez.: You don't say.
Kar.: I'm not going to put you on.
  It's an exceptional dish.
  That's why our whole neighborhood smells so sweetly.
Vez.: Oh, by Allah,
  that is truly an extraordinary dish,
  an exceptional appetizer.
Kar.: (*To himself.*) I'll say, you wretch; I'm even considering eating it raw before it
  has a chance to cook. (*Chuckles.*) [*Laughter.*]
Vez.: Listen here, baker.
Kar.: Yes sir.
Vez.: As soon as the goose is baked . . .
Kar.: Yes?
Vez.: Take it out immediately
  and bring it over to the serai.
Kar.: This goose that doesn't belong to me, my pasha?
Vez.: Yes.
Kar.: Where do I take it?
Vez.: To me.
Kar.: And what are you going to do with it?
Vez.: Eat it.
Kar.: Come on now, my pasha,
  are you kidding me?

You're going to eat someone else's goose, my pasha?
Is that possible when the food belongs to someone else?

Vez.:   Don't fret about it, baker.

Kar.:   But I'll get in trouble with my customer.
He'll take me to court as a thief
on the charge that I ate his food.

Vez.:   Don't fret.
Where will your customer who brought the goose bring you to
court?

Kar.:   To you, my pasha.

Vez.:   And I'll find you innocent.

Kar.:   And what kind of an excuse are we going to give, my pasha,
when I bring you the goose to eat?

Vez.:   What's your name, Karagiozis? (*Realizes he is asking what he
already knows.*)
Didn't we say your name is Karagiozis?

Kar.:   Yes.

Vez.:   Tell me, please,
when your customer comes to me
to complain,
do you know what excuse I'll give him?

Kar.:   What excuse will you give him?

Vez.:   Listen closely so you'll know what my excuse will be.
I'll tell your customer
that the baker is justified.

Kar.:   And he'll say, "How is he justified, since he ate my goose?"

Vez.:   I'll explain it to you right away.
I'll saaaayyyy that the Koran . . .

Kar.:   What's the Koran?

Vez.:   Our Bible.

Kar.:   Your Bible?

Vez.:   Yes.

Kar.:   Then what?

Vez.:   Our Koran says that one day
Muhammad will perform a great miracle.

Kar.:   Muhammad?

Vez.:   Yes.
A goose
plucked and butchered

will fly out from a bakery
and will get up and fly away.

Kar.:   (*To himself.*) WHyyyy THEEEE LIAAAARRRR.
Say, this guy's got me beat in lying.
I lie too, but not that big.
(*To Veziris.*) The goose, my pasha, butchered,
plucked,
will fly away?

Vez.:   Yes.
We'll say Muhammad performed a miracle
and that our Bible, the Koran, says so.
In this way
if your customer doesn't believe the Koran
I can also punish him
and have him pay a fine.
You have nothing to worry about, Karagiozis.

Kar.:   So that's how we're going to do it.

Vez.:   Yes.

Kar.:   Wonderful.
If I won't get in trouble
I'll be happy to do it, my pasha.
As soon as the goose is baked
I'll bring it to you to eat.

Vez.:   I thank you.
And to get up a good appetite,
baker Karagiozis,
I'll go now and have a brandy
to whet my appetite.

Kar.:   OK, go get yourself a panty to wet your appetite. [*Laughter.*]

Vez.:   Yes. As soon as it's baked, bring it to me.

Kar.:   Absolutely, don't worry.

Vez.:   Wonderful.
I'm off.

Kar.:   OK.

Vez.:   I'm going for a brandy. (*Exits.*)

Kar.:   Get your panty, and we'll see what happens. [*Laughter.*]
Get the hell out of here, you and your little tricks.
I should bring you the goose to eat because the Koran says so.
You're out of your mind.

The Koran says Karagiozis and his clan should eat it, you nitwit.
Wait and see what I have in store for you. (*Laughs.*)
Now I have an excuse to eat the goose and not get blamed.
And let him wear his panty to wet his appetite. [*Laughter.*]
Let's take another little nap again.
Attaboy . . . [5]

Nionios: (*Enters singing.*) A black ship,
A black ship I will become.
White sails,
white sails I will hoist.
OK-now,-deary-you-can-stop-your-crooning-You've-reached-the-
    bakery-deary-Hey-there,-you-good-for-nothing-ne'er-do-well-
    Hey,-you-baker-where-are-you-I-brought-my-stewpan-do-you-
    savvy?

Kar.:   Who the hell's preaching out there? [*Laughter.*]
Who is it?
What's this?
Why, it's Nionios.
Hey, Nionios.
Would you believe it, out of the clear blue sky.
Welcome, my friend Nionios

Nion.:   Say-help-me-out-son-Don't-tell-me-Karagiozis-that-you're-
    the-baker.

Kar.:   Yes, Nioniooos. [*Laughter.*]

Nion.:   Oh-no-save-me-Virgin-Mary-There-go-my-edibles-You-ate-
    them,-sly-boots.

Kar.:   How can you say I ate them?
I didn't get them in my hands yet, Nionios.

Nion.:   I-don't-know-If-I-knew-you-were-the-baker-here-as-I-can-
    see-you're-the-baker-here-how-can-I-leave-my-stewpan-you-un-
    derSTAND.

Kar.:   Why, Nionios?

Nion.:   Oh-come-now-you-good-for-nothing-ne'er-do-well-You'll-
    fuck-things-uuuuPPPP. [*Laughter.*]

Kar.:   Listen, you, I won't fuck you up.
What do you have in this stew?

Nion.:   Don't-you-see-Karagiozis-don't-you-see?

Kar.:   What?

Nion.:   Here-in-this-stewPAN.

Kar.: Did you hear that, he calls the stew a stewpan. [*Laughter.*]

Nion.: I-have-a-world-of-goods.

Kar.: Where?

Nion.: In-the-stewpan.

Kar.: Hey, can you fit a whole world in such a small stewpan?
What, are you crazy?

Nion.: Look-you-can't-you-see?

Kar.: What kind of food is this?

Nion.: Can't-you-see-what-I-got-I-got-tomatooooes-potatooooes-
Macedonian-chicks-the-lord-and-the-ol'-heiress-KaragioZO.*

Kar.: What kind of food is this you're talking about?
Let me look.
Squash, potatoes, eggplants, tomatoes.
Where is this lord and the ol' heiress?

Nion.: Can't-you-see-how-it's-swimming-around-there-the-lord-
and-the-ol'-heireSS? [*Laughter.*]

Kar.: Ah, he's put a lot of oil in there and calls it the lord and the ol'
heiress. (*Laughs.*)
OK, Nionios,
leave your stewpan right here.
You won't even get your stewpan back by the time I get through with
you; you have my word on it.

Nion.: Karagiozis-don't-you-spoof-me-and-eat-my-stewpaaaan.

Kar.: Hey, of course not, Nionios; I give you my word.
I'm now in business with Hatzatzari.
Don't you trust me?
I'm reformed now.

Nion.: Well-all-right-I'll-leave-my-stewpan-When-can-I-pick-it-
up-Karagiozo-When-will-it-be-reaDY?

Kar.: Come back in two hours and you won't find a thing.

Nion.: Bravo-But-be-carefUL.

Kar.: Eh?

Nion.: When-you-take-it-out-with-that-baking-paddleeee . . .

Kar.: Yeah.

Nion.: Uh,-uh,-straighten-it-straighten-it.

---

*Nionios refers to the lard and oil in his stew as *lardos ke ipolardia*. Lardos is a masculine form, while ipolardia is a feminine form. The words themselves have no meaning.

Kar.: Do what?

Nion.: Straighten-it-so-you-won't-spill-the-lord-and-the-ol'-heiress,-OK?

Kar. All right; I won't spill the lord and the ol' heiress. [*Laughter.*]
Wait a minute.

Let me straighten it out. (*Karagiozis places the stew on the baking
paddle.*) What the hell do you think I'm using here, you nitwit, a
leveler to straighten it out?

Watch it now. (*Karagiozis is here attempting to put the stew into the
oven.*)

Attaboy.

He's so fussy, this customer . . .

All right, Nionios, now leave it here.

Nion.: Watch-it-don't-tilt-it.

Kar.: What do you mean, don't tilt it?

Nion.: Straighten-it-out-so-you-won't-spill-the-lord-and-the-ol'-
heiRESS. [*Laughter.*]

Watch it.

Straighten-it-out,-straighten-IT-OUT-straighten-it-out-you'll-spill-
my-lord-and-the-ol'-heiress-I-tell-you.

Kar.: NIONIOS, GET THE HELL out of here.
YOU'RE DRIVING ME CRAZY.
I'M GOING TO BONK YOU OVER THE HEAD TONIGHT
WITH THIS STEWPAN. [*Laughter.*]

Nion.: Watch it, watch it,
straighten it.

You from the . . .

you-from-the-front-you'll-dump-my-lord-and-the-ol'-HEIRESS-
YOU-SLY-BOOTS.

Kar.: Ouch, you're driving me nuts tonight.
All right, Nionios, there.
Easy does it.

Nion.: You sly boots, go slow. You dumped my lord and the ol'
heiressss.

Kar.: Listen, you, I didn't spill your lord and the ol' heiress.

Nion.: Hey, I'm going, Karagiozo, and I'll be back to pick up my
stewpan.

Kar.: Go ahead. You're not going to pick up a thing.

Nion.: So long.

Damn this lowlife, I-hope-he-doesn't-botch-things-up. (*Exits.*)
Kar.: Good.
Just a minute now.
Why not go to the pasha
and see
what the Koran says about squash potato stew.
The Koran might say something of interest about this food too.
There he comes . . . [2]
Vez.: Are you still here, baker?
Kar.: I'm right here, pasha.
Vez.: Did you bring me the goose yet?
Kar.: Just a liiiitle bit longer before it's ready. [*Some laughter.*]
Vez.: Listen up, now.
You can't imagine how hungry I am.
I've already had two brandies.
Kar.: It's some feat to put on two panties. (*Laughs.*) [*Laughter.*]
Vez.: When will you send me the goose?
Kar.: Eh, it still needs to be turned a bit on the other side so it'll be
well cooked.
Vez.: Bravo.
Bake it well. I'll just have to be a little patient.
I'll have another brandy.
Kar.: (*To the audience.*) Good idea. Put on another panty, and we'll
see what happens. [*Laughter.*]
(*To Veziris.*) By the way, pasha,
someone from Zákinthos just came by.
His name was Dionisios.
Vez.: Yes, so?
Kar.: He brought a stewpan.
Vez.: What's a stewpan?
Kar.: A stew.
Vez.: Good.
What's in it?
Kar.: It has squash and potatoes,
eggplant, which he calls Macedonian chicks, and lord and ol'
heiress. [*Some laughter.*]
Vez.: What's a lord and ol' heiress?
Kar.: I didn't know either, but I found out.
A lot of oil.

Vez.: Good.

Kar.: Does the Koran concern itself with this dish?

Vez.: I'm not interested in squash and potatoes,
         Karagiozis.

Kar.: You're not interested, eh?

Vez.: No.

Kar.: Good.
         Can I eat them, then?

Vez.: If you like them, eat them. [*Laughter.*]

Kar.: And what excuse could I give my customer?

Vez.: Let's seeee.
         Tell him whatever you want; I'm going to say it's in the Koran.

Kar.: Pasha, could I say that
         the tomatoeeees and the potatoeeees had words between them,
         and the Macedonian drew a gun (*Gestures how gun is drawn.*)
             [*Laughter.*]
         and killed the chicks,
         and the lord and ol' heiress jumped out [*Laughter.*]
         and called the cops and an ambulance,
         and we had eighteen casualties and five homicides,
         and all my food was spilled and my bakery ransacked,
         and there was a big brawl?

Vez.: But that's an outright lie, baker.

Kar.: Why?

Vez.: How can squash and potatoes have a quarrel?
         It can't be; it's a lie.

Kar.: OK.
         So it's a lie.
         But what about your butchered goose that flew off and got away?
             Isn't that a lie?

Vez.: So OK, say it's in the Koran.

Kar.: So you want the goose for yourself, right?

Vez.: Yes.

Kar.: And the squash and potatoes?

Vez.: You'll eat those.

Kar.: Naturally, I'm observing Lent. How could I forget? (*Laughs.*)
         [*Laughter.*]

Vez.: Come on now, let me have the goose.

Kar.: It need just a little bit more baking.

Vez.: Fine.

I'll go have a brandy. (*Exits.*)

Kar.: Yes, go have a panty. (*To himself.*) I'll drive you wacky tonight. [*Laughter.*]

What does he mean, just the squash and potatoes?

I want everything.

I'm going to eat it all; I'm no dummy.

Let me take a little nap.

Attaboy [*Laughter.*] . . . [16]

Uncle George: Good gracious,

what a nosegay downs heres. Where's that baker?

I broughts m'kill

to get it baked . . . [4]

hey, wheres ya aaaatttt? [*Whistles long and loud.*]

Kar.: HEY, DRIVER, WATCH IT.

HEY, DRIVER, people are sleeping.

Watch it, driver.

What? Hey, it's Uncle George,

and here I thought some sixteen-wheeler was bearing down on me.

(*Laughs.*) [*Laughter.*]

Good God, what's he holding in his hands?

Let me see . . . [2]

Hey, Uncle, welcome.

Welcome to my good little uncle.

Unc.: Prais' th' Lord!

Ya heres, ya scrounger?

Kar.: Yes.

Unc.: (*Crying.*) YA BONEHEAD, ya tucked it away, ya mucker, ya tucked it away, ya scrounger.

Kar.: What did I eat, Uncle?

Unc.: M'kill, ya finished it off, m'boy.

Kar.: What of yours did I eat, Uncle?

Unc.: Hey ya, ya put away m'kill.

Kar.: What-kill-are-you-talking-about-Uncle-since-you're-still-holding-it-in-your-hands?

I-haven't-touched-it-yet-It's-not-time-yet-I-know-when-to-eat-it-It's-not-time-yet. [*Laughter.*]

Unc.: Karagiozis, are ya th' baker?

Kar.: That's right, Uncle.

Help us out.

My friend Hatzatzari and I own the bakery together.

Let me bake it for you, Uncle.

I'll do a nice job.

Unc.:   Hey ya scrounger, watch ya don'ts puts away m'kill an' haves me go hungry.

Kar.:   So? It wouldn't be the first time I let you go hungry, uncs. [*Laughter.*]

Come on now, nunky,

bring me your lamb to bake; you'll see how nice I'll bake it.

You'll, you'll never forget me.

You can't imagine how tasty I'll make it.

Unc.:   Karagioz,

watch outs ya don'ts tucks away m'kill.

Kar.:   Of course not, Uncle.

Listen,

have faith, and put it down right here.

Aaaaattaboy.

Come on, put it down, uncs.

That's the way.

Aaaaattaboy

(*Gleefully.*) And it's so plump. (*Laughs.*)

(*Greedily.*) You'll see how things come out. Aaaaattaboy. (*Puts the lamb in the oven.*)

Unc.:   Hey, tells me.

Kar.:   Eh?

Unc.:   Did ya push it in, ya?

Kar.:   What?

Unc.:   Did ya push m'kill in yet?

Kar.:   Where were you? Weren't you standing right here when I put it in?

Unc.:   Grubs it out again.

Kar.:   Why should I take it out?

Unc.:   Ya tucked it away.

Kar.:   What did I eat?

Unc.:   The kill, ya tucked it away.

Kar.:   What are you talking about, uncs? It's in there.

Unc.:   I SAID, GRUBS IT OUT, YA. (*Hits him.*) ○

Kar.:   WATCH IT, YOU.

What you hitting me for, Uncle?

Unc.:   Ya tucked it away, ya cuckold.

Ya tucked it away. Grubs it out. (*Hits him.*)

Grubs it out, I says. Ya tucked it away, ya BONEHEAD.

Grubs it out here, ya. (*Hits him.*)

Kar.:   Hold on there, Uncle.

Hold on.

Why do you hit me, Uncle?

I put it in. Wait now, wait, I'll show you. He doesn't believe me.

Waaaait a minute . . . (*Karagiozis takes the lamb out of the oven.*)

He doesn't believe me. Eeeeeasy does it.

There, you see, Uncle? Why hit me for nothing?

(*Sadly.*) I'm black and blue.

Unc.:   Gets on.

Push it in again.

Kar.:   What?

Unc.:   Push it in again.

Kar.:   Should I put it back in?

Unc.:   Ya, push it in again.

Kar.:   I'll put it back in.

Aaaaattaboy. (*Puts it back in the oven.*)

Unc.:   Hey ya,

get on.

Kar.:   What?

Unc.:   Did ya push it back in?

Kar.:   What's the matter with you? Have you gone blind, you gimp?

Didn't you just tell me to put it back in?

Unc.:   Grubs it out again.

Kar.:   What?

Unc.:   Grubs it OUT again. (*Hits him.*)

Kar.:   JUST a minute, Uncle.

Unc.:   Grubs it out again. (*Hits him.*) Ya tucked it away, ya BONEHEAD.

Kar.:   Hold-on-a-minute-because-you're-driving-me-crazy-tonight.

Move back a bit so you can see.

I don't believe all this work. (*Opens the oven and takes the lamb out again.*)

There it is, Uncle.

There's your lamb.

Unc.:   Ya.
          Gets on.
Kar.:   What?
Unc.:   Push it backs in again.
Kar.:   JUST A DAMN MINUTE, YOU GIMP.
          IS THAT WHAT I HAVE TO LOOK FORWARD TO? IN AND
          OUT?
Unc.:   Gets on, push it in, I tell ya.
Kar.:   OK. I'll put it back in.
          Easy does it. (*Puts it back in the oven.*)
Unc.:   Did ya push it in, Karagioz? (*Hits him.*)
Kar.:   Stop hitting me, Uncle. Didn't you just see me?
Unc.:   Comes out with it.
Kar.:   What?
Unc.:   Where's yore kids?
Kar.:   In school, Uncle.
Unc.:   Ya sure they're nots in the oven to tucks away m'kill?
Kar.:   What's with you, Uncle? They'd burn in the oven; there's fire
          in there. What are you, nuts?
Unc.:   Gets on.
          I'm pullin' out.
Kar.:   See you, Uncle.
Unc.:   Watch ya don'ts tucks away m'kill.
Kar.:   I won't, Uncle.
Unc.:   When I comes back,
          I'll cries out from 'far.
Kar.:   Yes.
Unc.:   And I'll cries out, "Did ya fizzle it out or gobs it up?"
Kar.:   And I'll respond, "Fizzlegob."
Unc.:   What's that?
Kar.:   That the lamb is ready? Got me?
Unc.:   Ya.
          You'll tells me, "Fizzlegob."
Kar.:   (*To himself.*) Yes, fizzlegob that I ate it and have done with it.
          Then you'll beat me up, and we'll be even. [*Laughter.*]
Unc.:   (*To himself, but Karagiozis overhears.*) Confound it!
          Ya know this kid's a thief.
          He'll eats up yore lamb for sure.

George, m'boy, ya mights as well goes butcher another one so ya
   don'ts go hungry t'night. (*Leaves the screen.*)
Kar.:   So you finally got it, did you, you clodhopper. (*Laughs.*)
   Let me see now what the Koran says about lambs. (*Laughs.*)
   [*Laughter.*]
   Let's see what the Koran says. (*Laughs.*)
   Oh, oh, oh, here comes the pasha . . . [2]
Vez.:   Have you brought me the goose yet, baker?
Kar.:   Just a liiiitle bit more baking.
Vez.:   Do you realize how hungry I am? Does it take that long?
Kar.:   What can I say, I'm making it a little crisper, my pasha.
Vez.:   Well, all right.
Kar.:   Did you have any panties?
Vez.:   Yes, I had a number of brandies.
Kar.:   Listen to this, my pasha.
   A shepherd came by, a villager
   called Uncle George,
   and he brought me
   a lamb,
   clubbed, tubbed, and scrubbed for the skewer.
   It's
   nice and plump.
Vez.:   You don't say.
Kar.:   Yes, I do,
   and I'm baking it.
   You wouldn't be interested in lamb, would you?
Vez.:   Absolutely.
   These villagers know how to bake their lambs.
   They know how to pick them plump.
   I would like to have both the goose
   and the lamb
   for my dinner, baker Karagiozis.
Kar.:   And the potatoes?
Vez.:   For you.
Kar.:   I see.
   Well, I'll bring them to you as soon as they're ready.
Vez.:   Yes.
Kar.:   And what excuse should I give?

Vez.:   Whatever you say
     I will assure the villager that it is according to your Koran.
Kar.:   And that a miracle occurred.
Vez.:   Yes.
Kar.:   Good.
Vez.:   When will you bring me the goose?
Kar.:   Innnn two minutes.
Vez.:   Bravo.
     I'm going inside then and expect you to bring it right away.
Kar.:   Yes, I'll bring it right away.
Vez.:   Bye now. (*Leaves the screen.*)
Kar.:   So long . . . [3]
     You just wait a second now. (*Opens the oven to remove the goose.*)
     Even raw it's good enough for my kids; it won't bother them a bit.
     Just a second now so I can take it over to my shack for them to eat.
          [*Laughter.*]
     Let's take out the goose.
     Attaboy.
     (*Gleefully.*) Hello there, missy. (*Laughs and sticks his finger in the
          goose.*)
     It's a bit softer than before. (*Spits twice and withdraws his finger*). I
          BURNED MYSELF, the dirty bum.
     I burned myself.
     Come out here. (*Takes out all the food from the oven and goes to his
          hut. Hums.*)
     Dah ta ra dah ta
     dah ta ra do
     dah ta ra dah ta
     dah tarado. [*Talking in the audience.*]
Kol.:   Wow, look there, that's what I call a thief.
     He just stole a chicken,
     Hey-you-where-did-you-steal-the-chicken-you? [*Laughter.*]
     Did you steal it from the baker?
Kar.:   Shut up, nitwit.
     Sit still, YOU.
     Leave a little for me to eat; I'll bring you more food.
     Stand back and let the poor Karagiozis clan eat.
     They're starving from hunger.
     Come to me,

you tomatoes and potatoes and lord and the ol' heiress [*Laughter.*] . . . [3]

Kol.: Oh, my good heavens!

Oh, oh my, good heavens.

Wow, squashes and potatoes.

Kar.: GET YOUR HANDS OUT OF THERE, YOU.

All of you sit still now.

Quiet down. I have more food.

Come over here. (*Puts the food on the table and serves.*)

Fizzlegob.

Get over here, now.

What a lamb. (*Laughs.*)

My kids will eat to their heart's content.

GET OVER HERE, YOU.

Kol.: GOOD HEAVENS!

LOOK AT THIS. HE BROUGHT A WHOLE HORSE. [*Laughter.*]

Would you believe it, a whoooole horse.

Kar.: Clam up, you nitwit, you and your horse.

It's Uncle George's lamb.

HEY YOU, SAVE SOME FOR ME TOO.

Wait now.

Let's put the baking paddle in here too (*Laughs and stores the baking paddle in the hut.*)

so Uncle George doesn't get a chance to murder me.

Attaboy . . . [10] (*Returns to the bakery.*)

Good.

Let me take a little nap, and God help me.

Dear God, please help me slip by from under Uncle George's clogs. [*Laughter.*]

I'm not worried about anything else: I can take care of Nionios.

The other one, Mr. Camel, can be toppled with a fart. [*Laughter.*]

But I'm scared of Uncle George.

He might let me have it with his clogs, and I'll wind up like Solomon's judgment. [*Laughter.*]

Let me take a little nap right here,

and God help me . . . [7]

Mukhtar Bey: Very strange,

I tell you.

This Arab boy of mine is something else again . . . [4]

Whatever errand I send him on,
he's always tardy,
and he gets in trouble
by annoying people.
I had complaints from a number of people
because he annoys people.
Well, anyway,
I believe he must have brought the goose,
and the baker should have it baked by now.
Where are you, baaaakeeeer?
Baaaakeeeer.

Kar.:   What is it?

Oh, it's Master Camel.

You poor soul, wait and see what the Koran says.

Bey: Greetings.

Kar.:   Welcome.

Bey: Say, baker, did the Arab boy bring you the goose?

Kar.:   Yes, yes master.

Bey: Would you have any idea where he went?

Kar.:   He didn't say.
He dropped off the goose and left.

Bey: Yes, he's a bit feisty, that boy,
and he annoys people.
I punish him, certainly,
but
I feel sorry for him. He's young yet.

Kar.:   Yes, you shouldn't mistreat the poor boy.
When he came by here
I was nice to him and gave him a chocolate.
I felt sorry for the boy.

Bey: Bravo.
You did well
to give him a chocolate.

Kar.:   Yes, I befriended him and let him have a few with the baking
paddle. [*Laughter.*]
He in turn threw some pinecones at my head. (*Laughs.*)

Bey: Baker, tell me . . .

Kar.:   Yes sir.

Bey: Is my goose ready so I can take my dinner home?

Kar.: What's that you say?

Bey: I said, is my goose cooked?

Kar.: What goose?

Bey: The goose you told me my Arab boy delivered to you.

Kar.: Tell me, Master Camel,
since you knew it was such a feisty goose,
why did you put it in the baking pan and bring it to the bakery?
Did you do it to give my business a bad name,
so I would lose my customers?

Bey: I don't understand, baker.

Kar.: You don't understand?
The goose you brought me was ill bred. [*Laughter.*]

Bey: What do you mean?

Kar.: SHE WAS TOO FEISTY.
As soon as I put her in the oven,
she got out of the baking pan
and went to all the neighboring baking pans and began to eat all the
food.

Bey: (*Laughs heartily.*) Bravo, baker.
You made me laugh.
You're a funny fellow, a regular comedian.
A goose,
roughed, plucked, and stuffed with spices,
just gets up and leaves the baking pan and goes and eats the other
food?

Kar.: Yes.
I turn around and see the goose eating the other food, and I say to
her,
"Mademoiselle-goose"-I-tell-her-"why-do-you-make-all-this-
fuss? ○
I'm-going-to-get-in-trouble-with-my-customers."
Just like this she got out and went out here in the square
next to the bakery.

Bey: The goose?

Kar.: Yes.
And I say to her,
"Get back in here, you. You're not wearing a sweater, and coming
from such heat you'll catch pneumonia," I tell her. [*Laugh-
ter.*]

And she right away began to mock me. (*In a sing-song manner.*)
  Hini, hini, hini, hini, hini, hini, hini, hini, hini."
Bey: The butchered goose?
Kar.: Yes.
  I tried to let her have it with the baking paddle, but she spread her
  wings and landed on the roof tiles.
Bey: The plucked and stuffed goose?
Kar.: Yup.
  I pick up a rock to throw at her,
  but she flapped her wings and flew away.
Bey: The goose
  left?
Kar.: Yes.
Bey: So there's no goose?
Kar.: How can there be a goose if she flew away?
Bey: For the sake of argument, let's say
  that I agree
  that the goose
  came to life and flew away.
Kar.: Yes.
Bey: Where's the baking pan, please?
Kar.: Let's seeee.
  She took the baking pan for a nest
Bey: The baking pan?
Kar.: Yes.
Bey: The spices?
Kar.: She took them for food; she said she had a long trip.
Bey: The sauce?
Kar.: She took that for water.
Bey: All right now, baker,
  enough kidding around.
  That was a cute joke,
  but now I want my goose
  because I have guests at home.
Kar.: What goose can I give you if she flew away?
Bey: ALL RIGHT NOW, MISTER.
  GIVE ME MY GOOSE.
Kar.: HEY,-GET-THE-HELL-OUT-OF-HERE,-YOU. [*Laughter.*]
  I already told you,

she was feisty and flew away.
How am I to blame?
I DON'T BELIEVE IT!

Bey: But-my-good-man,-how-is-it-possible-for-a-plucked,-stuffed-goose ◯
to-get-up-and-fly-out-of-the-oven?

Kar.: But she did fly away.

Bey: ARE YOU SERIOUS?

Kar.: SERIOUS.
AND I INTEND TO SUE YOU
FOR ALL THE FOOD SHE SPOILED.

Bey: ALL-RIGHT-NOW-GIVE-ME-MY-GOOSE.

Kar.: Get-the-hell-out-of-here-before-I-give-you-a-black-eye.
[*Laughter.*]
I DON'T BELIEVE IT.
You're very annoying.
You're heartless.

Bey: OK. If that's the way you want to play,
YOU FILTHY SCOUNDREL.
NOW I UNDERSTAND.
YOU'VE BEEN FEEDING ME ALL THIS NONSENSE ABOUT
THE GOOSE FLYING AWAY
SO YOU CAN EAT THE GOOSE YOURSELF.
I'LL SUE YOU.
I'LL GO TO THE PASHA.

Kar.: SO GO TO THE PASHA. WHY TELL ME ABOUT IT?

Bey: I'm going to sue you.

Kar.: Go ahead.

Bey: I'M GOING TO THE PASHA TO LODGE MY COM-
PLAINT. (*Exits.*)

Kar.: Go there and you'll see it's written in the Koran, you dope.
[*Laughter.*]
We agreed to that. (*Laughs.*)
Can you believe all that's happened to this man?
The other one is waiting to eat the goose, (*Chuckles.*) [*Child talking
in the audience.*]
but my kids haven't left a single bone from that goose. (*Chuckles.*)
And he's still waiting for the goose.

Veziris: Baker, what's happening?

I'm very hungry,
and I can't wait any longer.
Please,
let's not have any further delays.
Bring me the food as it is.

Kar.:   Just a little bit more baking, my pasha, and I'll bring you the goose.
Do you know
the-man-who-owns-the-goose-came-by-and-I-told-him-the-goose-flew-away-but-he-didn't-believe-me,
and he started shouting
and said he would come to sue you (*Checks his mistake and continues.*) to you to have me sued.

Vez.:   Let him come. I'll say it's written in the Koran.
Bring me the goose.

Kar.:   Just a little bit more baking and I'll bring it.

Vez.:   Wonderful
I'll be waiting.
Don't be afraid.
I'll take care of everything. (*Exits.*)

Kar.:   Yes, go-on,-go-on,-go-on.
(*Makes an obscene gesture.*) Take that!
That's that for the first one.
So far so good.
Now I have Uncle George to think about. (*Chuckles and coughs.*)
I don't know what's going to happen with Uncle George . . . [6]

Nionios: Halloo there! I've come to collect my stewpan. [*Laughter.*]
Halloo, Karagiozo.

Kar.:   Ah.
It's the Macedonian chick, the lord and the ol' heiress. [*Laughter.*]
(*We hear the faint sound of the performer giving orders to his helpers behind the screen.*) . . . [5]

Nion.:   Come, Karagiozo.

Kar.:   What's the matter, Nionios?

Nion.:   Come, Karagiozo, is my stewpan reaDY?

Kar.:   What?

Nion.:   Is my stewpan reeeeadYYYY?

Kar.:   Listen, Nionios,
and you're my friend besides.

Why did you do it? (*Tearfully.*) To make me look bad in the neigh-
borhood?

(*Crying.*) Listen, you, I had decided to go straight.

Nion.:   So-what's-wrong-KaragioZO?

Kar.:   Since you knew that the tomatoes didn't get along with the
potatoes,

why did you put them both in the stew?

And they got into a brawl in the oven,

and the Macedonian pulls out a gun, like this, and kills

the (*Performer loses his lines here.*)

the

the (*Performer recovers and continues.*)

lord,

and out jumps (*Performer gets tangled up here but recovers and
continues.*) the ol' heiress

and rushes out to get [*Laughter.*]

the cops, and the first (*Stumbles and recovers.*)

ambulance comes here

and took fifteen

injured

and took five dead.

The place was crawling with cops, people, commotion.

They spilled my foods.

Why did you do this to me, Nionios, why?

Did you do it to ruin my business?

Nion.:   Would you listen to him, people.

Why-the-crook-says-the-tomatoes-and-the-potatoes-DIDN'T-
GET-ALONG.

Listen, you, cut the crap

and give me my stewpan.

Kar.:   What stewpan? I just told you my whole world was spilled out.
Nothing is left.

I might even sue you.

Nion.:   Damn you, you crook. I knew you would eat my steeeewpan.
Why, you crook.

I'll go to the authorities to turn you in, KARAGIOZO.

Kar.:   WHAT'RE YOU TRYING TO DO, YOU,

FRIGHTEN ME?

GO RIGHT AHEAD TO THE PASHA AND TURN ME IN.

I'M INNOCENT.

THE TOMATOES HAD A BRAWL WITH THE POTATOES.

Nion.:   OK.

I'm going, you crOOK.

Just wait and see if you don't get in TROUble.

By-St.-Mary-why-did-I-leave-him-my-stewpan-And-he-ate-it-the-
crook. (*Exits.*)

Kar.:   Wonderful.

We're now finished with the lord and the ol' heiress. [*Some commo-
tion in the audience.*]

Now we have to wait and see what'll happen with Uncle George.

Uncle George: I'M COOOOMIIIING HEEEERE.

Kar.:   Oh, oh,

the clodhopper is coming down my way.

Unc.:   NEITHER FIZZLE NOR GOOOOB.

Kar.:   FIZZLEGOB, UNCLE . . . [6]

Welcome, Uncle.

Unc.:   Praise' th' Lord!

Kar.:   What did you say, Uncle?

Unc.:   He gulped it.

Kar.:   What?

Unc.:   YA GULPED THE LAMB, YA PINCH. (*Hits Karagiozis.*)
YA GULPED IT, YA

Kar.:   Wait a second, Uncle.

Let me explain, Uncle.

Unc.:   Ya mucker, ya gulped it. (*Hits him.*)

Ya gulped it.

Kar.:   (*Angrily.*) Wait a second, Uncle. Let-me-explain.-

Don't hit me.

Unc.:   Ya gulped it, (*Hits him.*) ya cuckold.

Ya gulped it.

Kar.:   WAIT A SECOND AND LET ME TELL YOU, UNCLE.

Unc.:   LISTEN, YA BONEHEAD, YA GULPED IT. (*Hits him.*)

Kar.:   WAAAAIT AAAA SEEEECOND. [*Laughter.*]

Wait.

I can't take any more tonight.

Wait and let me explain,

and if you don't believe me, beat me up.

Damn it, he won't let me say a word.

Listen, Uncle,
d'you know what happened?
Unc.:   Ya gulped it.
Kar.:   What?
Let me explain
Unc.:   Ya gulped it. ya bonehead.
Kar.:   What?
Unc.:   YA GULPED IT, (*Hits him.*) ya wretch.
Kar.:   Wait a second. (*Crying.*) Uncle.
I, I don't remember the Koran saying anything about this.
Oh, my goodness.
Listen, Uncle,
you know
just as I had placed the lamb in the oven,
a shepherd passed by with some sheep,
and the sheep were bleating,
and your lamb in the oven heard them,
and it hopped out here in front of the store and went
"baa, baa."
I tried to push it back inside,
but it jumped
and goes and gets mix . . . (*Performer loses concentration for a
   moment.*) mixed up with the shepherd's other sheep.
I begged the shepherd—
(*Crying.*) I was crying, Uncle—
to let me look for your lamb
(*Crying heavily.*) because I knew you wouldn't believe
(*Crying.*) that the lamb ran away.
The shepherd let me look, and I searched for hours,
but I couldn't make it out anywhere.
The shepherd was upset too, and he said to me,
"My good man, I can't do a thing for you,"
and he got up and left
with your lamb, Uncle, along with all the other sheep. (*Still
   crying.*)
Unc.:   Good heavens and prais' th' Lord!
What are ya saying,
th' butchered
lamb?

Kar.: Yes.
Unc.: Skinned?
Kar.: Yes.
Unc.: With its guts spilled out?
Kar.: Yes.
Unc.: Started t' bleat and wents with th' other sheeps?
Kar.: Yes.
Unc.: Takes thaaaat. (*Extends his open hand in Karagiozis's face and hits him twice.*)
Kar.: Oh, heaven help me. [*Laughter.*]
    Wait a second, Uncle, let me explain.
Unc.: Hey ya, tells me . . .
Kar.: What?
Unc.: The lamb lefts?
Kar.: Yes.
Unc.: Where's th' spit?
Kar.: The lamb gave the spit to the shepherd to use as a walking stick since he didn't have one.
Unc.: Takes thaaaat. (*Hits him.*) ○
Kar.: Oh, heaven help me.
    Oh, heaven help me.
    Wait a second, Uncle, let me ex . . .
Unc.: Karagioz,
    either ya gives me m'grub
    or I'll go to th' big boss,
    m'boy, to punish ya,
    and if he don't punish ya, I wills.
Kar.: Just go ahead, Uncle.
    You'll see I'm right.
Unc.: Huh.
    I'm goings.
    Ya crook, I knews ya'd gulps m'lamb. (*Exits.*)
Kar.: Praise God, I got out of that one. (*Chuckles.*) [*Laughter.*]
    I slipped by.
    I'll go to my shack for a little snack.
    I'll need my strength for the beating he's still bound to give me
      [*Laughter.*] . . . [7]
Mukhtar Bey: Come along with me, gentlemen.
    this baker is a true swindler . . . [2]

Whoever heard of such a thing
to claim that the goose flew away.
Nion.:   That's nothing.
What-about-me-He-said-the-tomatoes-and-potatoes-traded-
words. [*Laughter.*]
Uncle George: Would ya believes it, a butchered lamb, skinned,
ready for skewering,
he says started bleating and went with th' other sheeps?
Bey: No doubt about it, he's a big swindler.
Let's go before the pasha . . . [2]
Wait a minute, please,
so I can call the pasha.
Wait a minute . . . [10]
Kar.:   Good God,
they've all come here to see the pasha again.
Wait a second now, so I can see what's going on . . . [2] (*Climbs on
top of his shack.*)
Attaboy . . . [2]
Attaboy . . . [7]
Vez.:   Welcome, gentlemen.
Bey: Greeting, my pasha. We have a complaint,
and we came to tell it to you.
It's about the baker.
He is a big swindler
and stole all our food.
I brought him a goose
stuffed with a variety of spices,
and when I came back to pick up my goose, he lied to me that
the plucked, stuffed goose, my pasha, [*Children talking in the
audience.*]
flew away, got up and left.
He said she took the pan for her nest,
the stuffing for food, and the sauce, he says, for water.
Vez.:   Why, that swindler baker,
I'm going to punish him severely
for stealing your food.
Kar.:   (*From atop the roof*) Psst, hey, psst, hey [*Laughter.*] . . . [6]
Vez.:   Yes.
Gentlemen,

pardon me.
I just had a thought.
I remembered something.
I think the baker might be right.
Bey: Might be right, my pasha?
Vez.:   Yes.
EARLIER today
I was glancing at my Koran,
and I read
that Muhammad would perform a great miracle.
Wait just a bit until I consult the Koran, and I'll have an answer
    immediately [*Whispering in the audience.*] . . . [22]
Gentlemen,
don't blame the baker.
The baker
is right.
Bey: How is he right, my pasha?
Vez.:   Because just now I opened my Koran
and read
that one day . . . [2]
Muhammad
will perform a great miracle.
A butchered goose stuffed with spices
will come out of a bakery and fly away.
Bey: But is that possible, my pasha,
for a butchered goose
to get up and fly away?
Vez.:   LISTEN,
SIR,
YOU DON'T BELIEVE IN MUHAMMAD'S MIRACLE?
YOU DON'T BELIEVE IN OUR KORAN?
For this great sin you have committed,
I'm going TO PUNISH YOU, SIR.
Now go to the serai's cashier
and pay ONE POUND STERLING.
Bey: Please forgive me, Veziris.
Vez.:   NO SIR,
I WILL NOT FORGIVE YOU,
because you DO NOT BELIEVE

in Muhammad's miracle.
Go straight to the serai's cashier
and pay ONE POUND STERLING
before I put you in jail.
The baker is innocent.

Bey: Then, my pasha, I had better go pay my fine.

Vez.: DO YOU BELIEVE, THEN IN MUHAMMAD'S MIRA-
CLE?
Yes or no?

Bey: (*Cowering.*) I believe, my pasha.

Vez.: DO YOU BELIEVE THAT THE GOOSE FLEW AWAY?

Bey: (*Cowering.*) I believe, my pasha.

Vez.: Good, then.
Go in and pay the fine.

Kar.: (*To audience from atop the roof.*) So you think I work in this
bakery for you, you nitwit? [*Laughter.*]

Vez.: AND THIS GENTLEMAN?

Nion.: What-can-I-say-excellency-now-that-we-even-have-to-
paaaay . . . [2]

Vez.: What's your name, sir?

Nion.: I'm-named-Dionisios-Fringos,-and-I-hail-from-Zákinthos-
Let-me-tell-you-my-king-I-brought-the-baker-a-stewpan-and-he-
ate-my-stewpan-all-my-food-d'you-follow-me?

Vez.: Just a second, sir. Let me glance at my Koran.
Wait here.

Nion.: What a bummer.
D'you think I'll have the same luuuuck? . . . [3]

Vez.: Mr. Dionisios, you also don't have a complaint
against the baker.
Muhammad performed this miracle also. The potatoes and squash
had an argument
and left the bakery.
The baker is innocent.

Nion.: Oh, damn this liFE.
He's-giving-me-the-same-story-He-must-be-in-it-with-Kara-
gioZO. [*Laughter.*]

Vez.: IF YOU DON'T HAVE ANY FAITH, SIR,
you'll go inside and pay a pound sterling.

Nion.: Oh-no-I-lost-my-stewpan-and-I'm-paying-beSIDES?

Vez.: GO INSIDE, I SAID, AND PAY YOUR FINE.

Nion.: Oh, Karagiozo, you're in this with this Mr. Veziriiiissss.

Vez.: GET INSIDE, I said.

Nion.: Oh my goodness gracious, what has happened to me?

Vez.: And this gentleman, what does he want?

Unc.: The one looking at ya they calls Giorgos Vlatsaras.
  And in order to makes m'complaint
  th' baker must be heres.

Vez.: Yes.
  I'll call him.
  BAKER.

Kar.: (*From atop the roof.*) Hey you, no, no . . . [3]

Vez.: BAKER, COME HERE.

Kar.: Hey you, I said no . . . [4]

Vez.: BAKER.

Kar.: I said no, no.

Unc.: (*Turns and sees Karagiozis on the roof with his feet dangling.*)
  Come out here, ya crook.
  Yur on the roof like an alley cat.
  Gets down heres.

Kar.: Uncle.

Unc.: Gets down heres before I gets my shooter.

Kar.: Oh my heavens,
  he's going to kill me.
  Here I am, (*Jumps down.*) Uncle.

Unc.: Gets over heres, ya bonehead.
  Gets in front of th' big boss.

Kar.: OK . . . [4]

Vez.: All right,
  sir,
  here's the baker. What's your complaint?

Unc.: Yore big wheel, sir,
  I broughts him m'grub t' bake.

Vez.: What do you mean by *grub?*

Unc.: A lamb.

Vez.: Fine.

Unc.: Whens I goes t' gets it, he tells me a shepherd passes by
  and th' lamb starts t' bleat and goes with th' other sheeps. (*Karagiozis tries to get away from Uncle George.*)

(*To Karagiozis.*) Gets over heres and stops trying t' runs away, ya
   blockhead. (*Hits him.*)

Kar.:   Oh, I can't stand it. I'm going to get it again. [*Laughter.*]

Vez.:   Don't be afraid, Karagiozis.

Kar.:   Just wait and see what's coming to us any minute now.

Unc.:   Listen, crackbrain,
   if ya don't punishes this boy, who's a crook,
   I'll do it m'self.

Vez.:   Sir,
   just a moment so I can see (*Stumbles.*) glance at the Koran.

Kar.:   You're not going to fool Uncle George with Korans.

Unc.:   Gets back heres and stops tryin' t' squirm out. (*Hits him.*)
   Blockhead.

Kar.:   Oh my heavens, how did I get into this mess? (*Laughs.*)
   [*Laughter.*]
   And I can't wiggle out of here.

Vez.:   SIR,
   THE BAKER IS INNOCENT.
   Our Koran says one day there will be a miracle,
   and a lamb will bleat
   and will leave with the other sheep,
   and because you don't believe in the Koran
   and you bother the baker,
   you'll go inside and pay a one-pound-sterling fine.

Unc.:   Who me?
   He eats m'lamb, and I pays?

Vez.:   YES, YOU.
   WHO DO YOU THINK YOU ARE?

Unc.:   Ya comes over heres NOW. (*He grabs Karagiozis and begins
   to hit Veziris with him. A lot of clapping and shouting is heard.*)

Kar.:   Wait.
   STOP, UNCLE,
   UNCLE,
   COME ON, STOP NOW, UNCLE.
   Oh my heavens,
   Uncle,
   stop.
   Ohhhh. (*All this is now done in rhythm to the beating Karagiozis is
   receiving.*)

Un-cle,
let-me-tell-you,
Un-cle,
let-me-tell-you,
Un-cle,
(*Begins to sing.*) let-me-tell-you. [*Laughter.*]
Unc.:   Ya crook,
Ya bonehead,
ya ates m'grub.
Oh, I knews ya'd leaves me hungry. (*All exit screen.*)
Kar.:   (*Hurt and beaten he comes out of the serai followed by
Veziris.*) Ouuuuch.
Ouuuuch.
Oh, why oh why did you call me here, pasha?
I know this clodhopper.
I know what a wild man he is.
Ouuuuch, my God, I don't believe what happened here.
(*To the audience.*) But the pasha got his too, when Uncle George
started pounding me against him. (*Chuckles.*)
Vez.:   Oh, you poor wretch, Karagiozis.
What a wild man that Uncle George is.
Couldn't you have gathered up your feet a bit? You made me black
and blue.
Kar.:   You think I had time to do anything? He was tossing me around
like an octopus. (*Chuckles.*) [*Laughter.*]
Vez.:   We played our little game well, don't you agree?
Kar.:   To the limit.
Vez.:   So, when are you going to bring me the goose?
Kar.:   What?
Vez.:   The goose, I said. When are you going to bring it?
Kar.:   What goose?
Vez.:   The goose we lied about to your customer when we said it got
up and flew away.
Kar.:   That was a lie?
Vez.:   Of course it's a LIE.
Kar.:   Wasn't there a miracle?
Doesn't the Koran say so?
Vez.:   No, it's a LIE.
I said that so I could eat the goose.

Kar.: Soooo, it's a lie, is it?

Vez.: Yes.

Kar.: OK then, I should go find my client and tell him that it's a liiiie and that you wanted to eat the goose.

Vez.: What are you talking about, you nitwit?
You want to make a fool of me
and put the whole town in an uproar?
YOU DON'T INTEND TO BRING ME THE GOOSE?

Kar.: But didn't it fly away?

Vez.: I told you, we lied.

Kar.: What lie?
It's in the Koran, my pasha.
So WHAT can I do if the goose flew away?
How am I to blame?

Vez.: So you're not going to bring me the goose?

Kar.: What can I do if it flew away?

Vez.: And the lamb?

Kar.: What?

Vez.: The lamb?

Kar.: Didn't the lamb start to bleat and then run away with the other sheep?

Vez.: The pan full of squash and potatoes?

Kar.: Didn't they get into an argument and run away?

Vez.: Listen, you, are you bringing me anything or not?

Kar.: But if it says so in the Koran, how can it be my fault?
If you don't believe in the Koran, it's a sin, and you'll have to go inside and pay a fine, did you know that? [*Laughter.*]

Vez.: All right, let's cut the nonsense and get serious.
WHY, YOU SWINDLER,
YOU'RE CLEVER, KARAGIOZIS.
YOU ALWAYS
make the world laugh
and you always
end up
the cleverest one.
I DON'T CARE that you got the best of me.
Congratulations,
and I extend my hand to you.
Thank you

because
you entertained US and all our theatergoers
with your beautiful comedy.
Karagiozis,
I salute you,
and may you always
entertain the people.
Kar.:   Thank you, my pasha.
Thank you.
At this point, my dear friends,
our comedy *Karagiozis Baker*
is over.
Thank you very much for honoring us with your presence, and a
    good night to you
from here all the way to your homes.
Our theater
performs nightly.
Good night. [*Audience talking.*]

THE END

Notes

ONE: Official and Unofficial Culture

1. In these terms, two alternate societies exist: the traditional, stable status quo of a conservative ideological force opposed to change, identified with rural popular ideology, and the individualistic, unstable culture of the new elite, which capitalizes on change and sponsors the absolutism of the state, identified with the urban ideology of the learned elite (Underdown 1985).

2. In his discussion, Kiurtsakis has viewed Karagiozis as a parodic presentation not of the illusion of the truth of life but of symbolic truth. Using the medieval image of a continually turning wheel, Kiurtsakis sees that which is high up on one turn being cast down on the next and that which is low being brought up. Turning things upside down, as Karagiozis does, is thus the normal order of things as seen from a broader perspective. Recognition of this truth represents knowledge at the hub of the wheel. It means the victory of man over his subjugation at the end, the symbolic victory of life over death.

3. The phallus, behaving as an independent life, has symbolic meaning identified with fertility and the indomitable spirit of its possessor, according to Kiurtsakis (1985). Like the phallus and as a surrogate for it, the hand embodies instinct uncontrolled by the will of the ego and conscious thought. The most complex body part, the hump, expresses both subconscious enslavement and the contrary value of male pregnancy as a sign of the upside-down swollen belly. A sign of cleverness, the hump signifies the double nature of the grotesque body, its ability to construct another body, and its ability, thus, to separate from death. In this way, the grotesque body denies boundaries as a form ever transforming itself into new elements. Such a principle of fertility is physically exemplified by the phallus as well as by the phallic use of the figure's long arm—Karagiozis, for example, shoots his arm between his legs to greet people—and is metaporically indicated by the continual shifting of roles, which, like masks, Karagiozis constantly takes on and off.

4. Kiurtsakis explains that through his voracious appetite, Karagiozis ties his deathlessness to his insatiable hunger. Warned that when he dies the earth will eat him, Karagiozis answers, "The earth will eat me, or I will eat the earth," expressing the mythic-heroic nature of the comic demon in his dealings with death. In carnival terms, Karagiozis, as a life force, eats death; that is, he eats up his own death, bringing himself again to life in a metamorphosis. In this, he symbolizes the continuity and growth of life, the victory of biological renewal.

5. Karagiozis appears antisocial in the city, according to Kiurtsakis, an organic symptom of a society in which the poor must steal to survive and hunger is the only form of protest against the denial of collective identity. Alienated, fated, exiled to the

lower social strata in an anonymous interaction of a multitude of individuals, man suffers nostalgia for the lost maternal society of a more familiar world. In the urban comedies, man is hungry, in danger of dying by starvation, and he chooses only between different forms of defeat. Preoccupied with mere physical individual survival, he is engaged in a life struggle without issue. The lack of food in the oppressed class imprints class antagonim within an impersonal and fragmented social environment of haves and have nots. The central theme, hunger, expresses above all the instinct for self-preservation and the powerlesness of the underclass in a hostile environment to which it must accustom itself as if imprisoned.

6. The level of discourse is that of a dialectic between above and below, a confusion of antithetical elements, and a reversal that replaces sense with nonsense, the source of which is the marketplace and its humor. Through the reversal, Karagiozis leads us to the realization that our truth, experienced reality, does not represent all truth, but only one aspect. In terms of the dialectic, contradiction in a utopian sense should not require a choice of "either" but should be seen in terms of "both" to create a new irony or oxymoronic synthetic meaning. Thus Karagiozis's description of himself as "timios lopoditis" and "Milordos Patsavoros" requires that we understand the dialectic just as one understands social experience, as a context, not separated into opposed categories of a schematic, simple antithesis divorced into two parts, each of which must remain one-sided and relative.

7. The Eurocentric or official ideology of the new nation-state considered the Romeic or Ottoman-based culture of Greece as unclear or polluted. An exotic form, it was distanced in cultural space, just as ancestral Greece (the source in which official ideology found its origins) was removed in mythic time. Both cultural forms represented an "otherness" that failed to give priority to the actuality of present modern Greek social life, as Herzfeld (1982) explains.

8. From an official perspective, Herzfeld (1982) argues, the comic Karagiozis text's acceptance of an unsavory past led to its socially marginal status. That status arose largely from two sources: its association with female values and its derivation from Ottoman culture. Since the hero cannot transcend these sources, there can be no lasting comic victory. Since he does not accept the canonical rule of official discourse, there can be no celebration or sanctification. Herzfeld questions whether, given the intervention of elements of the comic world, even the history texts do not gloss over the pollution of their Ottoman source in their struggle to create a newly reconstituted beginning in the modern Greek world. These dialectical tensions between key images of Hellenism, the official culture, and Romiosini, the unofficial culture, pervade all of Greek society; Karagiozis merely represents one code or sign system through which elements of this opposition are balanced against each other.

9. Within the opposition represented by disemia (Herzfeld 1982), we find a key term, *egoismos,* expressed, in the first instance as a social stance of new beginnings in a hostile world and in the second as an enervating disunity that threatens social harmony. Herzfeld refers to it, on the one hand, as the European individualism of official history (personal heroism in defense of state interests), which one finds again in the Karagiozis history texts, insofar as one can sense there the appearance of a fledgling state interest. On the other hand, Herzfeld sees it as the Oriental self-interestedness of local experience, which one finds repeated in the Karagiozis comic texts. Thus, while ego is fundamentally an ideology that subverts order, it still represents a value of shared

concern between both official and unofficial cultures, a value that borrows elements from both cultures only to use them differently as strategies in the service of these differing ideologies.

10. Within the context of Herzfeld's argument, the Karagiozis performance can be seen as a confirmation of the human diversity of Babel, a threat to statist ideologies not only because it reminds us that divided Greece was in a state of fallen grace from which it must be raised and united. The pluralism of Babel sullied the ancestral purity of the Greek tongue and culture and by associating with the state of a fall from grace reproduced the sack of Constantinople, which led to the Ottoman predominance exhibited in the Karagiozis comedies. The passivity and fatalism of the comedies (discussed in Kiurtsakis 1985) becomes the justification for the Turkish hegemony.

11. The danger of discussing Karagiozis as a national expression is that such a discussion assumes the identity of official and unofficial ideological values in much the same way that generalizing about a national Greek character from local studies of rural village life assumes that local values mirror larger ideational structures. Nor is it useful to reduce discussion of the Karagiozis performance to the terms of an all-embracing official discourse that subordinates emergent and local truths to received absolute truths and thereby usurps what constitutes the alternative vision of the unofficial ideology of everyday practices. The two ideologies are in conflict, but they also interact, making a discussion of one irrelevant without reference to the other but leaving neither in a position of priority.

12. This identification of official and bourgeois values led to control and alteration of the performance. Nineteenth-century bourgeois forces did not rail against the heroic texts, for they were not developed until the last decade of the nineteenth century. Rather, the bourgeoisie railed against those texts, the comedies, that were most completely identified with Turkish Karagoz, the Ottoman progenitor of the Karagiozis performance, in spite of the fact (or perhaps because of it) that these were the texts in which Karagiozis's trickster role was most fully expressed and in which the elite urban influence was most strongly felt.

TWO: Karagiozis as Urban Folklore

1. The city resolves conflicts between urban and rural cultures in a way that enhances both their self-definitions and a common urban identity capable of acting as an intermediary form leading to a larger common or national identity (Moore 1975). Each level, from the family through the suprafamily to the nation, progressively holds values less deeply and becomes progressively more complex and therefore more in need of integration to tolerate conflicting values.

Building on this approach, we can see cities as interdependent with nonurban forms in the larger cultural context. Indeed, all levels of the larger cultural complex are interdependent. Survival at the national level depends on the unity of the nation's identity, or external face, in relation to other cultures.

2. Gender roles represent a key indicator of rural-urban change. The urban setting continues the same high differentiation and complementarity of the roles of husband and wife that are found in rural settings. Increased participation in urban industry as well as female role change attributable to urbanization have failed to present women

with role status similar to that of men (Hirschon 1978, 1981, 1983a, 1983b; Spinellis, Vassiliu, and Vassiliu 1970; Sutton 1978, 1983).

Women's participation in the work force is conditioned as well by an honor code that links women's economic activity negatively with the honor and reputation of the family (Cavunides 1983), for it suggests that a male family head is unable to support his family. Thus family status is enhanced if women do not work. Indeed, women appear to encourage the move to urban areas in order to be relieved of agricultural labor; viewing the domestic role as primary, they work only in order to provide temporary solutions to economic needs. Moreover, their earnings are twice as likely to be linked to family background as those of men, and they operate at a 50 percent earning disadvantage (Psacharopulos 1983).

The shift of emphasis from reproduction to production in the urban environment leaves women more rather than less devalued than they were in rural settings. Men's greater education, access to employment, and urban sophistication (they usually arrive in the city and become acclimated before their wives, sisters, and mothers) overshadow women's dowry contributions, as well as their productive labor outside the home, leaving male-female relationships in the urban setting even more asymmetrical than in the rural setting, particularly since the social importance of domestic power is diminished in the urban environment.

Female access to the in-group remains indirect through a male, either a father, son, brother, or husband. The proper female role is still fulfilled within marriage and not through pursuing individual goals. The major change has resulted from options being opened up to women through education, although even educated women are still less involved in decision-making and are less goal-oriented than men. There is even less personality differentiation in women than in men when they move from a simple to a complex milieu (Spinellis, Vassiliu, and Vassiliu 1970).

3. Gulick (1975) contends that heterogeneity is the distinguishing characteristic of cities.

4. The clearest force for urbanization was the migration of Greeks from the diaspora; most of these were from small urban areas of 1,000 or more (Dubisch 1977). Indeed, in the mid–nineteenth century there were more Greeks in Istanbul (120,000) and in Smyrna (60,000) than in Athens (36,000) (Vermeulen 1983). Until 1922 migration had greatly influenced the institutional life of the urban environment, whereas migration from 1922 to 1928 was transformational (Dubisch 1977; Vermeulen 1983).

5. Such essential urban characteristics as the interdependence of social and economic orders and the integration provided by a strong central government are not primary forces in Greek cities in this period. Like other poor cities in politically dependent countries, Greek cities differ from richer Western cities, growing up in the context of large bureaucracies, more traditional networks, and less intense patterns of social interaction (Southall 1973).

THREE: Gender in Karagiozis

1. The fullest understanding of male-female relationships ultimately requires that we see sexual oppositions as resulting from the politics and hierarchies of the larger

social process that creates binary perceptions of men and women. This approach leads us to see that the roles women play are only local forms of political and economic forms that liberate or oppress both men and women.

2. Women's inability to participate in productive aspects of the public sphere accounts for their lack of adult status (Sacks 1974) and thereby for their sexual inequality. Women's domestic work, having no exchange value, but only private use value, leaves women devalued. Property ownership or rights and control over resources contribute to the imbalance of power between men and women. Marriage, the turning point for the transmission of property, regulates woman's capacity to produce and provides the conditions for a productive role (Hirschon 1984). But while clearly specified women's ownership rights over the dowry equalize a woman in marriage, the dowry property is still given to a woman in the situational custodianship of her husband. A woman is thus not a fully acting subject even as a wife or mother (Whitehead 1984). Girls are seen as liabilities in a family (du Boulay 1983; Hirschon 1984), both for their costs to the family in requiring dowries and for the potential threat their sexuality represents to family honor.

In one view, it is not property ownership or control over resources but adult social status achieved through participation in the public sphere that is necessary for sexual equality (Sacks 1974). An alternate view (Hirschon 1984) sees property and property rights as the crucial indicator in the balance of power between men and women. Indeed, this view of property enables us to see that production and reproduction are part of the same process in which women play a central role through controlling the product of their labor, their dowry lands, and other forms of intangible property such as honor and reputation, which affect both a bride's marriageability and the prestige of a woman's house.

3. Women's power in the Romeic guise is variously described. It may exist in withholding sexual favors or in nagging (Friedl 1967; Herzfeld 1986), in submitting to men (Danforth 1983a) or to the cultural value system (du Boulay 1986), in fulfilling expectations of the female role (Salamone and Stanton 1986), in mediating within the community or between nature and culture (Ortner 1974), or in controlling property through the dowry (du Boulay 1983; Hirschon 1984). It may, equally, exist in socializing the family's children, in protecting as well as advertising family reputation (Dubisch 1974), in gossiping and even lying (du Boulay 1983), in controlling ideology (Dimen 1986), and in performing and maintaining religious rites (Caraveli 1986; Danforth 1983a; Hirschon 1983b).

4. We do not find the domestic sphere necessarily more highly prized in the urban setting. In urban situations, where the economic and social importance of the domestic sphere is diminished by the openings to the outside world offered by greater access to jobs in the public sphere, both family solidarity and domestic power have less influence, for they are isolated from that public world (Rogers 1975). Indeed, given the force of urbanization, shifts in the balance of gender power are likely to leave male-female relationships even more asymmetrical and in an even more hierarchical state than they were in the village.

The urban environment offers, as well, a clearer division between interior and exterior space as a territorial adaptation (Hirschon and Gold 1982). This form of urban adjustment provides the framework for everyday life, displaying clear ownership and further insulating the woman who keeps house, while providing privacy in the face of high population density. In addition, such a division operates as a communication of spatial messages that speak of identity, ownership, hospitality, and sociability, messages to be interpreted as a form of urban socialization.

5. Genovefa, the subject of a popular saint's tale, was accused of infidelity but was ultimately exonerated.

6. This may be a reference to the circles of hell.

7. Karagiozena does not appear in Giorgos Haridimos's version of *Karagiozis Baker,* translated in Part II.

8. Evzones are elite members of the Greek palace guard, noted for their bravery and chosen for their exceptional height.

9. Feminist anthropologists view women as actors, adopting a theory of rational choice that has long characterized the discussion of male activities. They assume that the female role is itself a negotiable cultural construct and that women are capable of redefining themselves as subjects rather than objects (Friedl 1976). But the ability of women to make choices is not free of the influence of male power and the larger structure of their society. Indigenous theorists, on the other hand, deny that women's activities are orderly and structured or that women do more than work for individual sons and husbands. Their work within families works against kinship units and community groups (Collier 1974). Indeed, feminist theorists who assert that women achieve power indirectly through and not directly toward finite goals (Alexiou 1987) themselves belie the usefulness of rational choice theory for understanding women's roles.

10. Moreover, appearances of power often obscure the realities (Friedl 1967); the separateness of women and their differential access to social space, positions of prestige, and resources merely represent external patterns behind which other realities of power operate. In the heroic texts, domestic complementarity serves as an analogue for the interdependence of men and women at the larger national level.

11. In firmly differentiated domestic-public dichotomies, women can use the very assertion of their anomalous position to assert the power that is uniquely their own and the solidarity of women that transcends domestic limits (Rosaldo 1974).

12. Insistence on dichotomies can, as a result, be conceived of as the hierarchical ideological intention to dominate one domain through the control of the other. In reality, the meanings of nature and culture shift in relation to one another depending on their shifting influence; thus male and female can be viewed both as complementary notions and as hierarchical oppositions (Strathern 1980), depending on their context. Dichotomies based on gender suggest a sense of wholeness or totality for concepts that, on the contrary, vary situationally and contextually (Tiffany 1984).

13. The listi texts profit from the more significant role played by women in the capitalist industrialist development of the 1920s, when women constituted 24 percent of wage earners in industry (Cavunides 1983), although they remained secondary providers and did not achieve economic independence. Educated women in the urban setting, moreover, act as a source of pressure for change by pursuing careers, as do upper-class urban women, who experience a more prominent female role, less role differentiation, greater equality, and more shared decision-making than do lower-class women (Vermeulen 1983).

14. Synopses of the Haridimos listi texts were provided by the player in an interview in 1987.

FOUR: Text and Context

1. In the entire recorded history of the Karagiozis performance, not a single female performer is noted. The use of gender-neutral references would therefore be misleading.

2. The problem that the contextual approach poses, however, is how to integrate such widely diversified data that, in itself, are not easily explained. Does one merely introduce general notions of context, treat contexts holistically as interactive systems, or objectify contexts into static and separable containers of thought that frame or shape meaning (Fine 1984)? The greatest danger, of course, is of falling into the trap of describing context as the functional relationship between text and society.

3. Both Herzfeld (1981a, 1981b) and Caraveli (1980) attack the notion of a complete or correct text based on an ideological assumption of correctness that is neither indigenously nor analytically located. Indeed, in Caraveli's view, performance itself is required to give the song the sense it sometimes seems to lack in its textual form. Context thus explains the apparent incompleteness of a text. The audience, familiar with the local repertoire, finds a line or two sufficient to recall the complete idea; each idea is complemented by contextual meaning. This approach assumes that the audience itself, serving as a passive bearer of a tradition, possesses sufficient knowledge of the performance to perform this function.

4. Herzfeld (1981a, 1981b) elaborates on contextual meaning through questions of perception and circumstantial knowledge, that is, through questions of semantic potential that suggest intertextual references, as well as moral, historical, and performance circumstances, questions of structural principles, and the "fit" of a song. He denies that a correct standard exists, as there would with an Ur-text, but rather holds that context, understood in its social, circumstantial, or verbal guise, either external or internal, is the means by which the meaning of a text is locally recognized.

5. Herzfeld (1977) studies the ritual context of a performance event as well. Inconsistencies in variant texts of Greek folk songs are explored not as the result of irrationality in the process of oral tradition, but as descriptions of structural principles underlying the ritual character of the event. Here ritual context limits the extent of possible variation, provides the basis on which texts achieve their form, and explains seeming irrationalities.

6. It is just this testimony that has the immediacy one needs to view the performative event directly, without the intervention of that kind of analytical reductionism that ascribes otherness to an object being viewed. Nevertheless, attempts on the viewer's part to examine the performance process, without being part of the discourse community that creates the meaning of the event, are in many ways spurious. Such efforts require that the folk community be allowed to speak for itself under its own authority but through the eyes of someone outside the community who imposes the language and perspectives of a formal analytical order on its informal world (see Derrida 1978; Foucault 1973, 1975).

For this reason, efforts to take an indigenous perspective have resulted largely in either examining local usage for its theoretical insights (Herzfeld 1979), using ethnographic evidence to test academic criticism (Herzfeld 1981a, 1981b), or mixing criticism and local insights in a shared discourse (Caraveli 1982; Herzfeld 1985). These efforts rarely, however, generate aesthetic based on indigenous testimony or theories (Herzfeld 1981a).

7. Player testimony for this chapter is taken predominantly from results of fieldwork, including thirty hours of taped interviews with Giorgos Haridimos conducted in 1973, 1979, 1984, 1986, and 1989. These interviews are supplemented by twenty hours of taped interviews with twenty-one players conducted by Mario Rinovolucri and Ms. Braithwaite, which are on deposit at the Center for the Study of Oral Literature, Harvard University (see Myrsiades 1983).

8. Folklore compositional theory (Lord 1981; Propp 1968) tends to treat influences outside the text itself as deviations from the compositional norm represented by an archetypal or original form or as predictable because of known compositional factors, thus placing them within the constraints of compositional controls. The underlying assumption of this study, by contrast, is that irrational forces produce dysfunctional consequences for an orderly compositional process. Thus, whereas the orderly approach suggests that the compositional process asserts itself actively (like an organism seeking homeostasis) to counteract disorderly outside forces, this study suggests that the compositional process interacts with irrational influences both to capitalize on and be changed by them.

9. One weakness of performance theory is that it does not account satisfactorily for irrationalities and inconsistencies that occur in text variants produced by the oral traditional process. It attributes these irrationalities to ideological assumptions or viewers' perceptions and explains them as incomplete expressions that require completion through the meaning found in forces in the outside world through a process of continuous interaction. Irrationalities are, by contrast, more productively viewed as a natural part of the developmental process of the oral tradition, as suggested to some extent by Marxist cultural theory.

10. Conventional views have held that traditional expressive devices act as steam valves for aberrant and potentially divisive forces and that antisocial and antinormative forces are handled by the community through control devices embedded in the structure of the form. Abrahams (1972) denies this view, arguing that control devices do not really control such social noise. He takes the position that whereas folklore calls for realignment of social misalignments and reunification of cultural and social imbalances, the equilibrium that is created is, nevertheless, not real. Folklore must thus be recited periodically, because factional, pluralistic interests continue to exist within the culture and the group senses the presence of a disequilibrating force that perpetuates an underlying conflict.

11. The nature of a form cannot be understood if the form is studied only through its stable constructs, which is what classical theory has largely done (see Burrell and Morgan 1979) on the premise that change is difficult to study except by comparison with stable constructs (Blau 1964). Bauman (1972a) makes the point that folklore may be as much an instrument of conflict as a mechanism contributing to social solidarity, which challenges conventional assumptions of a rational and orderly compositional process.

12. In compositional theory, the focus is neither the singleness of the composition of individual texts nor the unitary nature of performance composition as a general process, but the multiplicity of oral composition (Ortutay 9159) as expressed through numerous variants and the transformations represented by invariants (those that die

out). The focus is on the plurality of individual expressions and their impermanence rather than on the singularity of a text and its permanence. Indeed, texts that persist are not considered permanent, but merely tenacious. Finally, since our emphasis is on the renaissance of a tradition through its variants, it is a logical consequence that transformations and differences between individual variants of text types rather than identity or similarity have priority in this view.

FIVE: Giorgos Haridimos, Karagiozis Player

1. See Chapter 4, n. 7; Haridimos 1963.

References

Primary

Basios, Dimitris. 1947a. "O Karagiozis Don Zuan." *O Karagiozis,* 2 Aug., pp. 1-16.
———. 1947b. "O Karagiozis Eksoristos." *O Karagiozis,* 20 Sept., pp. 1-6.
Ianaros. 1969. *Markos Botsaris.* Rinovolucri 50. Center for the Study of Oral Literature, Harvard University.
Kareklas, Kostas. 1969. *To Kutsombolio.* Rinovolucri 35. Center for the Study of Oral Literature, Harvard University.
Xanthos, Markos. [1924a]. "O Karagiozis Furnaris." In *Ellinikon Theatron Tu Karagiozi.* Athens: Saravanos-Vuniseas.
———. [1924b]. "O Karagiozis Karvuniaris." In *Ellinikon Theatron Tu Karagiozi.* Athens: Saravanos-Vuniseas.
———. [1924c]. "O Karagiozis Psarras." In *Ellinikon Theatron Tu Karagiozi.* Athens: Sarvanos-Vuniseas.
Mihopulos, Panagiotis 1972a. "Astrapoyiannos Ke Lambetis." In *Pente Komodies Ke Dio Iroika.* Athens: Ermias.
———. 1972b. "O Kapetan Mavrodimos." In *Pente Komodies Ke Dios Iroika.* Athens: Ermias.
Mollas, Antonios. 1921. "Liga Ap Ola." In *Karagheuz; ou, Un Théâtre d'ombres à Athènes,* ed. Louis Roussel. Athens: Raftanis.
———. [1925a]. "I Arpayi Tis Oreas Elenis." In *O Karagiozis tu Mollas.* Athens: D. Deli.
———. [1925b]. "O Karagiozis Komis." In *O Karagiozis Tu Mollas.* Athens: D. Deli.
———. [1925c]. "O Katsandonis, O Ali Passas, I Kira Frosini, Ke O Karagiozis." In *O Karagiozis Tu Mollas.* Athens: D. Deli.
Mustakas, Ioannis. [1947a]. "O Karagiois Ke I Tris Spani." In *O Karagiozis Parastasis Aftotelis.* Athens: Ankiras.
———. [1947b]. "O Karagiozis Omiros Sto Haidari Ke Sti Germania." In *O Karagiozis Parastasis Aftotelis.* Athens: Ankiras.
———. [1947c]. "O Karagiozis Sti Zunkla." In *O Karagiozis Parastasis Aftotelis.* Athens: Ankiras.
———. [1947d]. "O Karagiozis, Ta Epta Thiria Ke O Megas Alexandros." In *O Karagiozis Parastasis Aftotelis.* Athens: Ankiras.
Vasilaros, Vasilis. 1969. *O Karagiozis Stin Ameriki (Baklaim Kukia).* Rinovolucri 62. Center for the Study of Oral Literature, Harvard University.

References 221

Secondary

Abadan, Nermin. 1963. *Social Change and Turkish Women*. Ankara: Basinevi.

Abrahams, Roger D. 1968. "Introductory Remarks to a Rhetorical Theory of Folklore." *Journal of American Folklore* 81: 143-58.

―――. 1970. "Creativity, Individuality, and the Traditional Singer." *Studies in the Literary Imagination* 3: 5-34.

―――. 1972. "Personal Power and Social Restraint in the Definition of Folklore." In *Toward New Perspectives in Folklore*, ed. Amerigo Paredes and Richard Bauman, 16-30. Austin: Univ. of Texas Press.

Akatli, Fusun. 1981. "The Image of Women in Turkish Literature." In *Women in Turkish Society*, ed. Nermin Abadan-Unat, 223-32. Leiden: Brill.

Alderson, A.D. 1956. *The Structure of the Ottoman Dynasty*. Oxford: Clarendon Press.

Alexiou, Margaret. 1974. *The Ritual Lament in Greek Tradition*. Cambridge: Cambridge Univ. Press.

―――. 1984. "Folklore: An Obituary?" *Byzantine and Modern Greek Studies* 9: 1-28.

―――. 1987. Review of *Gender and Power in Rural Greece*, edited by Jill Dubisch. *Modern Greek Studies Yearbook* 3: 385-88.

And, Metin. 1975. *Karagoz*. Ankara: Dost Yayinlari.

Andromedas, John. 1963. "The Enduring Urban Ties of a Modern Greek Folk Subculture." In *Contributions to Mediterranean Sociology*, ed. Jean G. Péristiany, 269-73. Paris: Mouton

Ardener, Shirley. 1981. "Ground Rules and Social Maps for Women: An Introduction." In *Women and Space: Ground Rules and Social Maps*, ed. Shirley Ardener, 11-34. London: Croom Helm.

Aswad, Barbara C. 1978. "Women, Class, and Power: Examples from the Hatay, Turkey." In *Women in the Muslim World*, ed. Lois Beck and N. Keddie, 473-81. Cambridge, Mass.: Harvard Univ. Press.

Bakhtin, Mikhail. 1968. *Rabelais and His World*, trans. Helene Iswolsky. Cambridge, Mass.: MIT Press.

―――. 1981. *The Dialogic Imagination*, ed. Michael Holquist. Austin: Univ. of Texas Press.

Banton, Michael. 1973. "Urbanization and Role Analysis." In *Urban Anthropology*, ed. Aiden Southall, 71-106. New York: Oxford Univ. Press.

Basgoz, Ilhan, 1975. "The Tale-Singer and His Audience." In *Folklore: Performance and Communication*, ed. Dan Ben-Amos and Kenneth S. Goldstein, 143-203. The Hague: Mouton.

Bates, Ulku U. 1978. "Women as Patrons of Architecture in Turkey." In *Women in the Muslim World*, ed. Lois Beck and N. Keddie, 245-60. Cambridge, Mass.: Harvard Univ. Press.

Bateson, Gregory. 1972. *Steps to an Ecology of Mind*. New York: Ballantine.

Bauman, Richard. 1972. "Differential Identity and the Social Base of Folklore." In *Toward New Perspectives in Folklore*, ed. Amerigo Paredes and Richard Bauman, 31-40. Austin: Univ. of Texas Press.

―――. 1972b. Introduction to *Toward New Perspectives in Folklore*, ed. Amerigo Paredes and Richard Bauman, xi-xv. Austin: Univ. of Texas Press.

———. 1977. *Verbal Art as Performance*. Rowley, Mass: Newbury House.

———. 1986. *Story, Performance, and Event: Contextual Studies of Oral Narrative*. Cambridge: Cambridge Univ. Press.

Beaton, Roderick. 1980. *Folk Poetry of Modern Greece*. Cambridge: Cambridge Univ. Press.

Becker, Howard. 1974. "Art as Collective Action." *American Sociological Review* 39: 767-76.

Ben-Amos, Dan. 1972. "Toward a Definition of Folklore in Context." In *Toward New Perspectives in Folklore*, ed. Amerigo Paredes and Richard Bauman, 3-15. Austin: Univ. of Texas Press.

Benedict, Peter. 1976. "Aspects of the Domestic Cycle in a Turkish Provincial Town." In *Mediterranean Family Structure*, ed. Jean G. Péristiany, 219-42. Cambridge: Cambridge Univ. Press.

Berleant, Arnold. 1970. *The Aesthetic Field: A Phenomenology of Aesthetic Experience*. Springfield, Ill.: Charles C. Thomas.

Bjornson, Richard. 1980. "Translation and Literary Theory." *Translation Review* 6: 13-16.

Blau, P.M. 1964. *Exchange and Power in Social Life*. New York: Wiley.

Bristol, Michael. 1985. *Carnival and Theatre: Plebian Culture and the Structure of Authority in Renaissance England*. London: Methuen.

Burke, Kenneth. 1945. *A Grammar of Motives*. Berkeley: Univ. of California Press.

———. 1950. *A Rhetoric of Motives*. Berkeley: Univ. of California Press.

Burke, Peter. 1978. *Popular Culture in Early Modern Europe*. London: Temple Smith.

Burrell, G., and G. Morgan. 1979. *Sociological Paradigms and Organizational Analysis: Elements of the Sociology of Corporate Life*. Portsmouth, N.H.: Heineman.

Campbell J.K. 1966. "Honour and the Devil." In *Honour and Shame: The Values of Mediterranean Society*, ed. Jean G. Péristiany, 139-70. Chicago: Univ. of Chicago Press.

Caraveli, Anna. 1980. "Bridge between Worlds: The Greek Woman's Lament as Communicative Event." *Journal of American Folklore* 93: 129-57.

———. 1982. "The Song behind the Song: Aesthetics and Interaction in Greek Folksong." *Journal of American Folklore* 95: 129-58.

———. 1985. "The Symbolic Village: Community Born in Performance." *Journal of American Folklore* 98: 259-86.

———. 1986. "The Bitter Wounding: The Lament as Social Protest in Rural Greece." In *Gender and Power in Rural Greece*, ed. Jill Dubisch, 169-94. Princeton, N.J.: Princeton Univ. Press.

Cavounides, Jennifer. 1983. "Capitalist Development and Women's Work in Greece." *Journal of Modern Greek Studies* 1: 321-38.

Colby, Benjamin N. 1966. "The Analysis of Culture Content and the Patterning of Narrative Concern in Texts." *American Anthropologist* 68: 374-88.

Collier, Jane Fishburne. 1974. "Women in Politics." In *Woman, Culture, and Society*, ed. Michelle Rosaldo and Louise Lamphere, 89-96. Stanford, Calif.: Stanford Univ. Press.

Cosar, F.M. 1978. "Women in Turkish Society." In *Women in the Muslim World*, ed. Lois Beck and N. Keddie, 124-50. Cambridge, Mass.: Harvard Univ. Press.

Costa, Janeen Arnold. 1988. "The History of Migration and Political Economy in Rural Greece: A Case Study." *Journal of Modern Greek Studies* 6: 159-85.

Culler, Jonathan. 1982. *On Deconstruction: Theory and Criticism after Structuralism.* Ithaca, N.Y.: Cornell Univ. Press.

Damianakos, Sthathis. 1976. *Kinoniologia Tu "Rebetiku."* Athens: Ermia.

Danforth, Loring M. 1976. "Humour and Status Reversal in Greek Shadow Theatre." *Byzantine and Modern Greek Studies* 2: 99-111.

———. 1983a. "Power through Submission in the Anastenaria." *Journal of Modern Greek Studies* 1: 203-24.

———. 1983b. "Tradition and Change in Greek Shadow Theater." *Journal of American Folklore* 96: 281-309.

———. 1984. "The Ideological Context of the Search for Continuities in Greek Culture." *Journal of Modern Greek Studies* 2: 53-85.

Denglar, Ian C. 1978. "Turkish Women in the Ottoman Empire: The Classical Age." In *Women in the Muslim World,* ed. Lois Beck and N. Keddie, 229-44. Cambridge, Mass.: Harvard Univ. Press.

Denich, Bette S. 1974. "Sex and Power in the Balkans." In *Woman, Culture, and Society,* ed. Michelle Rosaldo and Louise Lamphere, 243-62. Stanford, Calif: Stanford Univ. Press.

Derrida, Jacques. 1978. *Writing and Difference,* trans. A. Bass. London: Routledge and Kegan Paul.

———. 1985. "Des Tours de Babel," trans. Joseph F. Graham. In *Difference in Translation,* ed. Joseph F. Graham, 165-68. Ithaca, N.Y.: Cornell Univ. Press.

Dimen, Muriel. 1986. "Servants and Sentries: Women, Power, and Social Reproduction in Kriovrisi." In *Gender and Power in Rural Greece,* ed. Jill Dubisch, 42-52. Princeton, N.J.: Princeton Univ. Press.

Dorson, Richard. 1971. "Is There a Folk in the City?" In *The Urban Experience and Folk Tradition,* ed. Amerigo Paredes and Ellen J. Stekert, 21-64. Austin: Univ. of Texas Press.

———. 1976. *Folklore and Fakelore: Essays toward a Discipline of Folk Studies.* Cambridge, Mass.: Harvard Univ. Press.

Dragumis, Markos. 1975. "The Music of the Rebetes." In *Rebetika: Songs from the Old Greek Underworld,* ed. Katharine Butterworth and Sara Schneider, 16-26. Athens: Komboloi.

Duben, Alan. 1982. "The Significance of Family and Kinship in Urban Turkey." In *Sex Roles, Family and Community in Turkey,* ed. Çiğdem Kağitçibaşi, 73-96. Bloomington: Indiana Univ. Turkish Studies.

Dubisch, Jill. 1974. "The Domestic Power of Women in a Greek Island Village." *Studies in European Society* 1: 23-33.

———. 1977. "The City as Resource: Migration from a Greek Island Village." *Urban Anthropology* 6: 65-81.

———. 1983. "Greek Women: Sacred or Profane." *Journal of Modern Greek Studies* 1: 185-202.

———, ed. 1986. *Gender and Power in Rural Greece.* Princeton, N.J.: Princeton Univ. Press.

de Boulay, Juliet. 1974. *Portrait of a Greek Mountain Village.* Oxford: Clarendon Press.

————. 1976. "Lies, Mockery and Family Integrity." In *Mediterranean Family Structure,* ed. Jean G. Péristiany, 389-406. Cambridge: Cambridge Univ. Press.

————. 1983. "The Meaning of Dowry: Changing Values in Rural Greece." *Journal of Modern Greek Studies* 1: 243-70.

————. 1986. "Women—Images of Their Nature and Destiny in Rural Greece." In *Gender and Power in Rural Greece,* ed. Jill Dubisch, 139-68. Princeton, N.J.: Princeton Univ. Press.

Dundes, Alan. 1964. "Texture, Text, and Context." *Southern Folklore Quarterly* 28: 251-65.

Fallers, Lloyd, and Margaret C. Fallers. 1976. "Sex Roles in Edremit." In *Mediterranean Family Structure,* ed. Jean G. Péristiany, 343-60. Cambridge: Cambridge Univ. Press.

Faroqhi, Suriya. 1984. *Towns and Townsmen of Ottoman Anatolia.* Cambridge: Cambridge Univ. Press.

Fine, Elizabeth C. 1984. *The Folklore Text: From Performance to Print.* Bloomington: Indiana Univ. Press.

Finnegan, Ruth. 1977. *Oral Poetry: Its Nature, Significance and Social Context.* Cambridge: Cambridge Univ. Press.

Fish, Stanley. 1980. *Is There a Text in This Class?: The Authority of Interpretive Communities.* Cambridge, Mass.: Harvard Univ. Press.

Flaubert, Gustave. 1958. *Voyage en Orient: Egypte, Palestine, Asie Mineure, Constantinople, Grèce, Italie (1849-1851),* vol. 2, *Constantine, Tunis et Carthage (1858).* Paris: Société Le Belles Lettres.

Foucault, Michel. 1973. *Madness and Civilization: A History of Insanity in the Age of Reason,* trans. R. Howard. New York: Vintage/Random House.

————. 1975. *The Birth of the Clinic: An Archaeology of Medical Perception,* trans. A. M. Sheridan. New York: Vintage/Random House.

Fox, William. 1980. "Folklore and Fakelore." *Journal of the Folklore Institute* 17: 244-61.

Friedl, Ernestine. 1967. "The Position of Women: Appearance and Reality." *Anthropological Quarterly* 40: 97-108.

————. 1976. "Kinship, Class and Selective Migration." In *Mediterranean Family Structure,* ed. Jean G. Péristiany, 363-88. Cambridge: Cambridge Univ. Press.

Friedrich, Paul. 1966. "Revolutionary Politics and Communal Ritual." In *Political Anthropology,* ed. Marc J. Swartz, Victor W. Turner, and Arthur Tuden, 191-220. Chicago: Aldine.

Frow, John. 1986. *Marxism and Literary History.* Cambridge, Mass.: Harvard Univ. Press.

Geertz, Clifford. 1973. *The Interpretation of Cultures.* New York: Basic.

————. 1983. *Local Knowledge: Further Essays in Interpretive Anthropology.* New York: Basic.

Georges, Robert. 1969. "Toward an Understanding of Storytelling Events." *Journal of American Folklore* 82: 313-28.

Glassie, Henry, Edward D. Ives, and John F. Szived. 1979. *Folksongs and Their Makers.* Bowling Green, Ohio: Bowling Green Univ. Popular Press.

Goffman, Erving. 1959. *The Presentation of Self in Everyday Life.* Garden City, N.Y.: Doubleday.

————. 1974. *Frame Analysis: An Essay on the Organization of Experience.* New York: Harper Colophon.

Good, Mary-Jo Del Vecchio. 1978. "A Comparative Perspective on Women in Provincial Iran and Turkey." In *Women in the Muslim World,* ed. Lois Beck and N. Keddie, 482-500. Cambridge, Mass.: Harvard Univ. Press.

Gouldner, A.W. 1955. *Patterns of Industrial Bureaucracy.* London: Routledge and Paul.

Gulick, John. 1975. "The City as Microcosm of Society." *Urban Anthropology* 4: 5-15.

Haridimos, Hristos. 1963. "Ezisa Me Ton Karagiozi." *Theatro* 2.10: 55-62.

Hatzipandazis, Thodoros. 1982 "I Isvoli Tu Karagiozi Stin Athina Tu 1890." *O Politis* 49: 64-87.

Hauser, Philip M. 1965a. "Observations on the Urban-Folk and Urban-Rural Dichotomies as Forms of Western Ethnocentrism." In *The Study of Urbanization,* ed. Philip M. Hauser and Leo F. Schnore, 503-17. New York: Wiley.

————. 1965b. "Urbanization: An Overview." In *The Study of Urbanization,* ed. Philip M. Hauser and Leo F. Schnore, 1-48. New York: Wiley.

Herzfeld, Michael. 1977. "Ritual and Textual Structurs: The Advent of Spring in Rural Greece." In *Text and Context: the Social Anthropology of Tradition,* ed. Ravindra K Jain, 29-50. ASA Essays in Social Anthropology no. 2. Philadelphia: Institute for the Study of Human Issues.

————. 1979. "Exploring a Metaphor of Exposure." *Journal of American Folklore* 92: 285-301.

————. 1981a. "An Indigenous Theory of Meaning and Its Elucidation in Performative Context." *Semiotica* 34: 113-41.

————. 1981b. "Performative Categories and Symbols of Passage in Rural Greece." *Journal of American Folklore* 94: 44-57.

————. 1982. *Ours Once More: Folklore, Ideology, and the Making of Modern Greece.* Austin: Univ. of Texas Press.

————. 1985. "Interpretation from within: Metatext for a Cretan Quarrel." In *The Text and Its Margins: Post-Structuralist Approaches to Twentieth-Century Greek Literature,* ed. Margaret Alexiou and Vassilis Lambropoulos, 197-218. New York: Pella.

————. 1986. "Within and Without: The Category of 'Female' in the Ethnography of Modern Greece." In *Gender and Power in Rural Greece,* ed. Jill Dubisch, 215-33. Princeton, N.J.: Princeton Univ. Press.

————. 1987. *Anthropology through the Looking Glass: Critical Ethnography in the Margin of Europe.* Cambridge: Cambridge Univ. Press.

Hiliotis, Thanasis. 1980. "Folklore of Marginal Types." *Andi* 147: 10-11.

Hirschkop, Ken. 1986. "A Response to the Forum on Mikhail Bakhtin." In *Bakhtin: Essays and Dialogues on His Work,* ed. Gary Saul Morson, 73-80. Chicago: Univ. of Chicago Press.

Hirschon, Renée. 1978. "Open Body / Closed Space: The Transformation of Female Sexuality." In *Defining Females: The Nature of Women in Society,* ed. Shirley Ardener, 66-88. New York: Wiley.

————. 1981. "Essential Objects and the Sacred: Interior and Exterior Spaces in an Urban Greek Locality." In *Women and Space: Ground Rules and Social Maps,* ed. Shirley Ardener, 72-88. London: Croom Helm.

————. 1983a. "Under One Roof: Marriage, Dowry, and Family Relations." In *Urban*

Life in Mediterranean Europe: Anthropological Perspectives, ed. Michael Kenny and David I. Kertzer, 299-323. Urbana: Univ. of Illinois Press.

———. 1983b. "Women, the Aged and Religious Activity: Oppositions and Complementarity in an Urban Locality." *Journal of Modern Greek Studies* 1: 113-30.

———. 1984. Introduction to *Women and Property—Women as Property*, ed. Renée Hirschon, 1-22. New York: St Martin's Press.

Hirschon, Renée, and John R. Gold. 1982. "Territoriality and the Home Environment in a Greek Urban Community." *Anthropological Quarterly* 55: 63-73.

Hymes, Dell. 1964. "Toward Ethnographies of Communication." *American Anthropologist* 66.6: 1-35.

———. 1967. "Model of the Interaction of Language and Social Setting." *Journal of Social Issues* 23.2: 8-28.

———. 1975. "Breakthrough into Performance." In *Folklore: Performance and Communication*, ed. Dan Ben-Amos and Kenneth S. Goldstein, 11-74. The Hague: Mouton.

Iliadis, Vas. 1925. "To Propolemiko Turkiko Theatro." In *Akropoleos*. Athens, n.p.

Jameson, Fredric. 1981. *The Political Unconscious: Narrative as a Socially Symbolic Act*. Ithaca, N.Y.: Cornell Univ. Press.

Jansen, William Hugh. 1957. "A Culture's Stereotypes and Their Expression in Folk Clichés." *Southwestern Journal of Anthropological Research* 13: 184-200.

Jason, Heda. 1972. "Concerning the 'Historical' and the 'Local' Legend and Their Relatives." In *Toward New Perspectives in Folklore*, ed. Amerigo Paredes and Richard Bauman, 134-44. Austin: Univ. of Texas Press.

Joyner, Charles W. 1975. "A Model for the Analysis of Folklore Performance in Historical Context." *Journal of American Folklore* 88: 245-65.

Kandiyoti, Deniz. 1982. "Urban Change and Women's Roles in Turkey: An Overview and Evaluation." In *Sex Roles, Family and Community in Turkey*, ed. Çiğdem Kağitçibaşi, 101-20. Bloomington: Indiana Univ. Turkish Studies.

Kayser, Bernard. 1976. "Dynamics of Regional Integration in Modern Greece." In *Regional Variation in Modern Greece and Cyprus: Toward a Perspective on the Ethnography of Greece*, ed. Muriel Dimen and Ernestine Friedl, 10-15. Annals of the New York Academy of Sciences no. 268.

Kenna, Margaret E. 1976. "The Idiom of Family." In *Mediterranean Family Structure*, ed. Jean G. Péristiany, 347-62. Cambridge: Cambridge Univ. Press.

Kenny, Michael, and David I. Kertzer, eds. 1983. *Urban Life in Mediterranean Europe: Anthropological Perspectives*. Urbana: Univ. of Illinois Press.

Keyser, James M.B. 1975. "Differences in Urban Adaptations: A Turkish Case." *Urban Anthropology* 4: 161-75.

Kiurtsakis, Giannis. 1985. *Karnavali Ke Karagiozis: I Rizes Ke I Metamorfosis Tu Laiku Geliu*. Athens: Kedros

Kiray, Mubeccel. 1976. "The New Role of Mothers: Changing Intra-Familial Relationships in a Small Town in Turkey." In *Mediterranean Family Structure*, ed. Jean G. Péristiany, 261-71. Cambridge: Cambridge Univ. Press.

Kongar, Emre. 1976. "A Survey of Familial Change in Two Turkish Gecekondu Areas." In *Mediterranean Family Structure*, ed. Jean G. Péristiany, 205-18. Cambridge: Cambridge Univ. Press.

Kristeva, Julia. 1980. *Desire in Language*. New York: Columbia Univ. Press.

Kuhn, Thomas. 1970. *The Structure of Scientific Revolutions*. 2d ed. Chicago: Univ. of Chicago Press.

Kuyas, Nilufer F. 1982. "The Effects of Female Labor on Power Relations in the Urban Turkish Family." In *Sex Roles, Family and Community in Turkey*, ed. Çiğdem Kağitçibaşi, 181-205. Bloomington: Indiana Univ. Turkish Studies.

Kyriakidu-Nestoros, Alke. 1972. "The Study of Folklore in Greece: Laographia in Its Contemporary Perspective." *East European Quarterly* 5: 487-504.

———. 1976. "Laikos Politismos." *Andi* 41: 44-45.

———. 1985. *I Theoria Tis Ellinikis Laografias: Kritiki Analisi*. Athens: Eteria Spudon.

Laba, M. 1979. "Urban Folklore: A Behavioral Approach." *Western Folklore* 38: 158-69.

Lambropulos, Vassilis. 1985. "Toward a Genealogy of Modern Greek Literature." In *The Text and Its Margins: Post-Structuralist Approaches to Twentieth-Century Greek Literature*, ed. Margaret Alexiou and Vassilis Lambropulos, 15-36. New York: Pella.

Lamphere, Louise. 1974. "Strategies, Cooperation, and Conflict among Women in Domestic Groups." In *Woman, Culture, and Society*, ed. Michelle Rosaldo and Louise Lamphere, 97-112. Stanford, Calif.: Stanford Univ. Press.

Leeds, Morton. 1971. "The Process of Cultural Stripping and Reintegration: The Rural Migrant in the City." In *The Urban Experience and Folk Tradition*, ed. Amerigo Paredes and Ellen J. Stekert, 165-76. Austin: Univ. of Texas Press.

Lévi-Strauss, Claude. 1963. "The Structural Study of Myth." In *Structural Anthropology* 1: 206-31. New York: Basic.

Lewis, Oscar. 1965. "Further Observations on the Folk-Urban Continuum and Urbanization with Special Reference to Mexico City." In *The Study of Urbanization*, ed. Philip M. Hauser and Leo F. Schnore, 491-503. New York: Wiley.

———. 1973. "Some Perspectives on Urbanization with Special Reference to Mexico City." In *Urban Anthropology*, ed. Aiden Southall, 125-38. New York: Oxford Univ. Press.

Limon, J. 1984. "Western Marxism and Folklore." *Journal of American Folklore* 97: 337-44.

Lomax, Alan, and Joan Halifax. 1971. "Folk Songs as Culture Indicators." In *Structural Analysis of Oral Tradition*, ed. Pierre Maranda and Elli Kongas Maranda, 235-71. Philadelphia: Univ. of Pennsylvania Press.

Lord, Albert Bates. 1971. *The Singer of Tales*. Cambridge, Mass.: Harvard Univ. Press.

Lukatos, Dimitris S. 1985. *Isagogis Stin Elliniki Laografia*. Athens: Morfotiki Idrima Ethnikis Trapezis.

MacCormack, Carol P. 1980. "Nature, Culture and Gender: A Critique." In *Nature, Culture and Gender*, ed. Carol P. MacCormack and Marilyn Strathern, 1-24. Cambridge: Cambridge Univ. Press.

MacCormack, Carol P., and Marilyn Strathern, eds. 1980. *Nature, Culture and Gender*. Cambridge: Cambridge Univ. Press.

Mangin, William, ed. 1970. *Peasants in Cities: Readings in the Anthropology of Urbanization*. Boston: Houghton Mifflin.

Merton, R.G. 1957. *Social Theory and Social Structure*. Glencoe, Ill.: Free Press.

Michembled, Robert. 1985. *Popular Culture and Elite Culture in France, 1400-1750*, trans. Lydia Cochrane. Baton Rouge: Louisiana State Univ. Press.

Miller, Julia E. 1985. *Modern Greek Folklore: An Annotated Bibliography.* New York: Garland.

Mollas, Antonios. 1963. "O Karagiozis." *Theatro* 2.10: 62.

Moore, Kenneth. 1975. "The City as Context: Context as Process." *Urban Anthropology* 4: 17-25.

Morson, Gary Saul. 1986. "Who Speaks for Bakhtin?" In *Bakhtin: Essays and Dialogues on His Work*, ed. Gary Saul Morson, 1-20. Chicago: Univ. of Chicago Press.

Muzelis, Nicos. 1976. "The Relevance of the Concept of Class to the Study of Modern Greek Society." In *Regional Variation in Modern Greece and Cyprus: Toward a Perspective on the Ethnography of Greece*, ed. Muriel Dimen and Ernestine Friedl, 395-409. Annals of the New York Academy of Sciences no. 268.

———. 1978. *Modern Greece: Facets of Underdevelopment.* New York: Holmes and Meier.

Myrsiades, Linda. 1976. "The Karagiozis Performance in Nineteenth-Century Greece." *Byzantine and Modern Greek Studies* 2: 83-99.

———. 1978. "Nation and Class in the Karagiozis History Performance." *Theatre Survey* 19: 49-62.

———. 1980a. "The Female Role in the Karagiozis Performance." *Southern Folklore Quarterly* 44: 145-63.

———. 1980b. "The Struggle for Greek Theatre in Post-Liberation Greece." *Journal of the Hellenic Diaspora* 7: 33-51.

———. 1982a. "Non-Theatrical Entertainments in Greece: Through the Eyes of Foreign Travellers, 1750-1850." *East European Quarterly* 16: 45-58.

———. 1982b. "Theatre and Society: Social Content and Effect in the Karagiozis Performance." *Folia Neohellenica* 4: 145-59.

———. 1983. "Karagiozis: A Bibliography of Primary Materials." *Mantatoforos* 21: 14-42.

———. 1985a. "Oral Traditional Form in the Karagiozis Performance." *Ellinika* 36: 116-52.

———. 1985b. "Traditional History and Reality in the View of the Karagiozis History Performance." *Modern Greek Studies Yearbook* 1: 96-108.

———. 1986a. "Adaptation and Change: The Origins of Karagiozis in Greece." *Turcica* 18: 119-36.

———. 1986b. "Historical Source Material for the Karagiozis Performance." *Theatre Research International* 10: 213-25.

———. 1988a. "The Karagiozis Performance in Its Performative Context: The Rural/Urban Dichotomy." *Modern Greek Studies Yearbook* 4: 51-81.

———. 1988b. Review of *Karnavali Ke Karagiozis: I Rizes Ke I Metamorfosis Tu Laiku Yeliu*, by Giannis Kiurtsakis. *Modern Greek Studies Yearbook* 4: 394-98.

Myrsiades, Linda, and Kostas Myrsiades. 1988. *The Karagiozis Heroic Performance in Greek Shadow Theatre.* Hanover, N.H.: Univ. Press of New England.

Mystiakidu, Katerina. 1978. "Comparison of the Turkish and Greek Shadow Theatre." Ph.D. diss., New York University.

Nida, Eugene A. 1964. *Towards a Science of Translating.* Leiden: Brill.

Ortner, Sherry B. 1974. "Is Female to Male as Nature Is to Culture?" In *Woman, Culture, and Society,* ed. Michelle Rosaldo and Louise Lamphere, 67-87. Stanford, Calif.: Stanford Univ. Press.

Ortutay, Gyula. 1959. "Principles of Oral Transmission in Folk Culture." *Acta Ethnografica* 8: 175-222.

Papagiannis, Nikos. 1977. "Psihopathologia Tu Rebetiku." *O Politis* 12: 46-52.

Penzer, N.M. 1936. *The Harem.* London: Spring.

Péristiany, Jean G. 1966. "Honour and Shame in a Cypriot Highland Village." In *Honour and Shame: The Values of Mediterranean Society,* ed. Jean G. Péristiany, 171-90. Chicago: Univ. of Chicago Press.

———. 1976. Introduction to *Mediterranean Family Structure,* ed. Jean G. Péristiany, 1-26. Cambridge: Cambridge Univ. Press.

Petropulos, Elias. 1968. *Rebetika Tragudia: Laika Erevna.* Athens, n.p.

———. 1975. "Rebetika." In *Rebetika: Songs from the Old Greek Underworld,* ed. Katharine Buttersworth and Sara Schneider, 11-15. Athens: Kombolio.

———. 1976. "O Karagiozis Ke I Manges." *Andi* 51: 34-42.

———. 1978. *Ipokosmos Ke Karagiozis.* Athens: Grammata.

Pollis, Adamantia. 1977. "The Impact of Traditional Cultural Patterns on Greek Politics." *Greek Review of Social Research* 29: 2-4.

Propp, Vladimir. 1968. *Morphology of the Folktale,* trans. L. Scott. Austin: Univ. of Texas Press.

Psacharopulos, George. 1983. "Sex Discrimination in the Greek Labor Market." *Journal of Modern Greek Studies* 1: 339-58.

Rogers, Susan Carol. 1975. "Female Forms of Power and the Myth of Male Dominance: A Model of Female/Male Interaction in Peasant Society." *American Ethnologist* 2: 727-56.

Rorty, Richard. 1979. *Philosophy and the Mirror of Nature.* Princeton, N.J.: Princeton Univ. Press.

Rosaldo, Michelle. 1974. "Woman, Culture, and Society: A Theoretical Overview." In *Woman, Culture, and Society,* ed. Michelle Rosaldo and Louise Lamphere, 17-42. Stanford, Calif.: Stanford Univ. Press.

———. 1980. "The Use and Abuse of Anthropology: Reflections on Feminism and Cross Cultural Understanding." *Signs* 5: 389-417.

Rosaldo, Michelle, and Louise Lamphere, eds. 1974. *Woman, Culture, and Society.* Stanford, Calif.: Stanford Univ. Press.

Sacks, Karen. 1974. "Engels Revisited: Women, the Organization of Production, and Private Property." In *Woman, Culture, and Society,* ed. Michelle Rosaldo and Louise Lamphere, 207-22. Stanford, Calif.: Stanford Univ. Press.

Safilios-Rothschild, C. 1976. "The Family in Athens: Regional Variations." In *Regional Variations in Modern Greece and Cyprus: Toward a Perspective on the Ethnography of Greece,* ed. Muriel Dimen and Ernestine Friedl, 410-18. Annals of the New York Academy of Sciences 268.

Salamone, S.D., and J.B. Stanton. 1986. "Introducing the 'Nikokyra': Ideality and Reality in Social Process." In *Gender and Power in Rural Greece,* ed. Jill Dubisch, 97-120. Princeton, N.J.: Princeton Univ. Press.

Sanday, Peggy R. 1974. "Female Status in the Public Domain." In *Woman, Culture, and Society,* ed. Michelle Rosaldo and Louise Lamphere 189-206. Stanford, Calif.: Stanford Univ. Press.

Schechner, Richard. 1977. *Essays on Performance Theory, 1970-1976.* New York: Drama Book Specialists.

Schein, Muriel D. 1975. "When Is an Ethnic Group?: Ecology and Class Structure in Northern Greece." *Ethnology* 14: 83-97.

Schulte, Rainer. 1979. "The Act of Translation: From Interpretation to Interdisciplinary Thinking." *Translation Review* 4: 3-8.

Sciama, Lidia. 1981. "The Problem of Privacy in Mediterranean Anthropology." In *Women and Space: Ground Rules and Social Maps,* ed. Shirley Ardener, 89-111. London: Croom Helm.

Selznick, P. 1979. *TVA and the Grass Roots: A Study in the Sociology of Formal Organizations.* Berkeley: Univ. of California Press.

Simic, Andrei. 1983. "Urbanization and Modernization in Yugoslavia: Adaptive and Maladaptive Aspects of Traditional Culture." In *Urban Life in Mediterranean Europe: Anthropological Perspectives,* ed. Michael Kenny and David I. Kertzer, 203-24. Urbana: Univ. of Illinois Press.

Southall, Aiden. 1973. Introduction to *Urban Anthropology,* ed. Aiden Southall. 3-14. New York: Oxford Univ. Press.

Spinellis, D.C., Vasso Vassiliu, and George Vassiliu. 1970. "Milieu Development and Male-Female Roles in Contemporary Greece." In *Sex Roles in Changing Society,* ed. G.H. Seward and Robert C. Williamson, 308-17. New York: Random House.

Starr, Jane. 1984. "The Legal and Social Transformation of Rural Women in Aegean Turkey." In *Women and Property—Women as Property,* ed. Renée Hirschon, 92-116. New York: St. Martin's Press.

Strathern, Marilyn. 1980. "No Nature, No Culture: The Hagen Case." In *Nature, Culture and Gender,* ed. Carol P. MacCormack and Marilyn Strathern, 174-222. Cambridge: Cambridge Univ. Press.

———. 1984a. "Domesticity and the Denigration of Women." In *Rethinking Women's Roles: Perspectives from the Pacific,* ed. Denise O'Brien and Sharon W. Tiffany, 13-31. Berkeley: Univ. of California Press.

———. 1984b. "Subject or Object? Women and the Circulation of Valuables in Highlands New Guinea." In *Women and Property—Women as Property,* ed. Renée Hirschon, 158-75. New York: St. Martin's Press.

Sutton, Susan Buck. 1978. "Migrant Regional Associations: An Athenian Example and Its Implications." Ph.D. diss., University of North Carolina at Chapel Hill.

———. 1983. "Rural-Urban Migration in Greece." In *Urban Life in Mediterranean Europe: Anthropological Perspectives,* ed. Michael Kenny and David I. Kertzer, 225-52. Urbana: Univ. of Illinois Press.

———. 1988. "What Is a 'Village' in a Nation of Migrants?" *Journal of Modern Greek Studies* 6: 187-215.

Suzuki, P. 1964. "Encounters with Istanbul: Urban Peasants and Rural Peasants." *International Journal of Comparative Sociology* 5.2: 208-16.

Tedlock, Dennis. 1971. "On the Translation of Style in Oral Narrative." *Journal of American Folklore* 84: 114-33.

———. 1977. "Towards an Oral Poetics." *New Literary History* 8: 507-19.

Tiffany, Sharon W. 1984. "Introduction: Feminist Perspectives in Anthropology." In

Rethinking Women's Roles: Perspectives from the Pacific, ed. Denise O'Brien and Sharon W. Tiffany, 1-12. Berkeley: Univ. of California Press.

Tsaussis, D.G. 1976. "Greek Social Structure." In *Regional Variation in Modern Greece and Cyprus: Toward a Perspective on the Ethnography of Greece*, ed. Muriel Dimen and Ernestine Friedl, 429-41. Annals of the New York Academy of Sciences no. 268.

Turner, Victor. 1968. "Mukanda: the Politics of a Non-Political Ritual." In *Local-Level Politics: Social and Cultural Perspectives*, ed. Marc J. Swartz, 135-50. Chicago: Aldine.

————. 1974. *Dramas, Fields, and Metaphors: Symbolic Action in Human Society*. Ithaca, N.Y.: Cornell Univ. Press.

————. 1986. *The Anthropology of Performance*. New York: PAJ.

Tziovas, Dimitris. 1985. "The Organic Discourse of Nationistic Demoticism: A Tropological Approach." In *The Text and Its Margins: Post-Structuralist Approaches to Twentieth-Century Literature*, ed. Margaret Alexiou and Vassilis Lambropoulos, 253-77. New York: Pella.

Underdown, David. 1985. *Revel, Riot and Rebellion: Popular Politics and Culture in England, 1603-1660*. Oxford: Clarendon Press.

Vermeulen, Cornelis J.J. 1970. "Families in Urban Greece." Ph.D. diss., Cornell Univ.

Vermeulen, Hans. 1983. "Urban Research in Greece." In *Urban Life in Mediterranean Europe: Anthropological Perspectives*, ed. Michael Kenny and David I. Kertzer, 109-34. Urbana: Univ. of Illinois Press.

Vlahogiannis, Giannis. 1943. "Tis Tehnis Ta Farmakis." *Nea Estia* 39: 853-60, 926-33, 1049-54.

Whitehead, Ann. 1984. In *Women and Property—Women as Property*, ed. Renée Hirschon, 176-92. New York: St. Martin's Press.

Williams, Raymond. 1977. *Marxism and Literature*. London: Oxford Univ. Press.

Zipes, Jack. 1979. *Breaking the Magic Spell: Radical Theories of Folk and Fairy Tales*. Austin: Univ. of Texas Press.

————. 1984. "Folklore Research and Western Marxism." *Journal of American Folklore* 97: 329-37.

Index